Ruling the Root

Ruling the Root

Internet Governance and the Taming of Cyberspace

Milton L. Mueller

The MIT Press
Cambridge, Massachusetts
London, England

First MIT Press paperback edition, 2004

© 2002 Massachusetts Institute of Technology

This book was set in Sabon by Graphic Composition, Inc., Athens, Georgia

Printed and bound in the United States of America.

Library of Congress Cataloging-in-Publication Data

Mueller, Milton.
    Ruling the root : Internet governance and the taming of cyberspace /
Milton L. Mueller.
        p. cm.
    Includes bibliographical references and index.
    ISBN 0-262-13412-8 (hc : alk. paper), 0-262-63298-5 (pb)
        1. Internet—Government policy.   2. Internet addresses—Government
policy.   3. Cyberspace—Government policy.   4. Telecommunication policy.
5. Right of property.   6. Institutional economics.   7. Organizational change.
I. Title.
TK5105.875.I57 M845 2002
004.67′8—dc21
                                                                2002020024

10 9 8 7 6 5 4 3 2

Contents

Ruling the Root

1

Introduction: The Problem of the Root

For two days in July 1998, one hundred and fifty people gathered in a windowless hotel convention room in Reston, Virginia. The crowd comprised techies in T-shirts, trademark lawyers in suits, academic and business people, and a small but significant number of Europeans, Latin Americans, and Asians. The meeting had an ambitious goal: to "prepare a model, a set of common principles, a structure and general charter provisions" for the formation of a global governance body for an Internet naming and addressing authority.[1] The meeting was compared to an Internet "constitutional convention" by some. But the delegates to this convention were not diplomats or legislators, and its participants held no formal credentials. There had been some attempts to encourage preregistration, but for all practical purposes attendance was completely open—anyone who walked in could participate. A call had been issued by a self-appointed, hastily assembled, and loosely defined steering committee, whose membership remained fluid and controversial for weeks afterwards. Aside from a few basic agenda and scheduling decisions, the process was made up on the spot. There were no formal committee chairs; facilitators either volunteered or were appointed. There were not even arrangements for breakout rooms for subgroups to work in, so the committees had to huddle in corners of the same noisy room and sometimes shout to make themselves heard.

The Reston meeting was the first in what turned out to be a series of four such conferences known as the International Forum on the White Paper (IFWP). Reston, Virginia, was an appropriate location for the inaugural meeting; it was ground zero of the commercial Internet explosion of the mid-1990s. The region was home to Network Solutions, Inc. (NSI), the government contractor that had turned domain name registration into a multimillion dollar business and that was the site of the critical A root server, the central source of data for coordinating the world's Internet names. Reston itself was the headquarters of the Internet Society. The Pentagon and the National Science Foundation, whose sponsorship of the Internet had pushed it to the brink of global critical mass, were only a few miles away. So was the Corporation for National Research Initiatives (CNRI), which hosted the secretariat of the Internet Engineering Task Force (IETF) and once served as the organizational home of Robert Kahn and Vint Cerf, the joint inventors of the Internet protocol. Commercial firms that had risen to prominence with the Internet, such as MCI, PSINet and America Online, located their headquarters nearby.

For several years it had been clear that the Internet was no longer a subsidized tool of education and research but a vibrant new global medium. The Internet was growing at exponential rates, and its importance to the economy was becoming increasingly evident. But key technical functions such as name and address management were still performed under contracts with the U.S. military and the National Science Foundation. Foreign governments were becoming increasingly restive about unilateral U.S. control of such an important part of the global communication infrastructure. Network Solutions' unplanned-for and increasingly lucrative monopoly over domain name registration was also a point of growing contention.

The transition process, everyone knew, would be risky and controversial. Domain names and IP (Internet Protocol) addresses stood at the core of the Internet's operation. If they were handled poorly, the Internet could break. As the stakes grew higher, however, the Internet community had fallen into rancorous battles over policy and control. The years of escalating tension became known as the domain name wars. Finally, in July 1997, the U.S. Department of Commerce initiated a formal proceeding to privatize the domain name system (NTIA 1997). The result was a policy document officially titled "Management of Internet Names and Addresses" but universally known in Internet circles as simply "the White Paper" (NTIA 1998b).

With the release of the White Paper on June 3, 1998, the U.S. government took an unusual approach to the transition. Instead of using its rule-making powers to settle issues, instead of creating an organization and specifying the rules it would follow, it threw the responsibility back to the warring parties, back to what it called private sector stakeholders. The government's announced intention was to "recognize . . . and seek international support for a new, not-for-profit corporation formed by private sector Internet stakeholders" (NTIA 1998b, 31749). That new corporation, not the U.S. government, would make the difficult policy decisions. It was up to the Internet community itself to form this organization and come to the U.S. government with a single proposal that commanded the unified support of the global Internet community. This had to be done in only four months.

1.1   A Constitutional Moment

Hence, the unusual gathering in Virginia. The IFWP was the response of those who took literally the U.S. government's call for private sector leadership. It was conceived as an open, neutral arena that would bring the key parties involved in the domain name wars together in face-to-face meetings. Tamar Frankel, a Boston University law professor who was expert in corporate governance structures but largely innocent of the Internet and its controversies, agreed to preside over the meetings. Many participants in the Reston meeting reveled in the government's willingness to keep its hands off and allow the "Internet community" to resolve the problems on its own. The words *consensus* and *self-governance* were on everyone's lips. Ira Magaziner, the Clinton administration policy adviser who had supervised the White Paper proceeding, gave the Reston gathering a kind of official blessing with an opening speech and then left to allow "the private sector" to do its work. Jon Postel, the respected Internet technologist who had managed the number space and domain name delegations for many years, sent a letter from California expressing his hopes that the forum would succeed. The Reston meeting was followed by quickly organized counterparts in Geneva, Singapore, and Buenos Aires. The ultimate result, for better or worse, was the Internet Corporation for Assigned Names and Numbers (ICANN).

The IFWP seemed to initiate a unique form of international organization. Normally, policy for global resources such as Internet names and numbers would be coordinated through established institutions, such as national governments, trade associations, standards bodies, international treaties, or formal international organizations. The Internet was different, however. It seemed to call forth an entirely new spirit for collective action. It had created a perplexing set of issues that eluded resolution by any one government or organization. There was no suitable legal or organizational framework in place. Various organizations—the Internet Society, the International Telecommunication Union (ITU), alternative "root server confederations"—had tried and failed to create one.

The type of problem that the White Paper set out to solve was not entirely unprecedented. The telegraph and postal systems, radio, satellites, air travel, and maritime transport all had raised similar issues in the past. These problems had been handled by collective action among nation-states through formal treaties or intergovernmental organizations such as the ITU. Something different was happening here. The intellectual, commercial, and political climate surrounding the Internet militated against the involvement of states and state-derived international organizations. True, the U.S. government had set the stage for the process by holding a formal proceeding and issuing a policy statement. It still held substantial power over who would be selected to administer the authority. But the method it was using deviated sharply from traditional ones. Indeed, at the initial IFWP meeting, Magaziner presented the White Paper as an epochal change in the nature of international organization. Drawing on a distinction between "industrial society" and "information society" that was popular at the time, Magaziner suggested that the White Paper's methods were more appropriate to the information age. "We believe that the Internet as it develops needs to have a different type of coordination structure than has been typical for international institutions in the industrial age. [G]overnmental processes and intergovernmental processes by definition work too slowly and somewhat too bureaucratically for the pace and flexibility of this new information age."[2] The Harvard professor Lawrence Lessig, on the other hand, a critic of the administration's private sector approach, complained that "we are creating the most significant jurisdiction since the Louisiana purchase, and we are building it outside the review of the Constitution."[3]

A scene from the International Forum on the White Paper is thus a fitting way to open this book. Although it was only one of many episodes in the process, it was perhaps the purest exemplar of what David Post (1998) has called "cyberspace's constitutional moment." The Internet's growth created a need for a new kind of social contract. Its crucial central coordinating functions needed governing arrangements that were both technically robust and capable of winning the support and cooperation of global, diverse, constantly expanding, and often conflicting groups of interested parties. The Internet's structure was so distributed, and the organizations that built it were so diverse and so informal, however, that no single group, not even the U.S. government, possessed the legitimacy and authority to pull it all together on its own. If the IFWP process seemed ramshackle and ad hoc, it was because it had the task of bootstrapping authority on a global scale in an absurdly compressed time span. There was, for precisely this reason, something exhilarating about the IFWP's brief moment. Like the first meetings of the Long Parliament in the English revolution of 1640,[4] the apparent power vacuum produced a heady feeling of self-determination. It encouraged idealistic pronouncements based on first principles. It fostered the illusion that the needed governance arrangements could be designed from scratch. And the IFWP, like the Long Parliament, was ultimately bypassed and superseded by more powerful forces impatient with the transaction costs of an open, democratic process. Yet, by creating expectations of open public participation and private sector consensus the IFWP had a lasting impact on the process.

1.2   The Root

What problem precipitated this constitutional moment? What great issue animated these global negotiations? The object of the controversy was control of a seemingly obscure set of technical functions related to naming and addressing computers on the Internet. Data communication on the Internet takes place by breaking messages into smaller units called packets and routing them from network to network. In order to know where to go, each packet must carry a numerical address, known as an Internet Protocol (IP) address. Every computer connected to the Internet must have a unique IP address. To supplement these numerical addresses, the computers, routers, and other resources connected to the network can be given user-friendly names like *www.yahoo.com,* known as domain names.

Many vital activities on the Internet, such as email or the World Wide Web, use domain names rather than IP numbers as addresses. But for packets to flow across the network, the user-friendly names must be translated into IP addresses. Both kinds of addresses—domain names and IP numbers—are valuable resources, a kind of virtual real estate that can be bought and sold.

It was name and address management that created the controversies that led to the IFWP. The specific set of functions at issue can be summarized as

• The authority to set policy for and to manage the allocation and assignment of Internet Protocol addresses

• The authority to add new names to the top level of the Internet domain name hierarchy

• The responsibility for operating root servers that distribute authoritative information about the content of the top level of the domain name space

These functions are defined more precisely and discussed in greater detail in chapters 2 and 3. Although they may sound uninteresting, they are the technical underpinnings of what the Internet is all about. We tend to speak of the Internet as if it were a *thing*, but in reality the Internet is entirely virtual; it consists of nothing but a software protocol suite known as TCP/IP.[5] The software enables any computer in the world to exchange information with any other computer, regardless of the particular physical networks to which they are attached or the hardware they use. It does this largely by giving computers addresses and names, and providing instructions about how to use them. Consistent and scalable naming and addressing protocols are at the core of TCP/IP's design. The functions enumerated previously are needed to ensure that the names and addresses will be unique. Throughout this book, I refer to that cluster of functions as "the root."[6]

The root is the point of centralization in the Internet's otherwise thoroughly decentralized architecture. The root stands at the top of the hierarchical distribution of responsibility that makes the Internet work. It is the beginning point in a long chain of contracts and cooperation governing how Internet service providers and end users acquire and utilize the addresses and names that make it possible for data packets to find their destinations.

Addresses and names must be globally unique. Ensuring uniqueness in an open, rapidly growing network with millions of users is a coordination problem of some magnitude. The root is the Internet's answer to the problem of coordinating unique identifiers.

The security and stability of the root server system is critical to the viability of any service or function that relies on the Internet. No one disputes the operational significance of the root, and hence no one disputes the need for the formation of permanent, stable organizational arrangements to control—to govern—those functions. But the word *governance* has wider implications.

1.3   Governance

During the debates over the formation of ICANN, an interesting dialogue evolved over the use of the term "Internet governance." To some, "governance" meant the legal and organizational arrangements for management of the root functions. This narrow construction of the term was analogous to the way we use "corporate governance" to refer to the articles and by-laws of an organization, how board members are elected, and so on.

To many others, however, "Internet governance" raised troubling questions. Aside from being a single point of failure, the domain name system (DNS) root is also, potentially, a single point for the surveillance of users and the control of access to cyberspace. The strategic lever of the root, many believed, could be used to enforce public policy and to regulate or control Internet users. "Internet governance" sounded a lot like "a government of the Internet." As David Post (1998) observed,

> If the person or entity controlling the root servers determines that a $1,000 fee (or a certificate of good standing from the California Secretary of State, or a pledge to abide by the laws of Uzbekistan, or a promise not to transmit encrypted messages, or . . .) is required to register a name-number combination and place it in these publicly accessible databases, those who cannot or will not pay the fee, obtain the certificate, or make the required promises, are effectively banished from the global system.

Indeed, the original creators of ICANN always attempted to distance themselves from the term "governance." They preferred to say "technical management." As Esther Dyson put it, ICANN "governs the plumbing, not the people. It has a very limited mandate to administer certain (largely technical) aspects of the Internet infrastructure in general and the Domain Name System in particular."[7]

The White Paper itself utilized *governance* in both senses, referring at one point to the "bottom-up governance that has characterized the development of the Internet to date" (NTIA 1998b, 31749) and claiming at another that "the U.S. government policy applies only to management of Internet names and addresses and does not set out a system of Internet 'governance'" (31743).

The two meanings define the fundamental dilemma of Internet governance: the intersection of technical management and regulatory control. Where does one end and the other begin?

It is clear that technical management decisions have direct and immediate economic consequences. Decisions made by those who control the root profoundly affect the structure of the rapidly growing market for domain name registration. At the beginning of 2001, that market was valued at about US$1.5 billion, and it had doubled annually for the preceding five years. As discussed in later chapters, it was the conflict over who would be assigned the right to register names under new top-level domains that catalyzed much of the global governance debate. It is a question a root manager cannot avoid making decisions about. The economic value of IP addresses is harder to estimate, because end users are not allowed to trade them in a market. (That, of course, is itself a policy decision of some magnitude that straddles the economic and the technical.) But most experts would view addresses as even more valuable assets than domain names. IP addresses are essential inputs into networked services. Their cost and availability will have a major impact on the business plans of telecommunication service providers and equipment manufacturers in the burgeoning digital economy.

The importance of root governance goes well beyond the dollar value of any real or imagined market for names and addresses, however. As unique identifiers, IP addresses can be used to identify and track users. Similarly, domain name registration records directly reveal to the world the name, email address, and physical address of the registrant. The domain name system establishes a mechanism for the identification and surveillance of the denizens of cyberspace. Consider, then, the security and privacy implications of the policies adopted by an Internet naming and addressing authority. Contradicting privacy concerns are demands by some government agencies to use domain name registration data to facilitate identifying and sanctioning Internet users who break the law. A domain name record can, in fact, function very much like an Internet "driver's license." Here is another policy tug of war that cannot be sidestepped by whoever administers the root.

A similar tension hangs over domain name–trademark conflicts. The domain name system allows almost anyone to think of a name, register it (if it is not already taken), and publish it globally. The brand equity of trademark holders often conflicts with the ability of individuals and small businesses to express ideas and achieve visibility in cyberspace. As discussed in later chapters, major intellectual property holders succeeded in linking domain name registration to the adjudication of trademark–domain name disputes. Indeed, they are trying to leverage the root's ability to monitor and police intellectual property in even more ambitious ways.

The assignment of domain names also intersects with content regulation, or what Americans call free-speech or First Amendment questions. Several interest groups and politicians have called for the creation of a *.xxx* top-level domain in order to clearly identify and segregate sexually explicit material. By the same logic, many businesses and consumers have called for a *.kids* domain that would only contain "child-appropriate" content. But if a domain name authority assigns a *.xxx* domain, is it encouraging governments to use their powers to force all sexual material into that domain? If so, who decides what is X-rated on a global basis? If the root administrator gives someone the *.kids* domain, is it taking responsibility that the sites under that label really are suitable for children? More broadly, should a domain name administrator be concerned with the authenticity of the content associated with a specific domain name?

The tendency for policy demands to be placed on the administration of the root cannot be dismissed. And that does not even begin to touch upon the geopolitical questions. For if one concedes that control of the root is economically, technically, and politically important, then one cannot avoid the issue of how that power is distributed among the world's nations, geographic regions, and cultures. Would Americans feel comfortable if the root of the domain name system were located in China? If not, how can they expect the Chinese to be happy about its location in the United States?

The uncomfortable fact is that the two meanings of "Internet governance" are inseparably linked. Centralization of control at the root does create levers for the intrusion of politics, policy, and regulation. If these powers are not to be expanded or abused, the governance structure (in the narrow organizational sense) must be designed to prevent this from happening. There is no way to institutionalize control of the root without confronting the larger governance issues. Investigating the nature of these issues forms the central theme of this book.

1.4   Institutionalization

The tools I use are drawn from institutional economics. Institutional economics looks at the interaction of law, economics, and politics; it examines how societies solve collective action problems by defining property rights and establishing governance arrangements. It is interested in technology insofar as it creates new resources that must be incorporated into legal and institutional regimes, or causes changes in transaction costs or relative prices that lead to a breakdown in a preexisting order.

The root—not specific people or organizations—is the protagonist of this story. The development of internetworking endowed the name and address spaces with enormous social value. The Internet's origins in informal, noncommercial, and relatively nonpolitical research and education organizations, however, placed these valuable resources outside the control of existing institutions. The root was essentially unowned, and its inherently global nature made it difficult for nation-states and traditional international organizations to respond. Consequently, as the Net became public and commercial, it fostered an international struggle over the definition of property rights and governance arrangements. The governance problem could only be solved through the development of new institutional arrangements. This is therefore a case study in institutional innovation, all the more interesting and complex because it happened on an international scale.

Admittedly, *institutionalization* is an ugly and seemingly unexciting word. How much more interesting to talk about the vast amounts of money that can be made from e-commerce or the exciting new capabilities of information technology. But *institutionalization* is the only word that gets to the essence of what happened (and continues to happen) to the Internet from 1996 to 2001.

When we ask who controls the Internet, the response typically takes one of two extremes. The first, favored by many technologists, is to say that no one controls it. The Internet is inherently uncontrollable. Technology is more powerful than governments, traditions, cultures; the Internet "routes around" censorship, and so on. The other extreme is to search for the names of a clique of people or corporations who are said to have overwhelming power to issue authoritative commands. The Internet is run by MCI, or AOL, or the U.S. government. Both responses, I think, miss the point. For any complex sociotechnical system, especially one that touches as many people as the Internet, control takes the form of *institutions,* not commands. Contending parties work out rules and procedures that make their interactions less costly, more stable and predictable. They supplement these rules with organizations that monitor compliance and sanction those who break the rules. In such a process, control is never perfect and no one gets exactly what he wants. But it is false and misleading to say that there is no control, no social constraint. Some parties have more bargaining power than others. Rules are never perfectly fair or neutral; they are always formulated and implemented in ways that favor some types of interests over others. Not everyone has the same amount of resources to devote to monitoring and enforcing their rights. Some people break the rules and get away with it. In short, there are winners and losers in any institutionalization process. And there is always continuing pressure for the modification of the rules in ways that reflect the special interests of various parties. The value of the institutional perspective is precisely that it provides a framework for understanding these kinds of interactions.

1.5 Goals and Plan of the Book

I have three related objectives in writing this book. One is to tell the story of Internet governance objectively and comprehensively, and in the process apply what we know about property rights economics and institutional analysis to the story. Another is to synthesize a technological understanding of DNS and IP addressing with the economic and institutional analysis. This is necessary if we are to understand how technical systems are shaped by political and institutional constraints, and vice versa, and how the development of technical systems can be frozen or diverted into unexpected paths by legal and political pressures. Finally, I want to assess what is really at stake in this matter, to discuss and evaluate contrasting claims about the significance of ICANN and its new regime.

The book is organized into three parts. Part I is framework and background: it analyzes name and number spaces in technical and economic terms, and then elaborates the theories of property rights and institutional change that can be applied to the issue. This part draws on the work of Gary Libecap (1989) on the initial formation of property rights, Elinor Ostrom (1990; 1994) on collective action to resolve common pool problems, and John Richards (1999) on international regimes.

Part II is historical. It traces the growth of the root, the development of property rights conflicts, and the emergence of a new institutional framework to resolve those conflicts. It shows how organized interest groups, particularly intellectual property holders, deliberately reached for control of the root, the centralized point of coordination and control, to impose an order upon the Internet more to their liking. They were joined by an entrenched technical hierarchy that wanted to solidify its role in the management of the Internet and lacked the vision to understand what they were giving up to get it.

Part III explores the stakes and the longer-term policy and social issues posed by the institutionalization of the Internet under ICANN. It characterizes ICANN as a new international regime, one that is likely to become more politicized and to attract more direct and formal participation by governments as it matures. The new regime is analogous to radio broadcasting regulation, in that it uses its exclusive control of a resource to regulate the economic structure of an industry and to sanction various forms of user behavior. Unlike broadcast regulation, however, this is an explicitly global regime and has been placed outside the normal institutional constraints of national governments. The book also explores the World Intellectual Property Organization's attempt to use the ICANN regime to create a new system of global property rights in names.

I

The Root as Resource

2

The Basic Political Economy of Identifiers

Certain aspects of the Internet governance debate are neither new nor unprecedented. We have decades of experience with the coordination of name and number spaces in other media such as the telephone system. Many of the policy and economic issues are analogous. This chapter attempts to put domain names and Internet addresses into a wider context by exploring some of the common economic and political features of address or name space management.

2.1 Uniqueness Requires Coordination

The fundamental starting point is that addresses must be unique. That is what makes it possible for them to guide the movement of data. Unique identifiers allow automated networks, such as telephone systems or the Internet, to distinguish among what may be millions of different parts.[1] The unique values needed by a large-scale public network cannot be created and assigned in a spontaneous and fully decentralized manner. Random or uncoordinated selection of values might lead to the selection of the same names or numbers by different people. Addressing thus requires some kind of coordinated action.

Coordination takes place at two distinct levels. First, a name space or address space representing a range of values must be defined and agreed upon as the basis for the identifiers. Second, individual values within that space must be assigned on an exclusive basis to specific devices or users. The first step in the process—defining the space—is basically a standardization process; it represents an agreement to use a specific architecture.

The second step—assigning values within the space to particular users or devices—is an ongoing responsibility and must be implemented by an organization.

2.2   Defining the Space

Name and number spaces are everywhere in our technology-saturated environment. Bank ATM cards and credit cards all have numbers assigned to them that must be unique within their particular technological system. Postal codes carve up countries into distinct, mutually exclusive regions. Bar codes in grocery stores are assigned to specific products. Books have their own international numbering standard (ISBN). Almost every durable good we buy has a unique serial number that is part of a number space defined by the manufacturer. The rise of the Internet and the digitization of all forms of information have fomented a great deal of research and experimentation on new ways of naming or identifying information content (Green and Bide 1997).

Depending on the technological, economic, and organizational circumstances, defining an address space can be very simple or very complex. Imagine a simple number space that starts with 1 and goes on to infinity. The first applicant would get the number 1, the next would be assigned the number 2, and so on indefinitely. Such a space would work like one of the "take a number" machines at a crowded delicatessen but with an infinitely large roll of tickets. Such an address space architecture makes it easy to assign values but imposes other costs. A few lucky people would get short, memorable, easy-to-use identifiers; those who came later would get increasingly long, unwieldy ones. In this hypothetical system, the identifier assigned to individuals would not yield information that was useful in running a communication network. All it would tell us is the particular sequence in which people received identifiers. It would tell us nothing about where they were located or how they might communicate with other people on the network. It would also make it difficult for computers or other automated methods to process such addresses efficiently, because they would never know exactly how long the number would be.

The hypothetical example is intended to illustrate some of the choices that must be made in defining a name or address space. Should the unique name or address merely *identify* an item, as a serial number does, or should it *locate* the item, as a Web URL (Uniform Resource Locator) or a telephone number does? Or should it try to do both? Should the address space be flat or hierarchical? A flat space may have difficulty adjusting to rapid growth, but a hierarchical space may impose limits on the mobility of the addressed objects and lead to less efficient use of the space. Should the address be purely arbitrary, or should it embed some intuitively accessible information about the object? There are operational advantages and disadvantages either way.

Table 2.1 provides a summary of some common name or address spaces and their basic features.

The structure of an identifier can be compared to a language that the network uses to talk to itself. The switches, routers, or other machinery on a network can "read" it to better handle the movement of information. A telephone number in North America, for example, has a syntax based on geography or function and the switching hierarchy. The number starts with a three-digit area code associated with a geographical region or special function. If the area code is 800, for example, the user knows that it is a toll-free call and the network knows to which database to go to find out how to connect the call. The area code is followed by a three-digit exchange number and a four-digit line number. The structure plays a vital role in telling the network how to route phone calls.

2.3 Assigning Unique Values

Once an address space has been defined, there must also be coordinated procedures for handing out unique values within that space and attaching them to users or objects. This process is known as assignment. Assigning unique values to individual users or machines can be viewed as an act of technical coordination. But it can have an economic and policy dimension as well. Figure 2.1 diagrams the relationship. Three distinct criteria that can be applied to the assignment of unique identifiers are represented as distinct layers. The first criterion is the technical coordination that ensures

Table 2.1
Summary of Common Name/Address Spaces and Their Features

Name	Owner/Root Administrator	Purpose	Capacity	Architecture
E.164	International Telecommunication Union (ITU), Geneva	To coordinate international telephone dialing	~1,110 country codes; permits 1 billion to 1 trillion national numbers per country	Recommends number prefixes for international calls (00) and domestic toll calls (0); assigns unique country codes (1–3 digits); fixes maximum digits for international numbers (15 digits, excl. international prefix)
"Handles" (Digital Object Identifiers)	Corporation for National Research Initiatives (CNRI), Virginia	To provide persistent unique identifiers for digital objects	No design limits on number of prefixes or suffixes	Two-part hierarchy: a prefix assigned by naming authority and a suffix created by user, separated by a slash "/"; separates location from identification to achieve permanent identifiers
Ethernet (EUI-64)	Institute of Electrical and Electronics Engineers (IEEE), Piscataway, New Jersey	To assign unique addresses for Ethernet Network Interface Cards (NICs)	16 million OUIs (Organizational Unique Identifiers); 1 trillion unique values per OUI	Two-part hierarchy: a 24-bit OUI and a 40-bit Ethernet Unique Identifier (EUI)
ISBN (International Standard Book Number)	International ISBN Agency, State Library, Berlin	To make processing and handling of books more efficient for publishers and booksellers	Number of unique IDs available depends on how much space is consumed by higher-level identifiers. Group ID max = 5 digits; publisher ID max = 7 digits; title ID max = 6 digits	10-digit number divided into 4 parts (separated by spaces or dashes) representing codes for group ID, publisher ID, title ID, and a check digit for error control Convertible into optical bar codes

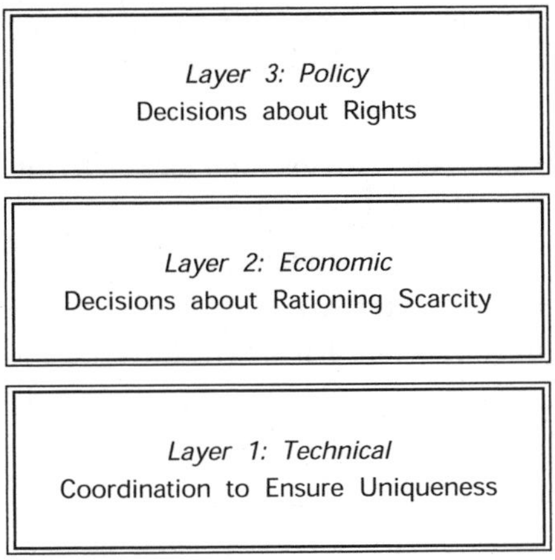

Layer 3: Policy
Decisions about Rights

Layer 2: Economic
Decisions about Rationing Scarcity

Layer 1: Technical
Coordination to Ensure Uniqueness

Figure 2.1
Three-layer model of assignment

the uniqueness of the assignments. The second layer is economic rationing, that is, the imposition of rules or procedures designed to conserve the resource space. The third layer consists of rules or policies defining or adjudicating rights to names.

2.3.1 The Technical Layer

Because of the uniqueness requirement, names and addresses in technological systems are almost always exclusive resources, that is, the assignment of a name or address to one thing necessarily prevents another thing from using the same name or address at the same time. Assignment processes must be organized to maintain this exclusivity. Two or three people cannot be given the same Social Security number without disastrous consequences. Multiple computers on the Internet cannot utilize the same IP address or domain name if they are to communicate reliably with the rest of the Internet. Thus, the assignment process must ensure that the process of giving out addresses or names to users is coordinated to preserve uniqueness and exclusivity.

2.3.2 The Economic Layer

An identifier space is a finite resource; it can be used up if it is not conserved properly. In addition to preserving the exclusivity of assignments, there may be a need to control the distribution of identifiers to make sure that the resource is not wasted. Are there enough to go around? Should prices or administrative methods be used to ration the resource space? These are important decisions that must be made by an assignment authority (or someone else). Let's call this the economic layer.

In many respects, decisions about economic rationing methods could also be considered policy decisions. Because the size of address spaces is fixed for a long time by standardization decisions that are costly to change, it is not easy to determine what conservation principles to use or how stringently they need to be applied. However, an economic rationing policy deals with a restricted set of issues. Machine-readable identifiers such as IP addresses, credit card numbers, or Ethernet addresses can be thought of as an undifferentiated pool—all the assignment authority needs to worry about is whether the supply of identifiers is sufficient to meet the quantity demanded for the foreseeable future.

As our society has become increasingly information- and communication-saturated, virtually all the major public network address spaces have had to be expanded. The size of the Ethernet address space (see section 2.5) is being expanded from 48 bits to 64 bits. Internet addresses are (we hope) being expanded from 32 bits to 128 bits. North America altered the syntax of its telephone number plan to make room for many new area codes.[2] Since 1996 the toll-free number space in North America has been given four new toll-free codes to keep pace with demand.[3] Many countries, including China, have moved to eight-digit local telephone numbers.

Often, the reason for expanding the supply of numbers is not that the available space is fully consumed but that assignment practices delegate large chunks of the space in an inefficient manner. U.S. telephone numbers provide a prime example of inefficient assignment practices. The United States was forced to add 119 new area codes between 1995 and 1999 despite the fact that only 5 percent of the 6.4 billion unique numbers supported by the numbering plan were actually assigned. The problem was that numbers were assigned to the telephone companies' geographic subdivisions in groups with a minimum size of 10,000, even when the areas had only a thousand or so telephone lines. Thus, it is difficult for most assignment authorities to avoid using economic criteria in their practices.

2.3.3 The Policy Layer

Assignment procedures may be designed to solve policy problems as well as economic and technical problems. If the identifiers are semantically meaningful, an assignment authority may need to make policy decisions about how to resolve competing claims for the same assignment.

The economics of assignment are profoundly affected by who uses the identifier: is it people or machines? As noted before, machine-readable identifiers such as IP addresses, credit card numbers, or Ethernet addresses are an undifferentiated pool. But when people directly interact with identifiers and when the values identifiers take can be meaningful, the market dynamics become far more complex. It is no longer just the quantity of identifiers but their *quality* that dominates the assignment process.

Think of the difference between two Internet domain names, *df5k67tlh.com* and *music.com*. Both are perfectly functional as Web site addresses, but the semantic features of the latter make it far more desirable. People will pay significant sums of money for vanity license plates on their cars. Businesses will sue each other over toll-free telephone numbers that spell words. Households prefer local telephone numbers that are easy to remember. In Hong Kong the Telecommunications Authority holds auctions for local phone numbers that contain lucky numbers. Domain names in the dot-com space based on common words have changed hands for millions of dollars. Semantics can produce huge variations in the economic value of different identifiers in the same space.

Meaning totally subverts the homogeneity of an address space. No two words or symbols mean exactly the same thing. Hence, no two identifiers are perfectly good substitutes for each other in an economic sense. Furthermore, meaning itself varies with the eye of the beholder. The domain name *df5k67tlh.com* does not seem very valuable, but this assumes that your company's name is not df5k67tlh or that df5-k67-tlh isn't the name of a new wonder drug or a leading rock band. Any apparently meaningless string of characters can become meaningful to some people or acquire secondary meaning through its association with something.

If identifiers are both public and meaningful, legal and policy issues surrounding consumer confusion, fraud, intellectual property, and freedom of speech cannot be avoided. Disputes over who "deserves" a name or who has a legal right to use it will arise. If you have registered the toll-free telephone number 1-800-COLLECT, and a new toll-free code, 888, is introduced, do you have a "right" to 1-888-COLLECT or should someone else be allowed to get it? Would the coexistence of these two numbers confuse customers? Similar issues arise in domain names. Is it legitimate for someone who is not French to register *france.com* or to run a top-level domain *.france*? Even if we agree that the domain should be limited to the French, how does the assignment authority decide which French organization or person "deserves" the name?

Or perhaps the technical coordinating body should not be involved in such decisions at all? In the toll-free number space, the U.S. Federal Communications Commission (FCC) decided *not* to impose trademark protection criteria on the assignments under new toll-free codes, instead leaving such protection to litigation under trademark law.[4]

A few technologists have proposed to solve the policy problems created by semantics by eliminating the meaningfulness of the identifiers. For example, proposals to replace meaningful, memorable Internet domain names with meaningless character strings occasionally are put forward in the domain name debate (Vixie 1995). Such "solutions" are attempts to avoid rather than to cope with the problem. People get involved in business and legal disputes over names because their meaning makes them valuable as identifiers. Eliminating the meaning eliminates the basis for disputes, true, but it also eliminates most of their value. It is like proposing to cure a headache by cutting off one's head.

2.3.4 Portability and Switching Costs

We have seen how the value of an address assignment can be affected by two economic factors: the scarcity of available unique values and the semantic features of a name or number. I now turn to a third economic factor, almost as important as semantics: the equity a user might have built up in a particular identifier. By *equity* I mean the investment a user makes in associating her business or organization with a particular public identifier.

Equity, like semantics, is only an issue when the address is part of the human interface. A business's telephone number or Internet domain name may appear on official stationery, business cards, and in directories or Web site links. Equally important, the name or number will be mentally associated with the business or become a part of the personal records of customers and other contacts. This association is economically valuable and tends to accumulate over time. A user who changes or loses an identifier may sacrifice some of that equity or put it at risk. Most of the money put into publicizing an identifier is a sunk cost; it cannot be recovered.

If an identifier is controlled by a service provider, users who want to change service providers will not only risk losing some or all of the equity in the old identifier; they will also have to promote the new address and compensate for temporary confusion and misdirection among their contacts. These are known as switching costs in economics (Shapiro and Varian, 1998). Switching costs may act as a deterrent to competition by making it more difficult for customers to switch service providers.[5]

Regulators and policymakers have tried to minimize consumer switching costs by promoting the portability of address assignments across service providers. Various forms of number portability are now being implemented in the telecommunication industry around the world (ITU 1999). Toll-free telephone service in North America was the pioneer of number portability.[6] Portability is not an absolute but a quality that is achieved in various degrees. Addresses can be portable across service providers but not across different geographic regions (e.g., you cannot use a North American toll-free number in Europe). Internet domain names have always been portable in the sense that the telecom industry is trying to achieve. That is, the addresses have always been entirely software-based, and assignments have been performed independently of the services provided by infrastructure providers. However, many consumers of Internet services get their domain names from Internet service providers (ISPs) instead of registering them themselves. In those cases, end users are burdened with major switching costs if they attempt to change ISPs. Every time they change their ISP, they must alter their email address, and notify friends and business associates.

2.3.5 Rationing Methods

How then does an assignment authority distribute identifier resources? The economic techniques that can be used to assign identifiers are the same as those that can be used to ration any resource. The economic literature on this issue is vast, but it is rarely applied specifically to name and address assignment, so it makes sense to recount the techniques here.

First-Come/First-Served One common rationing method is first-come/first-served: whoever gets there first can grab whatever he likes. That may seem unfair and inefficient, but it has the advantage of extremely low transaction costs. No one has to monitor behavior or enforce any rules (other than the exclusivity requirement, of course). Thus, first-come/first-served is a rational way to govern access to abundant, relatively low-value resources, such as parking positions in a suburban shopping mall or domain names back when the Internet was small and noncommercial. First-come/first-served is much less problematical when the assignments are homogeneous, that is, when they have no semantic properties. Lawsuits over which organization receives a particular Ethernet identifier are unlikely.

Administrative Fees Administrative fees are another form of rationing. They are charges for identifier assignments imposed on a periodic or one-time basis. The fee amount is basically arbitrary but is used by an assignment authority to discourage those who might consume too much if the assignments were free. The fees may also be used to support the operations of the assignment organization. First-come/first-served methods can be and often are combined with administrative fees.

Market Pricing Market pricing is another common rationing method. Auctions can be used in the initial assignment as a method of resolving contention for resources and to allow the price paid for the assignment to reflect its true scarcity value. A full-fledged market pricing regime goes beyond auctions and allows assignments or entire blocks of the identifier space to be owned and traded. This requires private ownership of parts of the resource space and the freedom of owners to trade those portions in a market. Trading allows the price of the resource to reflect continual variations in supply and demand, thereby creating incentives to use the resource efficiently. Higher (or lower) prices will not only encourage users to find ways to limit (or expand) their consumption but also induce those who might otherwise hoard assignments to release them when the price is right. The transaction costs of creating a market are much higher, but the efficiency characteristics are much better.

Administrative Rules   Some assignment authorities will use administrative rules rather than markets to ration scarce number or name assignments. The use of administrative rationing criteria is easier for an assignment authority to implement and more controllable than a market, but it is less able to reflect and adjust to actual supply and demand conditions. As an example, applicants for address block assignments might submit information documenting their "need" for the assignments, and the assignment authority will evaluate that need. This assessment may be guided by simple administrative rules of thumb or by more complex criteria. At best, administrative rules are a low-transaction cost method of conserving a resource. At worst, they create a growing disconnection between the assignment authority and the actual needs and conditions of users. Some country domain name registrars, for example, imposed a rule that only one domain name should be assigned to an organization. That rule made life easy for the domain administrator but was very frustrating to domain name consumers and completely out of touch with the way domain names have come to be used on the Internet.

Merit Distribution   Yet another rationing method is merit distribution. Merit-based assignments occur when the authority in control of the space takes it upon itself to base its assignments upon some extrinsic standard of worthiness. Merit assignment can be considered an extension of the administrative rules method. The authority reviews applicants and decides which ones will best fulfill some policy objective. Procedurally, it is a relatively costly method. It requires extensive documentation to accompany an application for an assignment. Competing, mutually exclusive applications may go through quasi-judicial hearings or be put before the public for comment and criticism. Determinations are more discretionary. The process is often referred to disparagingly as "beauty contests." Merit assignments were used by the FCC to assign local broadcasting licenses, and are used by localities to award cable television franchises. Regardless of the efficiency or desirability of merit-based assignment, political reality dictates that it is likely to be used when there are severe constraints on the supply of assignments. If there were only ten telephone numbers to be awarded in the entire world, for example, the process of deciding who got them would be intensely political. Political lobbying and jockeying for influence would almost certainly push the assignment authority into imposing some merit criteria on the awards.

2.4   Governance Arrangements

Assignment requires an ongoing organizational apparatus. Decisions must be made, the organization's full-time staff must be supported, and policies must be defined. This raises all the familiar governance issues: How should that organization be controlled and held accountable? Should it be private or public, profit or nonprofit, regulated or unregulated? Where will its money come from? There is no common pattern, but there is a marked difference between the ways the telecommunication world and the computer/Internet world have approached the governance arrangements surrounding identifier resources.

Traditionally, telephone number spaces were controlled by national post, telephone, and telegraph monopolies. As liberalization of the telecommunication industry introduces multiple telephone companies into most countries, the trend is to take control of the number space away from the telephone companies and make it a "national resource" under the administration of national regulators (ITU 1999). The purpose of nationalization is to equalize competition between incumbent telephone companies and new competitors. National regulators try to achieve numbering parity among the competitors and ensure that all competitors who enter the market have equal access to number blocks, without which they cannot function. Although frequently the actual administration of the number space will be delegated to industry-run self-regulatory agencies, such as the Association for Telecommunications Industry Solutions (ATIS) in the United States, the policies they must follow are defined by law and extensively regulated by public authorities.

There is a different tradition in data communication. Identifier spaces tend to be administered by private sector nonprofit standards organizations, such as the Institute of Electrical and Electronics Engineers (IEEE), the Internet Engineering Task Force (IETF), the World Wide Web consortium, or the regional address registries of the Internet. The policies of these organizations mostly are not subject to specific national laws and regulations regarding identifier policy. Furthermore, the data world tends to operate on a global basis. In the voice communication world, global coordination of numbering was conducted by a specialized international organization, the International Telecommunication Union (ITU). The ITU achieved global compatibility in a bottom-up fashion, interconnecting the otherwise incompatible number spaces of different nation-states by adding higher levels of hierarchy to the number space (e.g., country codes and special signals for international gateways) (Rutkowski 2001). The Internet and the Ethernet, on the other hand, started with a global address and name space; coordination was achieved top-down, through international acceptance of the same address space. Their standards have no territorial dimension.

2.5 An Example: The Ethernet Address Space

Thus far we have looked at the political economy of identifiers in the abstract, with a few examples thrown in for illustration. It might be helpful at this point to discuss a specific example in more detail. Most local area networks use what are commonly called Ethernet addresses. Compared to the political drama surrounding Internet names and numbers, Ethernet addressing has thrived in obscurity. Officially, Ethernet addresses are called Ethernet Unique Identifiers (EUIs).[7] These addresses are burned into the network interface hardware during manufacture.

Ethernet was a standard formalized by the IEEE's 802 Committee, so it is the IEEE that "owns" the Ethernet address space and takes responsibility for managing it. EUI addresses are divided into two parts. The first, 24-bit part is an Organizational Unique Identifier (OUI), a distinct code given to a manufacturer of the hardware in which the Ethernet address will be embedded. The second part is the 40-bit extension (24 bits in the older number space) that is assigned to a particular piece of hardware by the manufacturer. Address blocks are assigned to network component manufacturers by a one-person Registration Authority within the IEEE. The IEEE Registration Authority controls only the assignment of the company identification numbers. It imposes a one-time charge of US$1,250 for the OUI assignment. Once a company receives its own 24-bit identifier, it assigns the remaining 40 bits (or 24 bits in the older space) to hardware components. The full Ethernet address is thus formed from the concatenation of the unique company ID and the company-assigned value. It is a simple, two-part hierarchy.

The older, 48-bit Ethernet addresses gave manufacturers 16 million unique addresses for every organizational identifying number they received. The new EUI-64 space will give them 1 trillion (10^{12}) unique addresses. As a simple conservation rule, the IEEE Registration Authority requires that organizations must have used up at least 90 percent of the available numbers under an existing OUI before they will be assigned another one: "It is incumbent upon the manufacturer to ensure that large portions of the unique word block are not left unused in manufacturing."[8] IEEE does not explain how this rule is monitored and enforced.

The Registration Authority imposes few restrictions on the redistribution of EUI-64 values by third parties. The two most significant restrictions are that only one address value can be assigned to a physical component, and organizations that received OUIs must indemnify IEEE against any damages arising from duplicate number assignments. Other than that, anything goes.

The Ethernet addressing scheme is an organizationally lightweight, technically focused form of address management. The costs associated with using the address space are very low and nonrecurring. Policy for the Registration Authority is set by a Registration Authority Committee composed of about a dozen people, mostly delegates of manufacturers, within the IEEE's 802 Committee. The policy component attached to the assignment of numbers is minimal. Assignment policies are not designed to regulate the market for networking products or to control the behavior of users; they are driven entirely by the need to conserve identifiers, to properly identify the source and type of addresses, and to indemnify the assignment organization against ancillary damages.

Why is Ethernet addressing so uncomplicated? Because there is no human interface. Ethernet addresses are an undifferentiated lot of meaningless numbers. No manufacturer and no individual consumer of a Network Interface Card cares which particular numerical value is on it as long as it is unique. OUIs are addresses of and for machines. Along with this total absence of any human interface goes a near-total absence of politics.

2.6   Review of the Framework

The previous discussion was meant to identify a basic analytical framework for identifier resources. The coordination of unique identifiers takes places at two distinct levels: once when the address space is defined and then on an ongoing basis as specific values within the space are assigned to users. The assignment methods used by an organization can perform three essential tasks:

• Maintain the uniqueness of identifiers by making sure that assignments are exclusive (the technical layer)

• Prevent the resource from being consumed in an inefficient manner (the economic layer)

• In some cases, resolve competition or disputes around particular assignments (the policy layer)

The discussion introduced an important distinction between identifiers that are publicly visible and meaningful and those that are not. The combination of public visibility and semantics makes the policy layer decisions potentially contentious. It also allows end users to acquire equity in the name or address, raising issues of portability and switching costs. Various methods that assignment authorities might use to perform economic or policy functions were surveyed, briefly noting some general performance characteristics of each. Finally, some basic features of the governance arrangements that have been used to control assignment organizations were presented.

In subsequent chapters, the comparative framework will clarify two key questions in Internet governance: What was it about the process of assigning unique values to Internet identifiers that created a major global controversy? and Why did the organizational responsibility for the assignment process become such a ferocious point of contention?

3

The Internet Name and Address Spaces

As far as this book is concerned, the interesting questions about the Internet's name and address spaces are economic and political. How much real control over the Internet and its users does management of the root yield? Is the root a source of power that can be seized and exploited for political or economic gain, or is its unique status a product of consensus and cooperation that would vanish the moment anyone tried to use it for such purposes? Are there important reasons for nation-states to worry about who controls the root? These questions are central to the Internet governance controversy. But any attempt to answer them leads to more specific questions about how the Internet works:

• How costly and technically difficult would it be to start an alternative, competing domain name system (DNS) root? Can the root of the DNS be easily bypassed, or are there economic factors that lock us into a single supplier? What would be the economic and technical consequences of an attempt to bypass it?

• Is a single, centralized root under the control of a single body technically necessary, or can this function be decentralized and distributed without sacrificing effective coordination?

• How robust is the root? Is its status as the global nexus for computer interconnection so fragile that its management must be carefully sheltered from any disruptive influences, perhaps by being placed in the hands of a technical priesthood or government supervisors? Or is the Internet's architecture so flexible and distributed that failures in a few locations can be easily routed around?

• How are domain names and Internet Protocol (IP) addresses related to each other in the Internet's operation? Do domain name assignment and IP address allocation need to be handled by the same organization?

To proceed along these lines we must know more about naming and addressing protocols on the Internet. This chapter describes in some detail IP addresses, the DNS, and the way they interact. The description of their technical structure is mostly abstracted from the organizations that implement them; later chapters fill in the organizational and historical dimensions. The purpose of this chapter is to establish the technical vocabulary needed to engage in an informed discussion of the political economy of the root.

Throughout this chapter I will refer to "RFCs." The Request for Comment (RFC) series archives and codifies Internet protocols and standards. It is the permanent document repository of the Internet Engineering Task Force. Begun informally in 1969 when Steve Crocker of ARPANET circulated a document that he wanted others to comment on, it now constitutes the official publication channel for Internet standards and other statements by the Internet research and engineering community (including the occasional poem and humorous spoof). Draft RFCs go through a review process supervised by the RFC Editor and the Internet Engineering Task Force's governing hierarchy. Officially adopted RFCs are numbered and are available free of charge to anyone via the Internet. A number of sites on the Internet contain complete collections of the RFC series, including <http://www.rfc-editor.org> and <http://community.roxen.com/developers/idocs/rfc/>.

3.1   The Internet Address Space

Internet Protocol breaks data transmissions into smaller chunks called packets. Communication takes place by forwarding these packets from one network to another. Every time it creates a data packet, Internet Protocol attaches a header with the IP address of the source and the destination. Thus, IP addresses are completely virtual, software-based identifiers. To the network, they are a string of thirty-two 1s and 0s, but people commonly represent them as four numbers from 0 to 255 separated by dots;

for example, 128.28.10.248. With 32 bits available, the IP address space yields a theoretical maximum of about 4.3 billion unique numbers.

The classical IP address has two basic parts. The first encodes a network to which a computer is attached; the second identifies a specific device attached to that network. The first part is often referred to as the network prefix, the second part as the host ID, where *host* refers to a computer or some other connected device. As in Ethernet addressing, the two-part structure helps to distribute the responsibility for address assignment. The central authority for IP addresses only needs to hand out network prefixes; the recipients then perform the task of assigning host IDs on their own networks. The original IP addressing structure defined three primary classes of address assignments, with the classes based on the number of bits used by the network prefix.[1]

3.1.1   Routers and IP Addresses

Unlike telephone numbers or postal addresses, IP addresses are completely independent of geography. The address structure itself tells you nothing about where the addressed host is actually located, nor does it tell a packet how to find its destination from its starting point. Internetworking requires additional protocols capable of telling packets how to get from point A to point B. There must, in other words, be some way to use the software address to find a specific physical network in a specific location.

That task is performed by routers. Routers are specialized computers connected to two or more physical networks and programmed to make decisions about how to forward data packets to their destinations. Packets work their way across the Internet by jumping from router to router—what networkers call "hops." To choose a path for data packets, routers refer to tables that correlate the network prefix of the packet's destination with the IP address of the next hop, the next router along the path to that destination. These routing tables can be described as a road map of cyberspace from the point of view of a particular router (figure 3.1). Every network prefix known to a router is associated with pathways through which it can be reached and the number of hops from router to router it takes to get there. The two-part structure of IP addresses is intended to make the routing of packets more efficient. Routing tables only need to contain network prefixes; they can make decisions about how to forward packets

Network	Via Node	Via Port	Type	Age	
0.0.0.0	140.248.192.1	Network	Indirect	00:00:00	
140.240.0.0	140.248.241.201	Network	Indirect	00:00:02	
140.246.0.0	140.248.128.20	Network	Indirect	00:00:01	
140.247.0.0	140.248.128.20	Network	Indirect	00:00:01	
140.248.0.0	140.248.140.241	Network	Direct	00:00:00	
192.168.19.0	140.248.128.20	Network	Indirect	00:00:01	

For Help, press F1   NUM

Figure 3.1
A routing table

without the full address. Routers need to know the full IP address only of hosts on their own local network and of a few neighboring routers.

Every time a new network address is added to the Internet, the potential size of the routing tables increases. Furthermore, routers must constantly communicate with each other to update their routing tables as new networks are added and communication links or networks go down, return to service, or are renumbered. If routing tables become too long and complex, the performance of the Internet as a whole will deteriorate. By now it should be evident that the assignment of IP addresses is constrained not only by the limits on the number of addresses available but by the capacity of routers as well. Two important conclusions follow from this.

First, the primary users of IP addresses are routers, not people. The only people who see them are the technicians working for Internet service providers (ISPs) and enterprise networks who must divide the address blocks into subnets, assign unique addresses to individual computers, and configure local hosts and routing tables. Because the addresses are invisible to people, no one imputes any economic value to the specific numbers. All they care about is whether their address block is of sufficient size to give unique identifiers to all hosts on their network, and whether the routing tables make their network visible to the rest of the global Internet.

Second, while the specific number itself is a matter of indifference, the place of an address in routing tables matters a lot. An IP address has no value unless its network prefix appears somewhere in the routing tables. A network prefix that appears in the core of the Internet—directly in the tables of the backbone routers—is more valuable than one that appears in the periphery. The reason is the speed of connection. Networks listed in the core will have better performance because packets make fewer hops to find them. Access to and placement within the routing tables is a resource every bit as valuable as the IP addresses themselves.

3.1.2 Registration

If assignments of IP addresses (actually, network prefixes) are to be exclusive, someone must keep track of which address blocks are assigned and which are unoccupied. This implies a registration process and the maintenance of a database that keeps authoritative, current records about which blocks have been doled out to which organization and which are free for assignment. That function is performed by Internet address registries (IRs). The basic structure and policies of IRs are described in RFC 2050 (November 1996). In this chapter, I set aside discussion of organizational and governance arrangements and concentrate on describing the functions of IRs.

Internet address registries are responsible for assigning address space. They stand at the second level of a hierarchy of address delegation that begins with ICANN and goes down through major ISPs and end users. IRs run publicly accessible databases that document to whom address blocks have been assigned. They also define policies for distributing addresses. The policies are designed to conserve the address space and control the size of the routing tables. Address registrations can help in the process of solving operational problems, and in fact that was their original intent. If a failure or problem traceable to a specific host or network occurs, contact information about the organization using the addresses can be helpful. As addresses in the original IPv4 address space become scarcer, however, Internet registries have increasingly used the leverage of the registration record to facilitate rationing and policy enforcement. When a company applies for additional addresses, registration authorities can check to see how many addresses have been allocated to it already and can verify whether the current allocation has been fully utilized. Furthermore, registration serves as an important check on the ability to trade or arbitrage address allocations. Companies with excess address space could auction off their surplus to those with a shortage. This practice, for better or worse, is strongly discouraged by the Internet addressing authorities. The only real leverage they have to enforce an antitransfer policy, however, is that the transferred addresses will still show up in the records of the address registries as being assigned to the original owner. Many Internet service providers will not insert address blocks into their routing tables unless the organization listed in the address registry record corresponds to the organization they are routing to. So the address registration, coupled with the router bottleneck, becomes a policy enforcement mechanism.

3.1.3   Adjustments in IP Addressing

The classical IP addressing and routing structure described in the previous section has gone through major changes since it was formally specified in 1981 (RFC 790). It is easy to forget that the address space architecture emerged from the era of mainframes and predated the personal computer. The Internet's designers never expected the Internet to grow as large as it did. By 1991 it became evident that if something didn't change, the 32-bit IPv4 address space would be used up and the growth of the Internet would come to a screeching halt. There were two fundamental problems. Class-based addressing had created structural inefficiencies by restricting assignments to address chunks of three predetermined sizes.[2] Only 3 percent of assigned addresses were actually being used, yet projections suggested that the rate of address assignments would exhaust the unassigned number space by 1996 or so. The growth of routing tables was also setting off alarms. Studies done in 1993 indicated that the size of Internet backbone routing tables was growing at 1.5 times the improvement rate in memory technology. The projected size of the routing tables would have exceeded the capacity of router technology by 1994 (RFC 1752).

The response to the Internet addressing crisis took three forms:

- Tightened assignment policies
- Development of new protocols to make address utilization more efficient and to reduce the size of routing tables
- Creation of a new, larger address space (IPv6)

3.1.3.1   More Restrictive Assignment   Early assignment procedures were based entirely on the first-come/first-served principle. Allocations of gigantic class A address blocks were free, and given away on request rather "hops" are like train steps

than on the basis of any demonstrated need. As an address shortage loomed, the Internet community responded by implementing administrative rationing rules and later by imposing administrative fees. Organizations requesting address space were required to document their needs. Between 1994 and 1996 there was even some discussion of implementing auctions or full-fledged markets for address blocks, although these proposals were never implemented (Huston 1994; Rekhter, Resnick, and Bellovin 1997). Later, the assignment authorities began to charge annual fees for address blocks of various sizes.

3.1.3.2 Route Aggregation and CIDR Even more significant than the tightened assignment practices was the development of new protocols to make more efficient use of the address space and to curb the growth of routing tables. These changes started as early as the mid-1980s with the introduction of subnetting,[3] but most took place between 1991 and 1996.

In 1993 a new routing standard called classless inter-domain routing (CIDR) was created to make more efficient use of the available IP address space.[4] CIDR eliminated class-based address assignments. Instead of three fixed sizes of address block assignments, CIDR allowed network prefixes to be anywhere from 13 to 27 bits. This allowed the assignment of address blocks to be more closely matched to an organization's real requirements. CIDR also supported hierarchical route aggregation. Route aggregation is the practice of forwarding all packets with the same network prefix to the same next hop, allowing a router to maintain just one entry in its table for a large number of routes. Hierarchical route aggregation applies this method recursively to create larger and larger address blocks out of shorter and shorter network prefixes.

CIDR implementation led to an important shift in the economic structure of IP address assignment. In order to promote route aggregation, the Internet technical community needed to align the assignment of address blocks with the connection topology. As Hofmann (1998) observed, this led to an interesting debate over how to define the Internet's geography—would it be based on political territories or on Internet service providers? The provider-based model won. Usually, a service provider's network will be a topologically cohesive entity, which means that a single routing table entry can be used for all hosts served by that provider. The push for route aggregation led to a more hierarchical approach to address assignment. The central Internet addressing authorities would assign large blocks of numbers to the larger commercial ISPs. The larger ISPs would then allow end users to use parts of the assignment, but the ISP retained control of the assignment. In other words, addresses were loaned, not assigned, to end users such as business networks, organizations, and smaller ISPs. IP addresses were no longer portable across Internet service providers. End users who changed their service provider would have to renumber their networks—a costly and labor-intensive process. The change raised other concerns. As one Internet veteran put it, "Route aggregation tied to topology based allocation, although necessary . . . is leading us down a path in which today's arteries of packet flow are being hardened, deeply entrenching the current shape of the Internet."[5] The practice had tremendous success, however, at reducing the growth of the routing tables to manageable proportions.

3.1.3.3   Creation of a Larger Address Space   CIDR and related adjustments were originally perceived as stopgap measures to buy time for more fundamental changes. In 1992 the Internet Engineering Task Force (IETF) formed the Internet Protocol next generation (IPng) working group to develop a new Internet Protocol with an enlarged number space. The final specifications for IPv6, as IPng is now officially called, were adopted in mid-1995. Software implementations began in 1996. Portions of the IPv6 address space were delegated by IETF to address registries in 1999. IPv6 is designed to be an evolutionary step from the older Internet Protocol. It can be installed as a software upgrade in Internet devices and is compatible with the older version of IP.

The IPv6 address space is 128 bits, which allows for nearly 10^{39} unique numbers. That number is, as one writer put it, "so big we don't really have a convenient name for it—call it a million quadrillion quadrillion. This is many more than the number of nanoseconds since the universe began (somewhere around 10^{26}), or the number of inches to the farthest quasar (about 10^{27})."[6] Ironically, however, the measures taken to preserve the older IP address space have been so successful that the transition to IPv6 is taking place more slowly than anticipated. Dynamic address assignment, which allows addresses to be shared, and network address translators

(NATs), which allow entire organizations to hide behind a few addresses, are having a major impact. Some analysts insist that the widespread adoption and deployment of IPv6 is not a foregone conclusion.

To wrap up, between 1991 and 1996 the IETF developed a significant number of new standards that dramatically extended the life of the original IPv4 address space. It also developed an entirely new Internet Protocol with an enlarged address space. Most of this activity took place while the Internet was being commercialized and was exploding in size—a pretty remarkable record of achievement. The most interesting thing about these changes from the viewpoint of this book, however, is that they were defined and implemented entirely within the Internet technical community's established institutional framework. Major resource constraints, technological adjustments, and large shifts in the incidence of costs and benefits did *not* spark a visible political crisis of the sort that led to the White Paper and ICANN. The adjustments did bring with them some quiet evolution in the relevant institutions (mainly the formation of regional address registries), but it did not catalyze institutional innovations. This development will be explored in later chapters, when organizational and historical aspects of the story are considered.

3.2   The Internet Name Space

Domain names are higher-level identifiers used by computers on the Internet. They consist of hierarchically organized character strings separated by dots, such as *mail.users.yahoo.com*. Domain names are not used by routers to move packets; thus, the Internet could make do without them altogether. Why give names to computers at all, then? There are two reasons.

3.2.1   Naming Computers

The first reason for naming computers is simply mnemonics. As long as there is a direct interface between human beings and the devices attached to a network, devices will be given names that are recognizable to humans. The presence of some semantic content in identifiers makes them easier to type in, easier to distinguish, and easier to remember. It also facilitates the use of naming conventions, which can make the administration of a network more orderly. Names can, for example, reflect categories or hierarchies based on geographic regions (*europe.company.com*), functions (*router2.company.com*), or organizational units (*accounting.company.com*).

The second reason for naming computers is to provide a single, more stable identifier. The IP addresses assigned to groups of computers are determined by the topology and routing practices of a network. Both tend to change relatively frequently as networks grow, shrink, or are reorganized. If a company's network outgrows its IP address block or changes its ISPs, its hosts will have to be totally renumbered. A change in the identifier of a computer connected to a network could wreak havoc on connectivity if thousands of internal and external users have stored the old address in their routers or browsers or email address books. If domain names are used instead of IP addresses, however, the network only needs to change the mapping from the name to a new address. The change can be implemented seamlessly without disrupting users, without even requiring their participation. Also, some computers, known as multihomed hosts, have more than one IP address. Naming allows multiple addresses to be encompassed by a single identifier.

The second rationale for naming does not require that the names have any meaning. But as long as human beings are the ones defining and using the names, there is no reason not to take advantage of semantic features.

3.2.2 Names, Assignment, and Resolution

A price must be paid for the advantages of names. Their use creates the need for another assignment process; someone (or some process) must coordinate the names used on the network to ensure that each one is unique. Also, packets still have to use IP addresses, not names, to find their way across the Internet. So once names are superimposed over a device's real address, some process must match the names to addresses. In essence, one needs the equivalent of an automatic telephone directory that will look up the number for any given name. The process of mapping names to addresses is called resolving names, or resolution.

In the earliest days of the Internet, all applications for names went to a single, central authority known as the Network Information Center (NIC). The NIC accepted applications for names, weeded out duplications to ensure uniqueness, and put the names into a list called *hosts.txt*. The *hosts.txt* file served as a global directory for mapping names to IP addresses. All networks downloaded their own copy and used it to resolve names locally. But the Internet only connected a few hundred computers at that time, and its simple, flat name space could not scale up as the Internet grew. Each name of each machine had to be approved individually by a remote central organization. Every change in a name-to-address mapping in any part of the network had to be communicated to the central authority, entered into *hosts.txt,* and then downloaded by every other computer on the network. The larger the network became, the greater the likelihood that users would apply for the same name and hence the harder it became to assign unique names. The list itself became larger and larger, and the process of creating and distributing it consumed more and more resources. The list itself represented a single point of failure.

3.2.3   The Domain Name System

DNS was developed as a way to break out of the bottleneck created by *hosts.txt* and to prepare the way for unlimited increases in the scale of name assignment and resolution. Although its implementation is complex, the concept behind it is simple. The name space was divided up into a hierarchy. The responsibility for assigning unique names, and for maintaining databases capable of mapping the names to specific IP addresses, was distributed down the levels of the hierarchy. The DNS is a just a database—a protocol for storing and retrieving information that has been formatted in a specific way. The complex and interesting thing about the DNS database, however, is that it is highly distributed. Responsibility for entering, updating, and serving up data on request is assumed by tens of thousands of independently operated computers. Yet, through client-server interactions, any computer on the Internet can find the information it needs to map any name to its correct IP address. Robustness and performance improvements are achieved by replication and caching of the information (Albitz and Liu 2001, 4).

As a distributed database protocol, DNS consists of four basic elements: a hierarchical name space, name servers, resolvers, and resource records. DNS partitions the *name space* into a hierarchy or tree structure (figure 3.2). When the domain name is written out, the top of the hierarchy is at the right and each segment of the naming hierarchy is separated by dots.

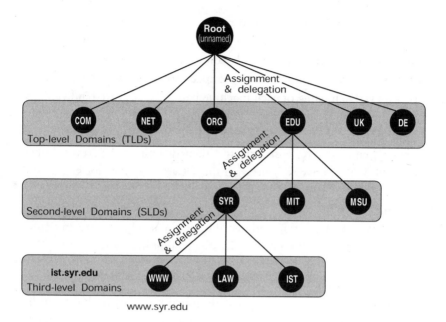

Figure 3.2
A hierarchical name space

At the top of the hierarchy there is an unnamed root. The authority in charge of the root assigns unique top-level domain names such as *.com* or *.uk* to an organization. That organization gains the exclusive authority to coordinate the assignment of second-level domain names under that top-level domain. The registrant of a second-level domain (such as *aol.com*) in turn has the exclusive authority to assign unique third-level domain names (*users.aol.com*) to users, organizations, or hosts under that second-level domain. And so on down the hierarchy. The protocol places certain limits on what characters can be used as names, and on the size of the character strings.[7]

The DNS name space provides a virtually inexhaustible supply of unique addresses. A domain name label (the string of text identifying a specific level of the hierarchy) can be up to 63 characters long. With 37 different characters available to use, the number of possible names is close to 37^{63}— an inconceivably large number.[8] Multiply that times the 127 levels of hierarchy possible under DNS and the vastness of the name space is evident.

Currently, there are 257 top-level domain (TLD) names listed in the root directory. Of these, 243 are two-letter country codes drawn from an international standard.[9] There are also seven three-letter suffixes originally defined to serve as a rough taxonomy of the types of users (*.com, .net, .org, .mil, .edu, .int,* and *.gov*). Both types of TLD were defined in an Internet standards document in 1984. Seven new generic top-level names were created by ICANN in 2001 (see chapter 9). The limits on the number and type of top-level domain names, however, are *social,* not technical. The top level is just another level of the DNS hierarchy and in principle could contain as many names as any other level.

Each organization that is assigned a domain name must provide *name servers* to support the domain. Name servers are computers that store lists of domain names and associated IP addresses (and other pertinent data) about a subset of the name space. Those subsets are called zones (figure 3.3). Every name server below the root must know the IP address of at least one root server, and it contacts a root server when it is first turned on. At least ninety percent of name servers run an open-source software called BIND to implement their name service.[10]

Resolvers are software programs that generate queries that extract information from a name server. They reside in the end user's computer and act as the client side of the client-server interaction. The software forms a domain name query that contains the name to be resolved and the type of answer desired. It then sends the query to a name server for resolution. A resolver must know how to contact at least one name server.

Resource records (figure 3.4) are the data or content stored in name servers. Zone files are the complete and authoritative resource records for a domain. The most commonly used resource record is the A (address) record, which matches domain names to IP addresses. There are several other resource record types, however, allowing DNS queries to return additional information. Resource records contain information about who is the authoritative source of information for a domain, how current is the copy of a zone file being used, and other important administrative information. As Steve Atkins put it, "DNS can do a lot of things besides name to address mapping if you ask it nicely." Figure 3.5 is a diagram of the domain name resolution process.

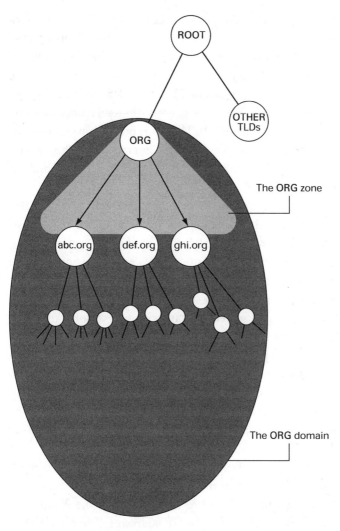

Figure 3.3
A DNS zone

Record type	input	output
A (Address)	shirley.ocis.temple.edu	129.32.1.64
CNAME	shirley.temple.edu	shirley.ocis.temple.edu
MX (Mail Xchanger)	shirley.ocis.temple.edu	fac.cis.temple.edu
PTR (PoinTeR)	64.1.32.129.in-addr.arpa	shirley.ocis.temple.edu
NS (Name Server)	temple.edu	comvax.ocis.temple.edu

Figure 3.4
A resource record

3.2.4   Names into Numbers: Inverse Resolution

The DNS intersects with the registration of IP addresses in the *in-addr.arpa* domain. Every time someone is assigned an IP address, it also receives a matching domain name delegation under *in-addr.arpa*. For example, if an organization received the IP address 2.3.4.5, it would also register the domain *5.4.3.2.in-addr.arpa* (the order of the numbers is reversed because the DNS hierarchy goes from right to left). The purpose of this rather odd practice is inverse resolution—instead of starting with a domain name and mapping it to an IP address, it allows one to use DNS to get the domain name of a machine when one knows the IP address.

Many sites, especially ftp servers and mail handlers, will check the source address on a connection to see whether it is coming from some address that properly reverse-resolves. If it doesn't, the connection will be rejected. The purpose of this practice is to act as a kind of certification that a communication is legitimate. If a name doesn't reverse-resolve properly it may be spam or some other kind of attempt to cover up the source of the message.

in-addr.arpa is significant to Internet governance because it is really the only place where administration of DNS and administration of IP addresses directly touch each other. The assignment and routing of addresses is otherwise completely independent of the assignment and resolution of domain names. The need to support inverse resolution means that whoever delegates IP addresses needs to have a special domain within the DNS where IP numbers can be registered as a domain. For all practical purposes, that means we are stuck with the *in-addr.arpa* domain for some time, because it is embedded in software implementations and changing it would cause a lot of trouble.

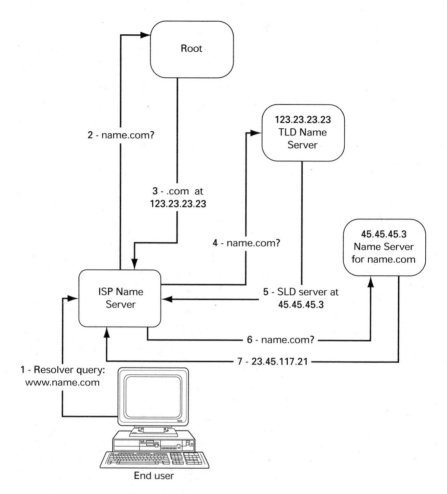

Figure 3.5
Domain name resolution process

3.3　The DNS Root

We are now in a better position to assess the technical, economic, and institutional significance of the DNS root. The term "DNS root" actually refers to two distinct things: the root zone file and the root name servers. The root zone file is the list of top-level domain name assignments, with pointers to primary and secondary name servers for each top-level domain. The root server system, on the other hand, is the operational aspect—the means of *distributing* the information contained in the root zone file in response to resolution queries from other name servers on the Internet. Currently, the root server system consists of 13 name servers placed in various parts of the world. (figure 3.6). The server where the root zone file is first loaded is considered authoritative; the others merely copy its contents. The additional servers make the root zone file available more rapidly to users who are spatially distributed, and provide redundancy in case some root servers lose connectivity or crash.

By now it should be evident that the real significance of the DNS root has to do with the *content* of the root zone file. The most important thing about

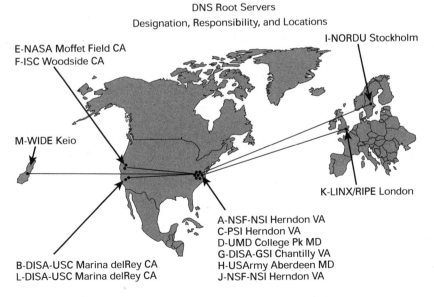

DNS Root Servers
Designation, Responsibility, and Locations

I-NORDU Stockholm

E-NASA Moffet Field CA
F-ISC Woodside CA

M-WIDE Keio

K-LINX/RIPE London

A-NSF-NSI Herndon VA
C-PSI Herndon VA
D-UMD College Pk MD
G-DISA-GSI Chantilly VA
H-USArmy Aberdeen MD
J-NSF-NSI Herndon VA

B-DISA-USC Marina delRey CA
L-DISA-USC Marina delRey CA

Figure 3.6
Location of 13 root servers

the DNS root is that it provides a single, and therefore globally consistent, starting point for the resolution of domain names. As long as all the world's name servers reference the same data about the contents of the root zone, the picture of the name resolution hierarchy in one part of the world will continue to match closely the picture in any other part of the world.

In many ways, the root zone file serves a function identical to the NIC in the old days of *hosts.txt*. It is still a central point of coordination, and there is still authoritative information that must be distributed from the central coordinator to the rest of the Internet. However, the central authority's workload has been drastically reduced, and as a corollary, so has the dependence of the rest of the Internet on that central point. The center doesn't need to be involved in every name assignment in the world, nor does it need to hold a directory capable of mapping every domain name in the world to the right IP address. It just needs to contain complete and authoritative assignment and mapping information for the top level of the hierarchy. And that information can be cached by any other name server in order to reduce its dependence on the root.

3.3.1   The Root and Internet Stability

The root server system, though vital to the domain name resolution process, is not that critical to the day-to-day operation of the Internet. As noted, all the root servers do is answer questions about how to find top-level domains. Reliance on the root is diminished by caching and zone transfers between primary and secondary name servers. As caches accumulate, more name-to-address correlation can be performed locally. With the sharing of zone files, many names can be resolved successfully without using the root even when the primary name server is down. Indeed, the root zone file itself can be downloaded and used locally by any name server in the world. The data are not considered proprietary or sensitive (yet), and with less than 300 top-level domain names in service, it is not even a very large file. The name servers of many large ISPs directly store the IP addresses of all top-level domain name servers, so that they can bypass the root servers in resolving names. Simple scripts in the Perl programming language allow them to track any changes in the TLD name servers.

To better understand the role of the root, it is useful to imagine that all 13 of the root servers were wiped off the face of the earth instantaneously.

What would happen to the Internet? There would be a loss of functionality, but it would *not* be sudden, total, and catastrophic. Instead, the absence of a common root would gradually impair the ability of computers on the Internet to resolve names, and the problem would get progressively worse as time passed. Users might first notice an inability to connect to Web sites at top-level domains they hadn't visited before. Lower-level name servers need to query the root to locate TLD name servers that have not been used before by local users. Worse, cached DNS records contain a timing field that will delete the record after a certain number of days, in order to prevent name servers from relying on obsolete information. When a cached record expires, the name server must query the root to be able to resolve the name. If the root is not there, the name server must either rely on potentially obsolete records or fail to resolve the name. Another major problem would occur if any changes were made in the IP addresses or names of top-level domain name servers, or if new top-level domains were created. Unless they were published in the root, these changes might not be distributed consistently to the rest of the Internet, and names under the affected top-level domains might not resolve.

Over time, the combination of new names, cache expiration, and a failure to keep up with changes in the configuration of top-level domain servers would confine reliable name resolution to local primaries and secondaries. There would be a gradual spread of entropy throughout the Internet's domain name system. The DNS would still work, but it would become balkanized.

That hypothetical disaster scenario, however, does not take into account the possibility that Internet users would *recreate* a common root server system or some other form of coordination. Users and service providers are not going to stand idly by while the tremendous value of global Internet connectivity withers away. The root servers are just name servers, after all, and there are thousands of high-performance name servers scattered throughout the global Internet. The critical information held by the root name servers—the root zone file—is not that hard to get. So it is likely that some organizations, most likely larger Internet service providers or major top-level domain name registries, would step into the breach. They could install stored copies of the root zone in their own name servers and offer substitute root name service. Operators of top-level domain name registries would have a powerful incentive to provide the necessary information about themselves to these new root servers, because otherwise their domains would be cut off from the global Internet. The most costly aspect of this transition would be getting the world's lower-level name server operators to reconfigure their software to point to the new name servers. BIND and other DNS software contain files with default values for the IP addresses of the root servers. New IP addresses would have to be manually entered into the DNS configuration files of hundreds of thousands of local name servers. That could take some time, and the process would likely result in some confusion and lack of coordination. Eventually, however, a new root could be established and functional.

If one imagines hundreds of thousands of local name server operators reconfiguring their DNS files to point to new sources of root information, the most interesting questions have to do with coordination and authority, not technology. Who would emerge as the operators of the new root servers? On what basis would they convince the world's ISPs and name server operators to point to them rather than to many other possible candidates? Would the world's name servers converge on a single, coordinated set of new root servers, or would competing groups emerge? Those questions are explored in the next section, where competing roots are discussed.

In short, DNS is fairly robust. The root server system is not a single point of failure; the hierarchical structure of the name space was designed precisely to avoid such a thing. In fact, the most serious potential for instability comes not from elimination of the root, but from software glitches that might cause the root servers or top-level domain servers to publish corrupted data. The only serious stability problems that have occurred in DNS have originated with the enormous *.com* zone file, a single domain that holds over 60 percent of the world's domain name registrations and probably accounts for a greater portion of DNS traffic.[11]

Figure 3.7 shows the number of queries per second received by a name server for *.com, .net,* and *.org* over the course of a single day (October 13, 2000). At its peak, the *.com* zone was queried about 2,500 times per second.

3.3.2 Competing DNS Roots?

DNS was designed on the assumption that there would be only one authoritative root zone file. That method of ensuring technical consistency

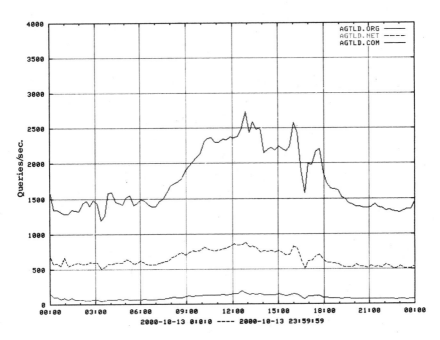

Figure 3.7
Number of *.com, .net,* and *.org* queries per second on a single day

creates an institutional problem. If there can only be one zone file, who controls its content? Who decides what top-level domain names are assigned, and to whom? In effect, some person or organization must have a monopoly on this vital decision. If top-level domain assignments are economically valuable, then the decision about who gets one and who doesn't can be contentious. Monopoly control of top-level domain name assignments can also provide the leverage needed to enforce regulatory policies. Assignments can be granted only to those who agree to meet certain regulatory obligations, taxes, or fees. And because each lower level of the domain name assignment hierarchy must get its names from the administrator of a top-level domain, the regulations and taxes imposed on the top-level assignments can be passed down all the way down. So political power, as well as economic benefit, is implicated in decisions about who or what is published in the root zone.

Some people believe that alternative or competing roots are the solution to many of the policy problems posed by ICANN. Others contend that such competition is impossible or undesirable.[12] That debate can be clarified by starting with a more precise definition of competition in this area and by applying known concepts from economics.

Competition at the root level means competition for the *right to define the contents of the root zone file*. More precisely, it means that organizations compete for the right to have *their* definition of the content of the root zone recognized and accepted by the rest of the Internet's name servers. As such, competition over the definition of the root zone is a form of standards competition. A dominant provider of root zone content (the U.S. Commerce Department and its contractor ICANN) publishes a particular set of top-level domains, while competing root operators strive to introduce additions or variations that will attract the support of other name server operators.

Economic theory has a lot of interesting things to say about how standards competition works. In standardization processes, user choices are affected by the value of compatibility with other users, not just by the technical and economic features of the product or service itself. A simple example would be the rivalry between the IBM and Apple computer platforms in the mid-1980s. During that time the two computer systems were almost completely incompatible. Thus, a decision to buy a personal computer had to be based not only on the intrinsic features of the computer itself but also on what platform other people were using. If all of a consumer's co-workers and friends were using Macs, for example, a buyer's choice of an IBM-compatible PC would lead to difficulties in exchanging files or communicating over a network.

There are many other historical examples of competition based on compatibility. Studies of competing railroad gauges (Friedlander 1995), alternative electric power grid standards (David and Bunn 1988), separate telegraph systems (Brock 1981), non-interconnected telephone networks (Mueller 1997), and alternative broadcast standards (Farrell and Shapiro 1992; Besen 1992) all have shown that the need for compatibility among multiple users led to convergence on a single standard or network, or to interconnection arrangements among formerly separate systems.

This feature of demand is called the network externality. It means that the value of a system or service to its users tends to increase as other users adopt the same system or service. A more precise definition characterizes them as demand-side economies of scope that arise from the creation of complementary relationships among the components of a system (Economides 1996).

One of the distinctive features of standards competition is the need to develop critical mass. A product with network externalities must pass a minimum threshold of adoption to survive in the market. Another key concept is known as tipping or the bandwagon effect. This means that once a product or service with network externalities achieves critical mass, what Shapiro and Varian (1998) call "positive feedback" can set in. Users flock to one of the competing standards in order to realize the value of universal compatibility, and eventually most users converge on a single system. However, network externalities can also be realized by the development of gateway technologies that interconnect or make compatible technologies that formerly were separate and distinct.

What does all this have to do with DNS? The need for unique name assignments and universal resolution of names creates strong network externalities in the selection of a DNS root. If all ISPs and users rely on the same public name space—the same delegation hierarchy—it is likely that all name assignments will be unique, and one can be confident that one's domain name can be resolved by any name server in the world. Thus, a public name space is vastly more valuable as a tool for internetworking if all other users also rely on it or coordinate with it. Network administrators thus have a strong tendency to converge on a single DNS root.

Alternative roots face a serious chicken-and-egg problem when trying to achieve critical mass. The domain name registrations they sell have little value to an individual user unless many other users utilize the same root zone file information to resolve names. But no one has much of an incentive to point at an alternative root zone when it has so few users. As long as other people don't use the same root zone file, the names from an alternative root will be incompatible with other users' implementation of DNS. Other users will be unable to resolve the name.

Network externalities are really the *only* barrier to all-out competition over the right to define the root zone file. A root server system is just a name server at the top of the DNS hierarchy. There are hundreds of thousands of name servers being operated by various organizations on the Internet. In principle, any one of them could declare themselves a public name space, assign top-level domain names to users, and either resolve the names or point to other name servers that resolve them at lower levels of the hierarchy. The catch, however, is that names in an alternative space are not worth much unless many other name servers on the Internet recognize its root and point their name servers at it.

There already are, in fact, several alternative root server systems (table 3.1). Most were set up to create new top-level domain names (see chapter 6). Most alternative roots have been promoted by small entrepreneurs unable to establish critical mass; in the year 2000 only an estimated 0.3 percent of the world's name servers pointed to them.[13] That changed when New.net, a company with venture capital financing, created 20 new top-level domains in the spring of 2001 and formed alliances with mid-sized Internet service providers to support the new domains.[14] New.net's top-level domains may be visible to about 20 percent of the Internet users in the United States.

An alternative root supported by major Internet industry players, on the other hand, would be even stronger. An America Online, a Microsoft, a major ISP such as MCI WorldCom, all possess the economic and technical clout to establish an alternative DNS root should they choose to do so. If the producers of Internet browsers, for example, preconfigured their resolvers to point to a new root with an alternative root zone file that included or was compatible with the legacy root zone, millions of users could be switched to an alternative root. It is also possible that a national government with a large population that communicated predominantly with itself could establish an alternative root zone file and require, either through persuasion or regulation, national ISPs to point at it. Indeed, the People's Republic of China is offering new top-level domains based on Chinese characters on an experimental basis.

Why would anyone want to start an alternative root? Defection from the current DNS root could be motivated by the following:

• Not enough new top-level domains

• Technological innovation, such as non-Roman character sets, or other features

• Political resistance to the policies imposed on registries and domain name registrants by the central authority

email Lorie about Rosenberg address

Table 3.1
Root Server confederations

Name	TLDs Claimed/Supported	Conflicts with
ICANN-U.S. Commerce Department root	ISO-3166-1 country codes, *.com, .net, .org, .edu, .int, .mil, .arpa, .info, .biz, .coop, .aero, .museum, .pro, .name*	Pacific Root (*.biz*)
Open NIC	*.glue, .geek, .null, .oss, .parody, .bbs*	
ORSC	Supports ICANN root, Open NIC, Pacific Root, and most New.net names plus a few hundred of its own, IOD's *.web*	Name.space
Pacific Root	27 names, including *.biz, .food, .online*	ICANN (*.biz*)
New.net	*.shop. .mp3, .inc, .kids, .sport, .family, .chat, .video, .club, .hola, .soc, .med, .law, .travel, .game, .free, .ltd, .gmbh, .tech, .xxx*	Name.space
Name.space	548 generic names listed	New.net, most other alternative roots
CN-NIC	Chinese-character versions of "company," "network," and "organization"	

Technological innovation almost inevitably leads to standards competition in some form or another. Furthermore, monopolies have a tendency to become unaccountable, overly expensive, or unresponsive. Competition has a very good record of making monopolies more responsive to technical and business developments that they would otherwise ignore. So even when competitors fail to displace the dominant standard or network, they may succeed in substantially improving it. New.net, for example, may prompt ICANN to speed up its introduction of new top-level domains.

Recall, however, that the value of universal connectivity and compatibility on the Internet is immense. Those who attempt to establish alternative roots have powerful incentives to retain compatibility with the existing DNS root and offer something of considerable value to move industry actors away from the established root. Whether the value that can be achieved by root competition is worth the cost in terms of disruption and incompatibility is beyond the scope of this discussion.[15]

3.4 Conclusion

The key question with respect to the DNS root is, Who (or what) gets to determine the contents of the root zone file? There are three distinct ways of answering that question. Two rely on market processes, the third relies on collective action.

• Firms can compete for the right to be the authoritative source of the DNS root zone information and accept some degree of fragmentation or incompatibility in exchange for a possible gain in innovation and functionality. Alternatively, the result may be a privately negotiated compatibility agreement among the multiple competitors, in which they agree to coordinate the contents of their root zone files to achieve a certain level of universal compatibility.

• Another possibility, which may be the inevitable outcome of the first, is to allow the private marketplace to converge on a single winner. In that case, the winner of the right to define the root zone file may be a private, for-profit firm that achieves lasting dominance, like Microsoft's command of the operating system. This could also produce a succession of "serial monopolies."

• A formal institutional solution could be created based on collective action. In this case the contents of the root zone file would be determined by a specialized authority, generally a nonprofit, controlled by specified governance structures and publicly formulated rules.

Subsequent chapters will show that, in the turmoil surrounding the institutionalization of the Internet from 1995 to 2000, all three options were on the table.

4

The Root and Institutional Change: Analytical Framework

The poster on the door of the departmental computer administrator said it all.

The Internet is like the ocean.

It is a great resource.

It is huge.

No one owns it.

It was 1991. The Internet had not yet exploded onto the world stage, but it was already linking hundreds of thousands of academics. The incredible power of global computer internetworking was beginning to dawn upon the higher education community. Instead of making US$3-a-minute phone calls or stuffing bulky papers into envelopes and waiting days or weeks for a response, one could transfer information almost instantly to any part of the world. The Internet was becoming a taken-for-granted part of our work infrastructure. It was just there. Most of us had no idea who ran it, how it worked, or who paid for it. Like prescientific cultures we deployed myths and metaphors to express our wonderment at this remarkable resource.

A huge ocean. No one owns it.

This attitude is typical of the kind of institutional naïveté that has characterized the Internet community. In fact, neither the ocean nor the Internet are free from contention. As the work of Ostrom (1990; 1994) and others has shown, common pool resources such as the ocean are more often than not the site of battles over the assignment and allocation of resource rights: to fish, to get minerals, and so on. Contention over value is unavoidable unless the resource is superabundant. Property rights, rules, and governance arrangements are tools to resolve those conflicts and to pave the way for more harmonious and profitable utilization of the resources.

We have now reached the conceptual core of the book. Internet names and numbers are resources; prior chapters outlined some of their distinctive economic and physical features. Internet governance will be now characterized as the institutionalization of those resource spaces. Framing the problem in this way is useful. First, it links the problem to some powerful, robust theoretical tools derived from the economic literature on property rights; second, it provides a direct, concrete linkage between the processes of technological and institutional change.

4.1   Formation of Property Rights

To those immersed in them, the political struggles over Internet governance may seem historically unique and too complex to categorize. But in hindsight the battles over the root fall unambiguously into a specific class of social phenomena: the formation of property rights. They are an example of what happens when a new resource is created or discovered and conflicts arise among individuals attempting to appropriate its value, forcing the affected community to define rules governing the economic exploitation of the resource. Gary Libecap (1989) calls this situation "contracting for property rights." *Contracting* is his term for the bargaining that takes place among private claimants "to adopt or to change group rules and customs regarding the allocation and use of property" (4). Ostrom, Gardner, and Walker (1994) describe essentially the same process as a "collective action situation" that prompts people to devise "institutional arrangements to regulate the use of resource systems shared with others" (23).

Contracting for property rights can be unpacked into three sequentially related parts: endowment, appropriation, and institutionalization.

Endowment is the development of new demand conditions that lend substantial value to a resource.[1] *Appropriation* refers to attempts by private actors to exploit the resource or establish claims to parts of it. If appropriation activity results in a significant number of mutually exclusive uses and conflicting claims, a need for formal property rights or governance rules is created. *Institutionalization,* the third stage in the sequence, is the working out of a set of rules or rights definitions that resolve the conflicts and provide a settled (but not necessarily efficient or just) basis for the exploitation of the resource. In developed societies, institutionalization processes typically take the form of litigation, lobbying, legislation, private bargaining, or the formation of new rule-making organizations. Most of the empirical literature on this topic examines the emergence of institutions governing shared natural resources, such as land claims, oil pools, fishing rights, groundwater basins, or mining rights. But the theory can be applied readily to technically constructed resources such as name and number spaces.

Part II of the book is based on this three-part sequence. It develops a thick historical narrative about the evolution of the root and the development and resolution of governance conflicts. The narrative begins with the growth and commercialization of the Internet and shows how it endowed the domain name space with value. Next, it examines how the governance wars emerged as businesses and individuals clashed over attempts to appropriate the name and number spaces; these conflicts were fueled by fundamental ambiguities about who owned the resource space. The narrative then moves to an analysis of the formation and structure of new property rights institutions, focusing on ICANN and its supporting organizations, its domain name dispute resolution procedure, and its quest for legitimacy.

There are several reasons why that process is worthy of sustained attention. The institutionalization of the root produced an institutional innovation rather than incremental modifications or adaptations of existing institutions. It was the product of a form of transnational collective action more or less outside the framework of the nation-state and the intergovernmental organizations that nation-states typically use to resolve such problems. The institutionalization of the Internet root thus raises important questions about the relationship between technology and institutional change, the role of nation-states, and the tendency of the Internet to globalize institutions. Also, the particular resource in which property rights are being established, global identifiers, raises a host of important and sometimes perplexing policy issues. These pertain not only to the relationship between technical assignment processes and trademark rights but also to the very nature of identity in cyberspace and the role of the state (or some other collective authority) in controlling the delegation and use of identifiers.

4.2 Property Rights

Why does this book base its analysis on property rights? Because the concept of property rights is a powerful analytical tool capable of synthesizing many of the economic, legal, and political dimensions of institutional change.[2] Property rights assign decision-making authority over resources to individuals or groups. They are defined by formal laws and regulations as well as by informal customs and norms that affect the way the formal specifications are put into practice. Colloquial usage tends to interpret a "property right" as a kind of absolute control over an asset, involving the right to use, the right to exclude others from use, the right to enjoy the revenue stream generated from its development, and the right to transfer or exchange it. In the real world almost all these aspects of property rights' are conditioned and limited by institutions. From the standpoint of property rights theory, for example, the grant of a broadcasting license is a kind of property right, but the licensee's conduct is regulated and the duration of the grant is limited. Ownership of a home may be conditioned by zoning regulations, rent controls, and so on. In this book, the concept of property rights is applied very broadly to include all forms of decision-making authority over assets.

The particular way in which rights are specified has a powerful impact on the performance of an economy and the distribution of wealth. It determines the degree to which economic actors are able to reap the rewards of their investment in the owned resource. In a simple but valid example, Posner (1972) observes that if a farmer plants and cultivates corn but his neighbor is entitled to harvest and sell it, wealth is transferred from the farmer to the neighbor, and the farmer's planting and cultivation work is likely to be minimized or abandoned. In the real world, of course, the choices are not always that stark. They may involve, for example, a choice between various ownership forms (private, public, nonprofit), what restrictions to impose on the use of the property, what limits to impose on its sale or transfer, and so on. Each of these choices will shape incentives, alter the relative distribution of wealth, and affect the ability of an economy to move resources to the highest valued and most productive uses.[3]

Creating and maintaining property rights is not free. Before one can claim ownership of a resource, one must first be able to define workable boundaries that separate one person's claim from another's. One must also be able to enforce that claim by excluding trespassers, either by fencing them out or by patrolling the borders and sanctioning them. These activities are costly. The costs of defining and measuring claims to resources and of monitoring and enforcing specified rights are known as transaction costs.[4] In many cases, such as land rights, the costs of surveying, mapping, fencing, and monitoring may be low relative to the benefits that can be reaped from control of the property. But there are many other resources, such as marine fisheries, that may not be fenced in without prohibitive expense (given prevailing technology). Transaction costs may prevent any attempt to create separable, transferable property rights in such a resource. In such cases, conflicts over appropriation may be handled by government regulation, international agreements among governments, or other forms of collective action.[5]

4.3   Technological Change, Endowment, and Appropriation

How property rights institutions come into being, and how and why they change, is a critical issue for social theory and public policy. It has been a topic in institutional economics at least since Karl Marx identified the enclosures of the common fields as a milestone in the transition from feudalism to capitalism. In the three-stage model just defined, the prime mover is endowment—a change in demand conditions that creates a quantum jump in the value of a specific resource. Particularly interesting is endowment that occurs as a result of technological development.[6]

The commercial development of a technological system can progressively bid up the value of certain components or inputs critical to the expansion of the system. Sometimes the affected resource is a natural substance, as when the development of a mass market for internal combustion engines transformed crude oil deposits from worthless goo into a prized commodity. More pertinent to our story, the commercialization of technologies may also create resources *internal* to the system—unnatural resources, as it were—that may need to be shared. Name and number spaces are examples of such resources. So are radio communication channels, satellite parking spaces in outer space, or airport gate slots. Demand for resources of this sort can intensify along with growth in the markets organized around the technical system of which they are a part.

Under certain conditions, technology-induced endowment can trigger major conflicts over appropriation activity. The change in the status of the radio frequency spectrum caused by the commercialization of broadcasting in the early 1920s is a good historical example of this phenomenon. The rapid diffusion of broadcast technology after the end of World War I suddenly endowed certain parts of the electromagnetic spectrum with great economic and political value. The airwaves could be used to deliver music and commentary to thousands of people. In the United States, the response was a monumental political and legal struggle over the control of the spectrum (Hazlett 1990; Minasian 1970). Hundreds of broadcasters occupied frequencies with little coordination by the U.S. government. Aside from the problem of coping with the land rush created by the sudden opening of an unoccupied frontier, the federal government also was faced with the problem of defining, allocating, and assigning rights to a new resource, the behavior of which was not well understood. While informal rights of precedence and coordination did develop among some private claimants, the nature and scope of property rights in the spectrum were unclear, and there were many conflicts. There was also significant ideological and normative opposition in some quarters to the notion of private ownership of the spectrum.

The encounter with this problem in the mid-1920s produced a new institutional regime for the regulation of communications in the United States. The airwaves were nationalized, and a new federal agency was created to assign highly regulated rights to operate and program broadcast stations for a limited time. A form of merit assignment (to use the terminology developed in chapter 2) governed the assignment of broadcasting licenses. In this property regime, resources were distributed according to a "public interest" standard (Krasnow, Longley, and Terry 1982). Assignment of spectrum licenses was explicitly linked to a set of regulatory obligations that gave a federal agency significant influence over the content of broadcasts, ownership of stations, and the geographic distribution of stations. Broadcasters were viewed as "public trustees," and the perceived scarcity of radio channels and the political problem posed by assigning them exclusively to privileged users became the regime's defining feature.[7]

The early history of broadcasting provides a vivid instance of how technological endowment can lead to significant and rapid institutional change. When an unowned resource space created by the commercialization of a new technical system increases in value, competition for access to it will intensify. As appropriation activity develops, the need to ration, own portions of, trade, or regulate the resource space to resolve conflicting claims and uses will also develop. In short, the need for institutional arrangements will become urgent, especially when the resource space created requires sharing or coordination to be used effectively. Precisely because the technical system is new, however, the resource space it creates may not fit readily into existing ownership models. In such a transition, there is likely to be rampant uncertainty about the gains or losses that might be caused by alternative property rights specifications. If conflicts develop, legal precedents are likely to be either absent or of debatable applicability. If endowment occurs quickly, the sudden rise in the financial stakes associated with possession of the resource, coupled with the creation of tremendous opportunities for first-mover advantages, can create a land rush that upsets institutional equilibriums. It is possible, even likely, that the social groups involved in the contracting for property rights will not be familiar with each other, further increasing the difficulty of finding a solution. Thus, when certain conditions are met, technological endowment can be a catalyst of significant institutional change.

4.4 Institutionalization

Institutionalization occurs when claimants attempt to resolve appropriation conflicts through collective action. The most relevant empirical literature on this process focuses on the privatization of common pool resources. Common pool resources are asset stocks that are unowned or collectively owned. If the resource, such as a village grazing field, is collectively owned, units of the resource are open to appropriation by any member of the group. If it is unowned, it is open to appropriation by any individual that comes along.

As demand intensifies and the number of appropriators grows, common property arrangements tend to break down. The absence of formal, exclusive property rights or enforceable rules governing appropriation leads to overdevelopment and exhaustion of the resource. Under common pool conditions, appropriators have an incentive to extract as much as they can from the common pool immediately, for if they restrain their withdrawal of resource units, they will simply lose out to others who do not. Common pool conditions thus tend to foster a race to appropriate, which in turn encourages costly and duplicative investments in extraction equipment. Readers may recognize in this a variant of the familiar "tragedy of the commons" story.

Technologically endowed resources may or may not possess common pool characteristics. Broadcast frequencies did; for a time, anyone who applied could obtain a license from the Commerce Department and broadcast signals regardless of their impact on other stations. The early stages of satellite communication also produced common pool conditions, because any country with launch capabilities could occupy a satellite orbit slot at will. The integrated circuit, on the other hand, was a revolutionary invention but did not directly create any interesting new institutional issues. The design and production methods could be patented, and thus fit into an existing property rights system. The chips themselves and the materials needed to make them could be owned and traded like other physical objects.

4.4.1   Political Constraints on Institutional Change

Unregulated appropriation can create huge economic losses.[8] Defining formal property rights or governance institutions can make society as a whole better off. But institutional change will not come about automatically simply because it is socially beneficial. As North (1981; 1990) and others have argued, economic institutions that are manifestly unproductive and dysfunctional do come into being and often remain in place for a long time. Most institutional economists now reject the view that the formation of property rights is guided by a kind of natural selection that ensures that inefficient institutions are eliminated and only good ones survive.

What then does social science have to say about the institutionalization process? Recall that it is political and legal processes that determine how property rights are assigned. Because of the intimate interdependence between the assignment of property rights and the distribution of wealth, any significant change in the definition of property rights is bound to produce winners and losers. Groups that would be made worse off by a proposed new property regime will resist it politically, and may hold enough power to prevent change or to lobby for an alternative regime more suited to their interests.[9] Political conflict over the distribution of wealth provides the controlling constraint on the creation or redefinition of property rights.

Libecap (1989) demonstrates that political bargaining over wealth distribution issues is the chief determinant of why there is such variety in property institutions, and why they can settle upon and maintain economically inefficient forms. The configuration of political power at any given time will be different, and the influence and level of organization of the various groups involved in contracting for property rights will vary widely. Drawing on historical case studies, he identifies several structural constants that will influence the outcome of the contracting process (21–26). These are worth recounting.

One significant structural variable is the size of the expected gains from institutional change. As a rule, the larger the expected aggregate gains from institutional change, the more likely it is that politicians will be able to devise a share arrangement that will win the consensus of the bargaining parties. Another important factor is the number and heterogeneity of bargaining parties. The larger the number of stakeholders involved in the contracting process, the more difficult it will be to reach an agreement. A heterogeneous set of bargaining parties also raises transaction costs, making it more difficult to achieve a stable, politically effective coalition. A third factor is the concentration of the current and proposed share distribution. Assuming a reasonably participatory political process, property arrangements that foster extreme concentrations of wealth are likely to be less successful in the political process than those that distribute wealth more broadly. Finally, there are "information problems." Uncertainty about the valuation of individual assets under current and proposed property rights regimes can increase the difficulty of coming to an agreement on share adjustments or compensation.

These factors prove to be useful in interpreting the history of Internet governance.

4.4.2   Property Rights and International Regimes

Institutions and rules are agreed upon and enforced by collective units. Most of the organizations that define, adjudicate, and enforce property rights and rules—courts, legislatures, regulatory agencies, and so on—are territorial in jurisdiction and derive their authority and legitimacy from sovereign national governments. Even the customs and norms that informally constrain uses of property tend to vary on a regional basis, and can be aligned (with varying degrees of success) with governmental jurisdictions. Thus, most of the theory of institutional economics takes the nation-state as the basic unit of analysis.

But a growing part of economic and social activity crosses national boundaries. Because there is no world government, contracting for property rights in these spaces requires collective action among sovereign nation-states. The rights and rules defined by agreement among national governments to institutionalize a specific sector are called international regimes (Young 1989). There have been several reasonably successful attempts to directly link property rights theory with international regime theory. Richards (1999), for example, describes international regimes as institutions that assign property rights in international markets. The national politicians who forge international institutions will favor arrangements that maximize their political support by benefiting important domestic constituents. Richards's theory also emphasizes the primacy of political bargaining over economic efficiency in determining the features of specific property regimes. Politicians assign rights in a way that transfers wealth to favored market participants, or they create international institutional arrangements that increase the amount of wealth available for domestic redistribution (3–4).

Applying this theory to the Internet and its name and number spaces is a challenging task. Although the Internet resources are global in scope, as it turned out, the collectivity involved in the institutionalization of the domain name system was not a group of nation-states bargaining as peers, either multilaterally or within the forum of an international treaty organization. Instead, a new, ostensibly private sector organization was created that would bring together the various stakeholders to formulate "consensus" policies. There were ideological as well as political and economic reasons for not turning the institutional problem over to traditional intergovernmental institutions. Internet governance thus led to the formation of a new arena of collective action. That process did, however, have to interact with the existing international system, and national politicians and international organizations played an important role in shaping the governance process.

4.5   Applying the Framework to Internet Governance

Subsequent chapters develop a narrative history of Internet governance that applies the theoretical framework described here. It is now possible to follow the structure of the argument in some detail. The following summary should provide the reader with a kind of road map through the historical detail of part II.

First, the growth and commercialization of the Internet created a new resource with substantial value. The resource in question was the domain name space. Second-level domain names acquired commercial value as global locators of Web sites. The policy of charging for domain names, instituted by the National Science Foundation and its contractor Network Solutions in 1995, proved that a significant revenue stream could be generated by the sale of registrations. The business value of second-level domains also heightened the significance of the administration of the root zone. Whoever controlled the definition of the root zone file would be able to authorize new top-level domain registries that could sell domain names to the public.

Second, the specific form that commercialization took turned the domain name space into a common pool resource. Although Network Solutions eventually charged annual fees for domain name registrations, they were relatively small and often uncollected, and it was too costly to discriminate among the thousands of applicants for names. A rule of first-come/first-served—essentially the same as a rule of capture in an open-access common pool resource—determined who got specific name assignments. This led to almost unrestricted appropriation activity, producing many conflicts over rights to particular names. Trademark rights began to be asserted as a principle for privileging certain claims over others, but the application of trademark law, which was national in scope and industry- and use-specific, to domain names, which were global in scope and were governed primarily by a uniqueness requirement, created as many conflicts as it resolved.

In addition to raising questions about the nature of global property rights at various levels of the domain name hierarchy, commercialization led inexorably to the problem of deciding who owned the root. The growing value of second-level domains produced strong and insistent pressures to create new top-level domains. When this demand could not be met because of the contested authority over policymaking for the root, alternative root servers arose that created their own top-level domains, threatening to make the top-level space another unrestricted common pool. In short, in the course of endowing the DNS root with value, the growth of the Internet created a new arena of appropriation activity that demanded a comprehensive institutional solution.

Third, the narrative explores three major barriers to the resolution of the property rights conflicts, which combined to prevent resolution of the problems within existing frameworks and pushed the actors into institutional innovations:

• There was no established, formal organization with clear authority over the root. Despite its origins in the work of U.S. government contractors, authority over the Internet's name and number spaces resided in an informal technical community that was distributed, unincorporated, and international in scope. Moreover, as the root's importance grew, the efforts of various domestic and international organizations to assert formal control over it failed because of attacks on their legal, political, and ethical legitimacy. Thus, the property rights conflicts were not resolved within established frameworks.

• Attempts to define property rights in domain names suffered from major conflicts over the distribution of wealth. The most wrenching of these was the conflict between trademark owners on the one hand and domain name registration businesses and domain name registrants on the other. Trademark owners viewed common pool conditions in the name space as diluting the exclusivity and value of their brand names. The regulation and protections they sought, however, would have increased costs and reduced the market of domain name registries. It also would have expropriated many Internet users and drastically reduced their freedom to employ ordinary words as domain names. The demand of prospective registries for new top-level domains threatened to further erode trademark owners' control over names and increase their costs of monitoring and policing the use of marks. New top-level domains also threatened the exclusivity of existing domain name holders as well as the monopoly privileges of incumbent registries. The conflicts were exacerbated by a lack of information regarding the real economic stakes for various actors.

• Contracting proved to be difficult because of the extreme heterogeneity of the groups involved. In addition to the U.S. government and Network Solutions, eight distinct stakeholder groups became involved: (1) the formally and informally organized Internet technical community, (2) domain name and address registries outside the United States, (3) prospective domain name registries and registrars seeking entry into the market, (4) trademark and intellectual property interests, (5) Internet service providers and other corporations involved in telecommunication and e-commerce, (6) civil liberties organizations concerned with freedom of expression and opposed to the expansion of intellectual property rights, (7) international intergovernmental organizations seeking a role in Internet governance, and (8) governmental actors in a few key nation-states.

New institutions emerged out of this contention. The narrative traces the formation of a dominant coalition among stakeholder groups that was capable of imposing its will on the other participants. The discussion focuses on the formation of the Internet Corporation for Assigned Names and Numbers (ICANN) and its at-large membership, and on a new global system of dispute resolution proposed by the World Intellectual Property Organization (WIPO) and implemented by ICANN.

The framework outlined in this chapter is able to provide a logical explanation for many aspects of the developments. It makes it clear why domain names rather than IP addresses were the point of conflict. It explains why the conflicts were focused on the open top-level domains operated by Network Solutions rather than on country codes or restricted top-level domains. It indicates why institutionalization took place at the global level rather than in the national arena. Finally, it is able to identify which groups were relative winners and losers in the particular property regime that emerged, and explain (retrospectively, of course) why certain proposed property regimes were rejected and others selected.

II

The Story of the Root

5

Growing the Root

The real domain authorities are going to be selected by some political processes that are not identified well enough, in any of the drafts we have considered, to allow us to seriously consider deciding on any of the top-level domains, ARPA included. . . . There just ain't no way that us techies are going to be allowed to dictate domain structures . . .
—Einar Stefferud, *namedroppers* list, May 1984

This chapter tells several interrelated stories.

One is the story of how the Internet's domain name and address spaces came into being in 1981. Another is a story of growth. In the decade following the formal specification of the Internet protocols, the number of host computers on the Internet increased exponentially. By the early 1990s, the Internet protocols and their name and address spaces had become the convergence point for the achievement of global interoperability in data networking.

Parallel to the narratives of growth and convergence is the emergence of a cohesive Internet technical community. Over a span of 20 years, the government programs supporting internetworking created a cadre of technologists committed to the promotion and development of the Internet protocols. It evolved into an internationally distributed community that conceived of itself as self-governing and developed its own norms and procedures. As the Net became a commercial mass medium, the senior leaders of this community, a technical priesthood backed by federal largesse, would struggle to retain control of the Internet's name and number resources. Their claim to ownership rights, however, would be made not in the name of the United States or its government, but in the name of a stateless, emergent "Internet community." The roots of institutional innovation

can be traced by examining this community's origins and its interaction
with established institutions.

5.1 Prehistory

John Quarterman described the Internet as the product of a "chaotic mé-
nage à trois of government, academia, and business."[1] The starting point
of this relationship was a very orderly research project, the ARPANET,
funded by the Information Processing Techniques Office (IPTO) of the
U.S. Defense Department's Advanced Projects Research Administration
(ARPA).

The ARPANET was an experimental backbone of leased lines connect-
ing research scientists in university, military, and industry sites. Its purpose
was to facilitate time sharing on mainframe computers. A request for proposals circulated in 1968 called for the construction of a packet-switching
device called an interface message processor, the development of software,
and the design of a physical network to connect them. A Cambridge,
Massachusetts, based research firm with longstanding personal and financial ties to ARPA, Bolt, Beranek, and Newman (BBN), won the
ARPANET contract in 1969 (Hughes 1998, 269–270).

The ARPANET was not the Internet. The Transport Control Protocol/
Internet Protocols (TCP/IP) had not been invented yet, and the word *Internet* was not used to describe it. The ARPANET was difficult to use and
connected at most about 200 people at 21 nodes. The project did, however, bring together the *people* who played a continuous role in the Internet's technical development and its governance for the next 30 years.
ARPANET created the nucleus of an Internet technical community.

Robert Kahn was one of the leaders of BBN's interface message processor project. He later co-authored the basic TCP architecture and helped to
form the Corporation for National Research Initiatives, which supported
the IETF in its early day. The site of the first ARPANET node, installed in
September 1969, was the ARPA-supported computer science research center at the University of California, Los Angeles, headed by Leonard Kleinrock, an inventor of queuing theory. At UCLA, Kleinrock's graduate
students Steve Crocker, Vinton Cerf, and Jon Postel were given most of the
responsibility for implementing the ARPANET protocols.[2] It was Crocker

who formed the Network Working Group and initiated the Internet's uniquely open method of developing and documenting standards, the Request for Comments (RFC) series.[3] Jon Postel eventually took over the task of editing the RFCs and gravitated to the administration of unique number assignments for ports and protocols. Cerf went on to become one of the principal designers of TCP/IP, the most persistent and effective advocate of the TCP/IP standard for internetworking, the founder of the Internet Society, and board chair of ICANN.

It was also the ARPANET project that brought Keith Uncapher, a RAND Corporation computer engineer, into contact with the military research agency. In 1972, Uncapher formed the Information Sciences Institute (ISI) as an affiliate of the University of Southern California (USC) but located it in Marina del Rey, apart from the main campus. ISI was conceived as a kind of West Coast BBN—a university-based research center focused on applications of computer science. Unlike BBN, however, it was nonprofit, and deliberately set up to obtain funding from ARPA exclusively. "I was totally captivated by the freedom that ARPA had, the excellence of the people, and their ability to commit to a good idea based on the back of an envelope drawing or a telephone conversation," Uncapher later said.[4] ISI became one of the main centers of Internet research and administration, supporting the work of Jon Postel, Robert Braden, Steve Crocker, Danny Cohen, Daniel Lynch, Paul Mockapetris, and others. Throughout the 1970s, many of the ARPANET principals moved seamlessly between the ARPA and ISI.

5.2   The Origin of the Root

The demand for research on internetworking followed quickly on ARPANET's heels. By 1973 the military agency, now named DARPA, was supporting two other packet-based networks (Abbate 2000, 121). Each of these networks used different, incompatible protocols. The military wanted to retain the advantages of specialized networks, but it wanted universal communication among them. It needed an internetworking protocol.

The task of developing such a protocol was taken up by Robert Kahn, who had moved from BBN to DARPA as a program officer in 1972. Kahn conferred with Vint Cerf, who had graduated and moved to Stanford University. In the spring and summer of 1973, Kahn worked with Cerf and others to develop a "universal host protocol" and common address space that could be used to tie together separate data networks. A basic architecture for a Transport Control Protocol was written by Kahn and Cerf in 1973 and published in 1974.[5] From 1975 to 1977 various versions of the proposed protocol were implemented in software and tested at BBN, University College London, and Stanford. It was during this period that David Clark, a computer scientist at the Massachusetts Institute of Technology (MIT), became involved.

The TCP was not yet ripe for full implementation. A key breakthrough came in 1978, when Cerf, Postel, and Danny Cohen proposed to split the protocol into two parts. A separate, connectionless Internet Protocol would be used to move packets between machines; a connection-oriented Transport Control Protocol would organize communications between hosts in an end-to-end fashion. With this basic conceptual issue addressed, intense work on a formal implementation proceeded. In September 1981, RFC 791 was presented to DARPA as the official specification of Internet Protocol.[6] The Internet address space had been created.

5.2.1   The First Address Assignments
RFC 790, released at the same time as RFC 791, documented the first IP address assignments to particular organizations. Forty-three class A network addresses were given out at that time. Most went to the local packet radio networks, satellite networks, and other ARPA-supported networks to be encompassed by the internetworking project. But local networks of universities (MIT, Stanford), research organizations (MITRE, SRI), and a few commercial carriers (Comsat, Tymnet, DECNet) also received assignments. Included, too, were several non-U.S. entities, such as the British Post Office, the French Cyclades network, University College London, and the British Royal Signals and Radar Establishments.

Jon Postel was listed as the author of both RFCs 790 and 791. During the formulation of the Internet protocols in the 1977–1981 period, Postel gained recognition as the person responsible for address and number assignments within the small DARPA community. RFC 791 states, with the informality typical of the early RFCs, "The assignment of numbers is . . .

handled by Jon. If you are developing a protocol or application that will require the use of a link, socket, port, protocol, or network number, please contact Jon to receive an assignment."

After completing graduate school at UCLA in 1973, Postel had moved to the MITRE Corporation (1973–1974), then to SRI International in Northern California (1974–1977), and in 1977 to ISI, where he stayed until his death in 1998. By October 1983 documents indicated that the responsibility for day-to-day assignment tasks had been delegated to Postel's ISI colleague Joyce Reynolds.[7]

5.2.2 The Invention of the Domain Name System

The spiral of growth began almost immediately after the successful implementation of internetworking among the military research networks. The Internet pioneers became aware that all planning had to take continuous increases in the scope of the network into account. The ARPA-Internet in 1982 consisted of only 25 networks and about 250 hosts. MIT's Dave Clark warned in RFC 814 (July 1982) that "any implementation undertaken now should be based on an assumption of a much larger Internet."[8] One of the weakest links in this regard was the ARPANET's approach to naming computers. As noted in chapter 3, up to this point the network had translated names into addresses by having each host store a specially formatted table, *hosts.txt*, containing the name and address of every computer on the network. The authoritative *hosts.txt* file was maintained on a Hostname Server by the Network Information Center of the Defense Data Network (DDN-NIC), operated by the private company, Stanford Research Institute (SRI) in Menlo Park, California, under contract to the Defense Communications Agency.

As early as September 1981, David Mills of Comsat noted, "In the long run, it will not be practicable for every internet host to include all internet hosts in its name-address tables" (RFC 799). Some concept of the domain name system was already hatching within the ARPA-Internet community. Mills wrote of a "hierarchical name-space partitioning," while Clark in RFC 814 mentioned plans to create a "distributed approach in which each network (or group of networks) is responsible for maintaining its own names and providing a 'name server' to translate between the names and the addresses in that network."[9] The basic concepts underlying the domain name system (DNS) were published only a month later by Su and Postel (RFC 819, August 1982). More detailed specifications and some early implementation software were written by Paul Mockapetris, who also was working at ISI (RFCs 882 and 883, November 1983).

Electronic mail was one of the first networking applications developed by the ARPANET community. The real push for network growth came not from the need to share mainframes but from email, which presented an opportunity to exchange ideas and gather comments from peers. At least since 1975, ARPANET participants had begun to deploy this newly developed capability to create virtual communities capable of collaborating on the development of protocols and standards. One of the first such email lists, if not the first, was the *msggroup* list moderated by Einar Stefferud.[10]

The implementation of DNS, which took place over the next six years, put to work the techniques for virtual collaboration by email list. In 1983, Postel inaugurated the *namedroppers* mailing list, "to be used for discussion of the concepts, principles, design, and implementation of the domain style names."[11] The group was used to review the documents describing DNS and discuss implementation of the system. Postel had already developed a transition plan. The first top-level domain of the DNS implementation was to be *.arpa,* a "temporary" top-level domain. All the names in *hosts.txt* would take the form *hostname.arpa* (RFC 881, November 1983). The next step was to define new top-level domains.

5.2.3   Top-Level Domain Controversies

That step (defining top-level domains) proved controversial. Indeed, the criteria for creating top-level domains and the semantics associated with them immediately raised many of the issues that later made domain name conflicts the catalyst of international institutional change.

DNS was organized around the principle that a "responsible person" would be delegated the authority to assign and resolve names at each level of the hierarchy. Names at all levels were conceived as names for network resources—primarily host computers—not for people, organizations, documents, or products. The designers of DNS had a good idea who they expected to take responsibility for second- and third-level names. Second-level domain names were thought of as names for major organizations whose networks contained 50–100 hosts.[12] Third-level domains would be administered by divisions of those organizations, or by organizations with only one host. The fourth level would be smaller subdivisions of the organizations. The DNS was anticipated to be "deeply hierarchical" (Klensin 2000).

If the second level consisted of organization names, the top level had to be broader categories or groupings of organizations. What then should those categories be?[13] Who was the appropriate "responsible person" for them? That issue was hotly debated on the email lists.

In a draft memo issued May 1984, Postel proposed six initial top-level domains: *.arpa, .ddn, .gov, .edu, .cor,* and *.pub.*[14] Einar Stefferud immediately voiced a deep criticism of the whole proposal: "It seems to me that this new draft has gotten us into the troublesome turf of semantic definitions, wherein we attempt to carve up the world and assign responsibility and authority to non-existent entities for large, ill-defined clusters of users and their service hosts."[15] Inadvertently corroborating Stefferud's argument, another list participant complained, "I have yet to run into ANYONE outside the United States who is interested in the EDU/COM/GOV domains. Without exception, they all want the top-level domains to be based on geography and international boundaries."[16] The British quickly expressed a desire to use a country designator rather than one of Postel's proposed names, although there was disagreement over whether to use *.gb* or *.uk*. Eventually *.uk* was assigned to Andrew McDowell of University College London—the first country code delegation.

Postel was interested in the design and implementation of the DNS, not semantics. Sensing the annoyances inherent in taking responsibility for naming political entities such as nations, Postel looked for an established, fixed list of country names. He found just what he was looking for in a recent standard issued by the International Standardization Organization, "Codes for the Representation of Names of Countries," designated as standard ISO-3166. The list, developed to guide interchanges among national postal, transport, and communication authorities, assigned two-letter alphabetic codes to countries and territories. (Unfortunately, the official designation for Great Britain under this standard was *.gb,* not *.uk,* but it was too late to alter Postel's original assignment.) In the final version of RFC 920, issued in October 1984, the ISO-3166 list was incorporated as a set of top-level domains.[17]

Reflecting the still unsettled criteria for selecting top-level domains, RFC 920 also authorized a category of the top-level domain that Postel referred to as a "multi-organization," a catch-all that would include large clusters of organizations that were international in scope and did not fit into any of the other categories. It seems to have been Postel's response to pressures on the Internet community to give other data networks their own top-level domains.

The DNS-inspired need to impose categories on the networking world raised other controversies as well. Some commentators criticized the proposed top-level domain names because they might confuse users as to which domain a particular organization could be found under. Would Stanford Research Institute be *sri.edu, sri.cor,* or *sri.org*? An exasperated Postel replied, "This is a naming system, not a general directory assistance system." It was not the job of DNS, he argued, to make domain names guessable by creating unique and intuitive assignments at the top level. "The whole point of domains, he wrote, "is to subdivide the name assignment problem. To try to preserve some higher-level uniqueness would require the very central coordination we are trying to eliminate!"[18] Similar assumptions about guessable names, however, played a big role in later debates over trademarks and domain names, and in resolving that problem, the ICANN Uniform Dispute Resolution Policy, as Postel predicted, had to recentralize authority over second-level name assignments (see chapter 9).

Some of the later problems associated with the delegation of Internet country code top-level domains also were dimly anticipated at this time. On the *msggroup* list, Postel drew a contrast between the Internet world and the more formal and regulated X.400[19] naming conventions under development by a committee of the International Standardization Organization (ISO) and the International Telecommunication Union (ITU). Postel noted that domain names were generally delegated to "the first [responsible] person who asks for the job," whereas the ISO/ITU approach was to give assignment authority to "some bureaucrat that does not really want to do it, but is assigned the job by the government-run PTT."[20] A more pessimistic perspective on this topic was voiced by Stefferud: "The real domain authorities," he wrote, "are going to be selected by some political processes that are not identified well enough, in any of the drafts we have considered, to allow us to seriously consider deciding on any of the TOP-level domains, ARPA included. . . . There just ain't no way that us techies are going to be allowed to dictate domain structures beyond the current bounds of the ARPA and DDN sub-nets." Stefferud proved to be wrong in the short term: the Internet community *was* able to define its own domain-naming structures before the "political processes" he feared caught up with it. But the comment was prescient (see chapters 9 and 11 on the political controversies that emerged over the delegation of country codes).

It was apparent that the meaningfulness of name assignments under DNS had opened up a new world of policy issues. As Steve Kille complained on the *namedroppers* list, "Eternal arguments about what everyone is called . . . [have] already filled far more network bandwidth than any of the design discussions."[21] Even so, the policy debates at this time were not animated by the possibility of economic gains or losses. Once commerce in names entered the picture, these latent controversies became explosive.

Beginning in November 1985, Postel banished semantic issues from the *namedroppers* list altogether, directing them to *msggroup*.[22] In 1987 he formally revised the *namedroppers* list charter to prohibit debates over semantics.[23]

5.2.4 Early Administrative Arrangements

Who actually maintained the DNS and IP address roots? In the mid-1980s, as far as the available evidence indicates, this was not a question that generated much interest or controversy.

Postel's involvement in the definition of the new top-level domains made it clear that he and other researchers at ISI had been given by DARPA what would later be called the *policy authority* over name and number assignment. That is, they established the initial procedures for assigning and keeping track of protocol and network numbers, and decided what top-level domains would be defined. A long-term contract between DARPA and ISI, which listed Postel as the principal investigator, contained a list of five or six work items, some of which were related to assignment functions but included other functions such as the RFC editor.[24] Postel's funding support from DARPA for those tasks would last until 1997.

The actual mechanics of registering domain names and addresses—the *operational authority*—was in different hands. Since 1971 the Stanford Research Institute (SRI) had maintained the *hosts.txt* file for the original

ARPANET and the ARPA-Internet under the pre-DNS naming system. The services were performed under contract to the Defense Communications Agency and given the title Defense Data Network–Network Information Center (DDN-NIC). As domain-style names were introduced, the SRI-operated DDN-NIC retained its familiar role as the central point of coordination for the name space. It became the "registrar of top-level and second-level domains, as well as administrator of the root domain name servers" for both the military and civilian parts of the Internet (RFC 1032, November 1987).[25] In November 1987, SRI's DDN-NIC also took over the IP address assignment and registry function from Postel and Reynolds at ISI (RFC 1020, November 1987). Both transfers of assignment authority followed a precedent in the Defense Department. Once a new system was no longer experimental, control was routinely transferred away from researchers to a military agency and put to practical use. The military agency might then contract with a private firm to perform various functions.[26]

In October 1982, the Defense Communications Agency decided to split the ARPA-Internet into two: the ARPANET would continue to connect academically based researchers supported by the military, while a separate, more restricted and secured MILNET would link military users. About half of the old ARPANET nodes went to MILNET. A few hosts were connected to both, as gateways for intercommunication. Name and number assignment functions for both networks, however, remained centralized at the DDN-NIC.

5.3   Growth and Convergence

The TCP/IP protocol suite, including DNS, entered the data communication environment at a critical and strategic time. Computers and computer communication were just beginning to diffuse widely throughout the business world. Buyers faced a plethora of competing and incompatible networking standards and protocols, such as IBM's Systems Network Architecture (SNA), the ITU's X.25 protocol, Digital Equipment's DECNET, and a variety of local area network standards. Debates and negotiations over technical standards were complicated by the fact that data communication products and markets cut across a wide swath of industries and interest groups. Computer equipment manufacturers, telecommunication service providers, telecommunication equipment manufacturers, and major users all had a stake in the outcome. Inevitably, national governments viewed standardization negotiations as an extension of their industrial policies, adding political and economic considerations to the debate over technology choices.

During the 1980s the International Standardization Organization led a global effort to develop a standardized, open approach to almost all aspects of data communication. This effort became known as Open Systems Interconnection (OSI). The OSI effort had strong backing from the world's traditional standards bodies, telephone companies, and governments. TCP/IP, on the other hand, failed to gain international political backing outside the United States. And yet, by 1991 or so, it was evident that data communication had begun to converge globally on TCP/IP and Internet-style domain names. The Internet, not OSI, ultimately became the common ground upon which most networking initiatives met and achieved interoperability. In this book, I am more interested in demonstrating *that* this happened than in giving a detailed analysis of *why* and *how* it happened. But it is worthwhile to spend some time describing the ways in which the rise of the Internet fulfilled some of the key conditions for winning a standards competition.

5.3.1   Critical Mass: Research and Education Networking

The value of a networking standard depends on who else adopts it. No matter how technically advanced and efficient it may be, a communication protocol or piece of equipment is of little use if it is not compatible with one's desired communication partners. Technology adoption choices are thus powerfully shaped by the choices other adopters make. One of the prerequisites of establishing a standard, therefore, is what economists have called critical mass. This is the minimum threshold of other committed users required to make the adoption of a particular technology attractive to a given user. Networks that achieve critical mass can generate self-sustaining growth. Those that do not achieve critical mass wither and die. One common method of achieving critical mass is to subsidize initial adoption (Rohlfs 1974).

TCP/IP was virtually guaranteed a viable critical mass of initial users by DARPA's willingness to subsidize not only the development of the protocols but also the provision of network services utilizing the protocols. The original ARPANET community created a small but strategic cluster of engineers and scientists strongly committed to TCP/IP and DNS. From 1982 to 1987 this group was expanded to include thousands of users in the federally supported scientific research community.

Parallel to the formation of the ARPA-Internet, the U.S. government had supported several discipline-specific networks, such as Energy Sciences Net, NASA Science Internet, and the National Science Foundation's Computer Science Net (CSNET). From 1983 to 1986 all were linked to the ARPANET backbone using the TCP/IP suite and domain-naming conventions.[27]

In 1983, DARPA also created a $20 million fund to encourage commercial computer vendors to write TCP/IP implementations for their machines. That same year, the protocol was included as the communication kernel for the University of California's popular BSD UNIX software. The Berkeley version of UNIX software was distributed free to universities, thus boosting the dissemination of internetworking capability and ARPANET connectivity (Albitz and Liu 1998, 2).

5.3.2   Converging Networks

The Internet grew not by adding new users, but by interconnecting other networks. Contemporaneous with the rise of the Internet were many networks based on different standards and protocols (Quarterman 1990; Abbate 2000, 200–205). Usenet, for example, used the UUCP protocol to distribute text-based discussion groups, attracting tens of thousands of users around the world by the mid-1980s. BITNET and Fidonet were other networking initiatives, one grounded in academic institutions employing an IBM protocol and the other in IBM-compatible PCs using dial-up bulletin boards. Both brought thousands of people into computer networking. Other governments also began to support research and education networks in the 1980s (JANET in the U.K., GARR in Italy, the Korean National Computer Network, and JUNET in Japan). Probably the most important form of bottom-up networking was the local area network (LAN), using Ethernet and other standards.

In any competition for preeminence with alternative technologies, the Internet enjoyed a decisive advantage. The TCP/IP suite had been designed from the very beginning to interconnect networks using different, potentially incompatible protocols. The design assumptions underlying TCP/IP projected a world of thousands of heterogeneous, independently administered networks that needed to interoperate. This differed radically from alternative protocols such as X.25, which were based on the assumption that data communication would be dominated by a limited number of public data networks run by telephone companies.

Moreover, the ARPA research community aggressively developed gateways that allowed other networking protocols to communicate efficiently with networks using TCP/IP. As email capabilities became popular, for example, pressure grew to interconnect different email systems. Email gateways played a big role in promoting the spread of DNS as a naming convention. Networks with different naming schemes could register a domain name, and the resource records for the registration could point to a computer on the Internet that would act as a mail forwarder (RFC 1168, July 1990). Eventually the DNS became a common addressing syntax that allowed different networks to exchange email effectively (Frey and Adams 1990, 12–13). BITNET and UUCP began to use domain names in 1986; Fidonet followed in 1988.

5.3.3   The National Science Foundation Backbone

Another major step toward critical mass came in 1986, when the U.S. National Science Foundation (NSF) decided to expand Internet connectivity to the entire U.S. higher education community. Working through "cooperative agreements" instead of costly procurement contracts, NSF began to support an Internet backbone starting in 1987, the NSFNET. NSFNET was a virtual private network supplied by a partnership of Merit Networks, Inc. (a nonprofit consortium of university computer centers in the state of Michigan), IBM Corporation, and MCI Telecommunications under a cooperative agreement award from the National Science Foundation.[28] The project signaled a transition from a very limited military and research role to broader education-oriented support for networking.

Technically, the NSF backbone had a special role in the Internet hierarchy: it acted as a generic transit, routing, and switching network (NAS

Table 5.1
Number of Internet Hosts

Date	# Hosts
August 1981	213
May 1982	235
August 1983	562
October 1984	1,024
October 1985	1,961
November 1986	5,089
December 1987	28,174
October 1988	56,000
October 1989	159,000
October 1990	313,000
October 1991	617,000

Source: RFC 1296 (January 1992)

1994, 239). NSF also provided subsidies to "mid-level networks" that operated regional facilities to carry research and education traffic from universities and other eligible institutions to the backbone. During this period the Internet was not available to the general public, and it was accessible to businesses only under special conditions. The NSF-imposed "acceptable use policy" (AUP) limited service "to support [of] open research and education in and among U.S. research and instructional institutions, plus research arms of for-profit firms when engaged in open scholarly communication and research."[29] Still, the TCP/IP Internet was achieving a critical mass of users large enough to put palpable pressure on research and education networks in other parts of the world to become compatible with it. Table 5.1 shows the growth in the number of hosts connected to the Internet in the first decade after the formal specification of the protocols.

Though they were not part of the original ARPANET cadre, those who rose to prominence in research and education networking at this time became leaders in the broader Internet technical community. David Farber at the University of Delaware and Lawrence Landweber at the University of Wisconsin, founders of CSNET, later became board members of the Internet Society. BITNET and CSNET merged in 1989 under the Corporation for Research and Education Networking, which was run by Mike

Roberts, the director of Educom. Roberts also helped to found the Internet Society and later became the first president of ICANN.

As the civilian Internet grew, both the Internet technical community and civilian federal government staff members knew that something important and valuable was happening. "We were interested in the grand vision," one NSF official put it, "and it worked."

5.3.4 Internationalizing Name and Address Assignment

Along with the growth of the Internet came pressures to distribute internationally parts of the name and number assignment functions.

Local area networks were spreading throughout Europe, and scientists in fields such as physics and computer science often used Berkeley UNIX, which came equipped with TCP/IP for LANs. As LANs were connected into European wide-area networks using TCP/IP, a need for name and number coordination and other forms of cooperation arose. This was the rationale behind the formation of Réseaux IP Européens (RIPE) in Amsterdam in 1989.[30] Like many Internet-related organizations, it began as a volunteer effort. The RIPE name was chosen deliberately to tease the European Community funders, whose OSI initiative was named RARE.

RIPE was in a delicate position. European governments backed OSI over Internet standards, and many of the participants were engaged in publicly funded research.[31] One of the common arguments used by the OSI camp against the Internet was that IP addresses were too scarce, and their allocation was under the control of the U.S. government. Members of RIPE convinced the Americans that these complaints could be countered if some part of the address space was delegated to Europe so that locals would control their assignment.[32] The Americans knew that many networks around the world were joining, or attempting to join, the Internet. But the locus of administrative power within a single national government was becoming an obstacle to this growth.

The National Science Foundation's "acceptable use policy," for example, tried to prevent commercial use of the NSF-subsidized Internet backbone. The United States enforced the acceptable use policy primarily by controlling entries into the address registration and domain name system databases. Before registrations could be entered in the DDN-NIC databases, thereby enabling global connectivity, a registrant needed a "sponsor" from a U.S. government agency. Such a policy, however, required foreign networks to adhere to U.S. access and use criteria even if a large portion of their traffic didn't go through the federally sponsored networks.

Beginning in 1990 the Internet technical cadre proposed to make it possible to register a domain name (and *in-addr.arpa* entries) without a U.S. government sponsor (RFC 1174, August 1990).[33] The first non-U.S. address registry, the RIPE Network Coordination Center (RIPE-NCC), was established in April 1992. A few years later the Internet technical community in the Asia-Pacific region, following the European precedent, established AP-NIC to delegate addresses in that region.

Another critical metric of the internationalization of name and address administration was the delegation of country code top-level domains and the formation of domain name registries overseas. A top-level domain delegation meant that domain name registries capable of assigning and registering second-level domain names were being established in other countries. As the networks in these countries were entered into the DNS root, the networking community in those countries acquired a stake in Internet administration.

The first three country code delegations were made in 1985. From 1986 to 1990 about ten were added each year. That pace doubled from 1991 to 1993 (table 5.2).

It was Postel at ISI who filled the critical role of assigning country code top-level domains to specific applicants. From 1985 to 1993, Postel made these delegations using a commonsense application of the DNS concept of a "responsible person." Delegations were made on a first-come/first-served basis as long as certain basic administrative criteria were met. The administrative contact, for example, was expected to be located in the actual territory that the code symbolized. Significantly, that delegation method tended to bypass completely the institutions in other countries that historically had possessed authority over communication, such as government ministries or post, telephone, and telegraph monopolies. Almost none of these institutions were paying attention to the Internet at this time. Typically, the result was that delegations ended up in the hands of university computer science departments or education and research networking organizations in the named territory. Postel himself noted that the person

Table 5.2
Number of Country Code Delegations, 1985–1993

Year	No. of country code delegations
1985	3
1986	10
1987	19
1988	27
1989	35
1990	46
1991	68
1992	85
1993	108

Source: France–Network Information Center (FR-NIC).

in charge of assigning second-level domain names "is generally the first person that asks for the job (and is somehow considered a 'responsible person')."[34]

There was at this time no explicit policy for resolving competing applications for the same assignment. When conflicts occurred—and they began to after 1991 as governments opened up the Internet service provider market to commercial entry—Postel typically used subtle forms of pressure to prod the disputing parties to settle it among themselves, such as refusing to make any delegation until the disputants agreed on a solution.[35] Contention over country code delegations was one of the first indications of the growing value of top-level domains and the ensuing political and economic obligations of managing the root.

5.4   Growth and Governance

When the wave of growth hit, the ARPANET elite—Kahn, Cerf, Postel, Crocker, Clark, and a handful of other colleagues—had been working together on networking continuously for about 15 years. The group formed a tightly knit cadre with strong backing from U.S. government research agencies. As the infrastructure and user base expanded, however, their status as researchers began to blur into a new and very different role as the managers of a new international standards organization. Rising to meet this challenge, they succeeded in forming a robust and unusually open protocol development community. As the importance and size of the Internet increased, they constructed more formal organizational structures around themselves to maintain their position as stewards of the Net. This process culminated in the formation of the Internet Society in 1992. It can be interpreted as an attempt by the Internet cadre to institutionalize their community. The latent contradictions in the process—most notably the ambiguous relationship to the U.S. government—set the stage for the Internet governance struggles of the late 1990s.

5.4.1   Internet Activities Board

The first step in the formation of a governance hierarchy was the creation of an Internet Activities Board (IAB) in late 1983, the precursor of today's Internet Architecture Board. The IAB replaced a standing advisory committee for DARPA's Internet program that had been around since 1979, back when Kahn directed the Information Processing Techniques Office and Cerf was working for him as the Internet program officer.[36] Cerf left DARPA in 1982 to join MCI Telecommunications. The initiative for a new arrangement came from Cerf's replacement, Barry Leiner, and MIT's David Clark, the chair of the earlier committee. The new board was set up as a ten-person panel, with each member supervising a task force devoted to different technical aspects of internetworking. Vint Cerf was designated the first IAB chair, and remained so for the next eight crucial years of Internet expansion. As chair, he decided who else could join the board. The members in turn elected a chair every two years.

The new IAB was just another DARPA committee, a self-selecting group of the original Internet people with no legal identity. According to one contemporary, Jon Postel was the "defacto Internet standards process" and "IAB served as his reviewing team."[37]

Things changed in 1986–1987, when the National Science Foundation became involved in funding the Internet backbone. The stimulus to growth led to increased scale and more complex engineering problems; Postel and the IAB alone could not keep up with the growth. In response to the pressing need for near-term Internet technical standards development, one of the original task forces, known as "Internet Architecture," evolved into the

Internet Engineering Task Force (IETF). Unlike the other task forces, which were limited to invited members, IETF began to hold public meetings four times a year starting in January 1986. At its fifth meeting at the beginning of 1987, 50 people showed up and spontaneously organized themselves into working groups. The channel into Internet activity created by IETF was entered by a growing number of computer scientists and engineers from the public and private sectors. Attendance exceeded 200 by July 1989; in 1992 more than 650 participants attended its summer meeting. The IETF had taken on a life of its own.

5.4.2   Internet Engineering Task Force

Where before engineers had spoken of a "DDN community"[38] or "ARPA community," it was now "the Internet community" or just "the community." IETF meetings and email lists were its social center. The IETF developed its own culture, a technical meritocracy where an informal dress code reigned and working groups could assemble or disband quickly and with minimal bureaucracy. In marked contrast to traditional standards organizations, participants were considered to be individuals and not representatives or delegates of organizations. The emerging community remained nonincorporated and mostly virtual. "There is no membership in the IETF. Anyone may register for and attend any meeting. The closest thing there is to being an IETF member is being on the IETF mailing lists" (RFC 1391, January 1993).

Unlike standards communities grounded in coalitions of vendors or carriers, the early IETF considered interoperability and empowerment of the end user to be basic norms. The standards themselves were nonproprietary. All documentation was open, noncopyrighted, and freely available online. The community "believes that the value of technical ideas should not be decided by vote but by empirical proof of feasibility or, in the language of the engineers, by running code" (Hofmann 1998). The community's political modus operandi was reflected in its famous credo, coined by David Clark in 1992: "We reject presidents, kings and voting; we believe in rough consensus and running code." IETF participants liked to draw unfavorable comparisons between themselves and traditional standards organizations, especially its global competitor, the OSI community.

"In the IETF world we produce running code that has documents that describe it. A lot of other standards organizations produce documents and that's the end of it."[39]

Within this emergent community, the DARPA/ISI veterans stood at the top of the informal pecking order and assumed the role of village elders. There was, in fact, a latent tension between the new participants pouring into the IETF meetings, who thought of themselves as self-governing, and the residual DARPA hierarchy, which thought of the IETF as a "subsidiary organization" under the control of the IAB. But this tension remained in the background until 1992. The relationship at this stage was symbiotic: the old guard provided a basic structure and process within which the others could work productively.

By the fourteenth IETF meeting in July 1989, the IAB/IETF reorganized itself to assume the basic structure that it still retains (although later some important changes were made in how the occupants of leadership positions are selected). The number of task forces was trimmed to two: Internet Engineering and Internet Research (IRTF). Simultaneous with this reorganization, a flurry of new RFCs issued forth from Cerf and Postel documenting the procedures and functional relationships among the elements of the Internet technical community.[40] The documents portray a hierarchical authority structure with the IAB on top, and below it the steering groups, area directors, and working groups of the IETF and IRTF. The notion of an "official IAB protocol standard" was first promulgated at this time (RFC 1083, December 1988).

Robert Kahn left DARPA and, together with Cerf and ISI's Keith Uncapher, formed in 1986 a new nonprofit organization, the Corporation for National Research Initiatives (CNRI) to "foster research and development for the National Information Infrastructure." Both the IAB and the IETF received funding support from the U.S. government. The IETF was supported by means of a cooperative agreement between the National Science Foundation and CNRI. As more federal government agencies were drawn into the TCP/IP Internet, a Federal Research Internet Coordinating Committee (FRICC) was created, in fall 1987. The committee's founding agencies were DARPA, NSF, NASA, the Department of Energy, and the Department of Health and Human Services. FRICC was described by Cerf as the "sponsor" of U.S. Internet research and the "source of support for IAB and its subsidiary organizations" (RFC 1160; see also GAO 1989).

5.4.3 Inventing the Internet Assigned Numbers Authority

RFC 1083 (December 1988), which defined a standards-making process for the new, extended Internet community, was also the first public document to mention an Internet Assigned Numbers Authority (IANA). IANA was said to be located at ISI, and Postel was listed as the contact. Under a longstanding contract between DARPA and ISI, IP address and protocol parameter assignment functions were listed as work items along with several other functions. The contract had been renewed in 1988, which may help to explain the sudden appearance of the IANA label. The contract itself did not use the label, however.

At any rate, the new RFCs made no mention of the DARPA contract. They claimed that IANA's authority was derived from the Internet Activities Board,[41] which was said to have given the IANA "policy-setting authority" over assignment functions.[42] The new documents further claimed that Postel, acting as "the IANA," had "delegated" the administrative aspects of the assignment function to SRI's DDN-NIC.[43] A new world was being defined by the RFCs. In that world, the IAB and Postel's assignment function, both established by DARPA, took on an independent existence. Cerf himself described the IAB at this time as "an unincorporated, volunteer organization, with support to participating individuals/organizations from the U.S. government or from the individual's own organization."[44]

These descriptions reflected the technical community's growing conception of itself as an autonomous, self-governing social complex. Explicit claims on the right to manage name and address assignment were being made by an authority structure that existed solely in Internet RFCs and lacked any basis in formal law or state action. The authority claims nevertheless had significant legitimacy within the technical community. Not only was Postel known, respected, and trusted within the IETF and the supporting government agencies but the RFC series was, for both old and new participants in IETF, the way reality was defined on the Internet. One former NSF official described the situation as an "enlightened monarchy in which the federal government funded the best brains. Their output was

RFCs, which were approved through a collegial, though sometimes brutal process of someone advancing an idea and everyone beating on it until the group consensus was that it would work. These RFCs became the 'law' of the Internet—'law' in the sense of operational practice, not legal jurisdiction. The federal 'managers' were personally involved and 'tracked' the activities as participants and partners. This participatory management model was so uniform and effective that many who were involved in the activity assert (even today) that the Internet was a 'working anarchy.'"[45] Mitchell and most other participants in this process emphasize the atmosphere of trust, collegiality, and cooperation that existed at the time. These halcyon days of the IETF were, of course, grounded in unique and irreproducible conditions. Once the original trust and collegiality were shattered, as they were in 1996, the whole model of a "bottom-up, consensus-based" assignment authority became a travesty.

5.4.4   The Internet Society

Beginning in 1991 the ARPA cadre did attempt to place an organizational and legal capstone around their efforts. They founded a private, nonprofit organization called the Internet Society, which some contemporaries say was inspired by the National Geographic Society (Comer 1995, 11). That step toward formalization immediately engendered conflicts over its authority and methods, however.

The initial impetus for the formation of the Internet Society was the need to protect IETF area directors and working group chairs against lawsuits. Noel Chiappa, whose design of the Proteon router had made him a millionaire, was one of the first members of the Internet Engineering Steering Group (IESG). Concerned about his potential liability, he asked his lawyer about the risk this position entailed and was told that IETF's unincorporated status made him personally liable for standards decisions. That uncomfortable fact was relayed to the IESG and to Cerf in spring 1990. The importance of IETF had grown to the point where its decisions could have economic consequences. Already, participants who felt they had been treated unfairly by the IAB hierarchy were threatening to take legal action.[47] An Internet Society could provide liability insurance to responsible parties in the IETF.

Funding seems to have been another consideration. As TCP/IP internet-working was now a well-developed technology, DARPA was winding down its support. NSF also had a well-defined policy of fostering self-supporting projects, and could not be counted on to fund Internet administration indefinitely. As early as November 1990, Cerf wrote to a colleague about his idea for "The Internet Society, which might be a way of funding the operation of the IAB/IETF/IRTF."[46]

A corporate identity also met the community's need for legitimacy in the international environment. Data networking and the telecommunication industry were beginning to converge. That brought with it a need for more extensive liaisons between the Internet world and the established international telecommunication standards organizations. Anthony M. Rutkowski, an American adviser to ITU Secretary-General Pekka Tarjanne, wanted to bring the Internet activity into the international standards community; at the same time, he saw the more open and flexible standardization processes pioneered by the Internet community as a model that the older institutions should imitate. In the traditional telecom world, as he was learning in Geneva, the idea of putting standards documents online and making them freely accessible was still a very radical one (Malamud 1992). Rutkowski proposed to get the Internet community recognized by international telecommunication standards organizations as a "major community of interest and a significant standards making forum with which liaison is required."[48] Cerf invited Rutkowski to join the IAB as its "international person" in October 1990.

The Internet Society (ISOC) was formed in January 1992. The initial board of trustees included Bob Kahn, Vint Cerf, Mike Roberts of Educom, Charles Brownstein of the National Science Foundation, Lawrence Landweber of the University of Wisconsin, Lyman Chapin, Geoff Huston, Frode Griesen, and Juergen Harms. All but three were Americans. Rutkowski was made executive director. Chapin was chair of the IAB at the time, and Cerf was still an IAB member. In June 1992, at a meeting in Kobe, Japan, the newly constituted Internet Society board prepared a draft charter for an Internet Architecture Board (IAB) that brought "the activities of ISOC and the Internet Activity Board into a common organization" (Cerf 1995). It can be seen as an attempt to self-privatize Internet governance in a way that finessed the issue of whether approval or any other action from the U.S. government was needed.

As soon as it was formed, the Internet Society exposed the chasm between the mindset of the IAB hierarchy that had created it and the rank and file of the IETF. As Brownstein mused later, "It proved to be difficult to convince the IETF itself that ISOC was its legal capstone."[49] In June 1992, only six months after it was founded, the IAB precipitated an outright revolt among IETF participants by announcing that an OSI technology, Connectionless Network Protocol (CLNP), would form the new standard for the Internet's routing and addressing in the future.

The Kobe incident was directly related to the pressures created by the Internet's growth. Classless interdomain routing (CIDR) had not been implemented yet, and the addition of large numbers of new networks to the Net threatened to deplete the IP address space soon. More worrisome, the rise of private, commercial Internet service providers (ISPs) alongside the single NSF backbone made routing much more complicated. With multiple, competing backbones and many new ISPs, as well as continual growth of other networks, routing tables were becoming too large for existing routers to handle.

The IAB chose CLNP because it would have provided a quick fix to the addressing and routing problems. It did so, however, in direct violation of established IETF bottom-up decision-making conventions. The IAB had discarded a recommendation of the IETF's steering group to allow further study and experimentation of the problem for six months. "The problems of too few IP addresses and too many Internet routes are real and immediate, and represent a clear and present danger to the future successful growth of the worldwide Internet," the IAB chair asserted. "The normal IETF process of let a thousands flowers bloom, in which 'the right choice' emerges gradually and naturally from a dialectic of deployment and experimentation, would in this case expose the community to too great a risk that the Internet will drown in its own explosive success before the process had run its course" (Lyman Chapin, July 1, 1992, cited in Hofmann 1998, 15).

The decision sparked a firestorm of protest that forced a full retraction at the next IETF meeting.[50] The controversy forced the IETF to confront fundamental questions about who made decisions within the Internet community and how the decision makers were selected. A new working group led by Steve Crocker was formed, the Process for Organization of Internet Standards, which became known as the POISED working group (RFC 1396). POISED redefined the nomination procedures for appointments to the IAB and the IETF's steering groups. Self-selection by the old Internet elite was no longer acceptable: "There was a strong feeling in the community that the IAB and IESG members should be selected with the consensus of the community" (RFC 1396, 3). The recommendations stopped short, however, of advocating formal elections of leaders. The most important reason the IETF didn't institute voting was that Jon Postel and several other senior figures vowed that they would refuse to run for office in any electoral system. The technical cadre's allergy to democratic methods and public accountability ran deep and would later play a significant role in the battles over the structure of ICANN. By many accounts, that fatal misstep of 1992 discredited the IAB for several years, tarnishing the Internet Society as well. It took until 1996 for ISOC and IAB to regain enough authority within the broader Internet technical community to be in a position to assert leadership.

ISOC also was hampered by incompatible notions about its mission and methods within the board. Rutkowski wanted an industry-based standardization organization that followed the telecommunication industry model in membership if not in procedure. He was particularly interested in forging stronger links to the regional address registries in Asia-Pacific and Europe. Cerf, Kahn, and Landweber, on the other hand, wanted a professional organization to promote the Internet with an emphasis on individual membership. Their model proposed to raise money through conferences, workshops, and fund-raising among "industry and other institutional sources" (Cerf 1995). These conflicts had not been resolved by 1995, and sharp personal differences began to develop between Rutkowski and other board members. Rutkowski was forced to leave. Lacking a clear purpose and method, the Society was not very successful at raising money. So while the IETF continued to grow in size and prestige, its meetings attracting over 2,000 participants, the Internet Society did not yet succeed in becoming its corporate embodiment (Werle and Lieb 2000). Figures 5.1 and 5.2 summarize some of the organizational relationships around 1993.

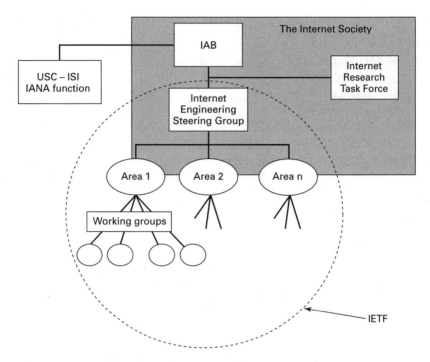

Figure 5.1
Internet governance circa 1993, private sector perspective

5.5   Who Controlled the Root?

Throughout all the growth and change that occurred between 1981 and 1991, most functions related to assigning names and numbers were still supported, directly or indirectly, by the U.S. military. Postel's putative IANA contract was funded by DARPA. The Internet root registry, name registration in all the generic top-level domains, and the address registry were operated by DDN-NIC, a Defense Department contractor. Yet, from 1983 civilian users were driving the growth of the Internet. Only about half of the domain name registrations were registered under the *.mil* top-level domain by 1990. The situation was not tenable in the long term, and between 1990 and 1993 important changes took place in the status of the root.

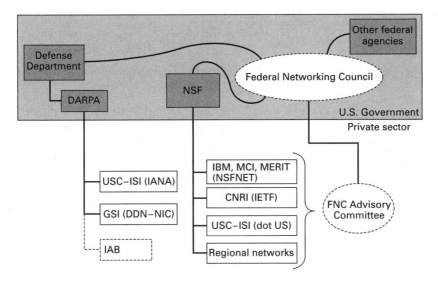

Figure 5.2
Internet governance circa 1993, U.S. government perspective

5.5.1 The Federal Networking Council

The coexistence of a military and civilian Internet raised delicate issues of policy and budget allocation. The U.S. government responded to these problems in a way that finessed agency and departmental boundaries.

Federal oversight of and support for Internet administration was handled by the Federal Networking Council (FNC), a coordinating committee of representatives from federal agencies that operated and used networking facilities and participated in defining the evolution of the federally funded portion of the Internet.[51] The FNC was created by the National Science Foundation in 1990, modeled on what was considered the successful precedent of FRICC. The most significant nonmilitary agencies in the council were the Department of Energy, NASA, and NSF. The FNC structure included an advisory committee of external scientists and network users, blurring the boundary between the public and the private sector.

The FNC became a kind of clearinghouse where the agencies worked out an informal set of quid pro quos to compensate each other for supporting various administrative activities required by the Internet, such as name and address registration, IETF meetings, BIND development, and so on. The military would allow the civilian Internet to use the address and domain name registry of the DDN-NIC; the Energy Department and NSF would fund other things that the military wanted. Generally, the agency that had some established relationship with the desired performer would fund the activity in question. The intra-agency transfers-in-kind were of dubious legality and obscured formal lines of authority, but they allowed the agency heads to proceed with the construction of the Net without getting bogged down in turf wars or legislation.

Throughout this period, there was lingering fear on the civilian side that the whole Internet could come to a screeching halt if the military flexed its muscles. Damage could be done to the collegiality of the Internet community, for example, if the Defense Department exercised its power to restrict access to various countries. The possibility was real, because name and address registration, which was run by the military, was already used as the choke point for the enforcement of acceptable use policies.

Given this situation, from the perspective of the government officials supporting the growth of the civilian Internet, Jon Postel was ideally positioned to guide the assignment functions. Postel was funded by DARPA and thus had roots in the U.S. Defense Department, the looming source of original authority. At the same time, Postel was friendly to the civilian Internet and wholly committed to its growth and expansion. It was in ISI/Postel's own interest to expand his role; as DARPA's interest in supporting the Internet waned, he needed to find new sources of support. In his capacity as an IAB member and administrator of the top-level country code domain for the United States (*.us*) he was also getting support from the civilian agencies. Thus, Postel's operation became the buffer zone between the civilian and military Internet. But the same characteristics that made him so useful in the federal ecology added ambiguity to the locus of policy authority over the root. Was IANA a military or a civilian function? Or was it really part of the IAB hierarchy, beholden to neither branch of government?

5.5.2   Demilitarizing the Root: The InterNIC Agreements

Sometime late in 1990 the Defense Information Systems Agency requested that civilian agencies begin to pay to support nonmilitary registration activity. The FNC decided that the burden of payment would be assigned to the National Science Foundation. The civilian agencies and Internet technical community pushed for the creation of separate contract awards for the civilian and military parts of the registry. Acceding, the Defense Department decided to open the DDN-NIC contract to new competition early in 1991 and make an award to a new contractor that would be concerned solely with registrations for the U.S. Defense Department.[52]

The winner of the new military NIC contract was a company called Government Systems, Inc. GSI simply subcontracted the registry function to a small Virginia-based enterprise named Network Solutions. On October 1, 1991, most of the services formerly provided by SRI, including hosting and distribution of RFCs and Internet-Drafts, registration of network numbers, and help desk services, were transferred to Network Solutions (RFC 1261, September 1991). The performance of domain name registration duties was delayed for nearly nine months, however, because SRI had used proprietary software and the Defense Information Systems Agency was unable to transfer it to the new contractor. Network Solutions subcontracted with Jon Postel to perform TCP port number assignments.

In the meantime, the National Science Foundation secured approval from the FNC to release a solicitation in 1992 for an NREN Internet Network Information Services (NIS) Center to take over key administrative functions for the civilian Internet.[53] The proposed center would include three distinct components: name and number registration services for nonmilitary Internet networks, directory and database services, and information services.

Network Solutions was one of the companies that submitted a proposal to the NSF.[54] The proposal touted the experience it had gained from one year of operating the military NIC. Once again, its proposal included a subcontract with the Information Sciences Institute. Jon Postel was put forward as part of the team with the title of IANA manager and chairman of the Advisory panel for the NREN NIS manager project. The proposal described his role as providing "services as an employee of USC's Information Sciences Institute (ISI), subcontractor to Network Solutions."[55] Joyce Reynolds, Postel's longtime collaborator at ISI, was tapped as "manager of coordination services." Most of the other proposals contained similar or nearly identical language. Network Solutions also proposed to officially designate RIPE as an Internet registry for European countries, and noted its commitment to "fostering development of a Pacific/Asia and other regional counterparts to RIPE."

The National Science Foundation announced its selections on January 5, 1993, awarding three distinct cooperative agreements totaling over US$12 million. Network Solutions was awarded the cooperative agreement for registration services.[56] AT&T's proposal won the directory and database services component, and General Atomics was awarded the information services component. At the request of NSF, the awardees developed a detailed plan to weave the three service components together into one collaborative project called the InterNIC. The Network Solutions part of the agreement was projected to cost US$4.2 million over a five-year, nine-month period.

In keeping with FNC guidelines on cost recovery, the cooperative agreements explicitly anticipated the possibility of charging fees for registration services. A news release announcing the award noted, "NSF expects to engage in an extensive discussion with the domestic and international Internet community on the motivation, strategy, and tactics of imposing fees for these services during the next fifteen months. Decisions will be implemented only after they have been announced in advance and an opportunity given for additional public comment."

At the beginning of the cooperative agreement between NSF and Network Solutions, there were approximately 7,500 domain names registered under the legacy generic TLDs.

5.5.3   Conclusion: The Creative Muddle

The Internet's fast and unexpected growth prompted a number of federal agencies on the civilian side to join the military agencies in supporting it. The ranks of the engineering and user communities swelled, and the technical challenges imposed by an expanding network multiplied. It was during this period (1986–1993) that the locus of authority over the root became unclear. Building the Internet was now an informal collaboration among three separate but interdependent authority centers: an Internet technical community centered in North America but international in scope; a diverse group of civilian federal government agencies interested in stimulating the construction of a national information infrastructure; and the U.S. Defense Department, which had created the protocols and still held residual authority over name and address administration. Among the first two groups, the guiding principle was to do whatever was necessary to promote and accommodate the interconnection of users as cost-effectively as possible. As a result, they were more than willing to delegate assignment authority to foreign entities, interconnect with foreign networks, and place a trusting reliance on the "amorphous network of geeks"[57] organized around the IETF to define policies and standards. Concerns about ownership, formal lines of authority, or jurisdiction over the name and address root were not evident at this time.

It is easy to see why those concerns were overlooked. Worrying about who owned the name and number spaces would not have promoted the Internet's growth at this stage; indeed, by arousing the U.S. military or sparking nationalistic debates it easily could have harmed it. Besides, identifier assignment was perceived as a minor part of the administrative overhead of the Internet. The cost of supporting registration was small compared to the subsidies required by network infrastructure or research and development. There was little anticipation of the potential commercial value of providing registration services. As for policy authority, there were hints of its significance in the early confrontations over top-level domains, and in the U.S. government's use of its control over the Internet registry to enforce the acceptable use policy. But in the huge excitement generated by an expanding new medium, those were minor blips on the radar screen. On most policy issues, the U.S. government was content to defer to the technical community, and the technical community deferred to Jon Postel when it came to names and numbers.

From a legal or organizational standpoint, the lines of policy authority were tangled or nonexistent. But informally, they converged on one man.

6

Appropriating the Root: Property Rights Conflicts

The Internet is no longer restricted to a small group of us who wrote some code. It's not ours anymore and we have to get over that.
—Paul Mockapetris, November 1995

From 1991 on, the Internet was opened to commerce. The growth and commercialization of the Internet, especially the World Wide Web (WWW), endowed the domain name space with a new kind of commercial value. The Web made second-level domain names global identifiers of organizations and locators of Web sites. The policy of charging for domain names proved that a top-level domain holder could generate a significant revenue stream from the sale of second-level registrations. The business value of second-level domains also heightened the significance of the administration of the root zone. Whoever controlled the definition of the root zone file could authorize new top-level domain registries that could sell domain names to the public.

As market forces began to swirl around the domain name space, the ambiguities surrounding its ownership and control became evident. A number of parties, most notably trademark owners, began to assert claims over domain name assignments. In addition to the intellectual property–based conflicts over second-level names, property rights conflicts emerged over the assignment of top-level names, and over the root itself. Ownership and control of the Internet Protocol (IP) address root also became an explicitly debated issue at this time. It was the domain name space, however, that catalyzed the most appropriation activity and the most difficult policy issues.

6.1   Endowment: Commercial Use and the World Wide Web

By mid-1990 it had become evident that the Internet was outgrowing its research and education roots. TCP/IP was becoming the long-awaited open platform for global data networking. Regional networks and the NSFNET backbone operator were beginning to eye a potential commercial market for Internet access. By 1990 some of the mid-level networks had formed commercial Internet service providers (ISPs) to operate alongside their subsidized regional networks.[1]

6.1.1   A Market for Internet Access

In May 1991, after much public and private discussion of commercialization and privatization, the National Science Foundation (NSF) permitted commercial traffic to cross the NSFNET, provided that certain stipulations regarding cost recovery, surplus revenues, and quality of service were followed.[2] But the commingling of commercial and noncommercial traffic and providers posed serious policy dilemmas for NSF.

In 1993, NSF responded to the problem by moving to an entirely new architecture for the Internet.[3] The agency withdrew from backbone support altogether and tried to facilitate a commercial marketplace for Internet access composed of multiple, competing backbone providers. Commercial ISPs would be interconnected at five NSF-designated and partially supported network access points (NAPs).[4] The new architecture went into effect in 1995, and NSFNET was decommissioned in April of that year. The transition was so successful that no one noticed; indeed, within a few years of the changeover the NAPs' role as interconnection points had been minimized because most ISPs began to rely on private contracting with backbone and transit providers for most of their interconnection.

The supply of Internet connectivity by a commercial market was a major stimulus to the demand for domain names. For the new ISPs, domain name registration and IP address assignment became required inputs into their service provision and thus acquired commercial value. Ordinary households and businesses joining the Internet brought a consumer mentality rather than a technical-engineering perspective to the selection and utilization of domain names.

6.1.2 The WWW: Domain Names Transformed

The most dramatic stimulus to the demand for domain names came from the emergence of the World Wide Web between 1990 and 1995. The World Wide Web was a client-server software application that made the Internet easier to navigate and more fun to use by linking and displaying documents (or other objects stored on networked computers) by means of a graphical user interface. The software code for Web servers and the first portable browser were created by European physicists at CERN in 1990 (Cailliau 1995). The Web was popularized by the public release of a graphical browser called Mosaic in early 1993 by the National Center for Supercomputer Applications in the United States.[5]

Only a year after its release, in January 1994, there were 20 million WWW users, 95 percent of them using Mosaic. The World Wide Web's hypertext transfer protocol (HTTP) had become the second most popular protocol on the Net, measured in terms of packet and byte counts on the NSFNET backbone.[6] After one more year, in early 1995, the World Wide Web passed the venerable file transfer protocol (ftp) as the application generating the most traffic on NSFNET. With the founding of Netscape in 1994, browsers and Web software became a commercial industry. Netscape released its first Navigator browser at the beginning of 1995 and quickly displaced Mosaic. Microsoft rushed Internet Explorer to market at the end of the year. With user-friendly, point-and-click navigation available, the Internet attracted a much broader base of users, including household consumers and small businesses. The Internet had suddenly become a mass medium for communication and commerce.

A quantum change now took place in the status of domain names.

The Web had its own addressing standard, known as Uniform Resource Locators (URLs). URLs were designed to work like a networked extension of the familiar computer file name. Web documents or other resources were given names within a hierarchical directory structure, with directories separated by slashes. In order to take advantage of the global connectivity available over the Internet, URLs used a domain name as the top-level directory. The basic syntax of a URL could be represented thus:

http://<domain name>/<directory or resource name>/<directory or resource name>/etc . . .

The hierarchy to the right of the domain name could be as shallow or as deep as the person in charge of the Web site wanted. URLs were never intended to be visible to end users. The Web's inventors thought they would hide behind hyperlinks.

By using domain names as the starting point of URLs, the Web altered their function in profound and unanticipated ways. As the term *resource locator* suggests, Web addresses were names for *resources,* which meant *any* kind of object that might be placed on the Web: documents, images, downloadable files, services, mailboxes, and so on. Domain names, in contrast, had been originally intended to name host computers, machines on the Net. And URLs were not just addresses but locators of content. A user only needed to type a name into the URL window of a browser and (if it was a valid address) HTTP would fetch the corresponding resource and display it in the browser. A URL included "explicit instructions on how to access the resource on the Internet" (Berners-Lee 1994). Domain names, in contrast, were originally conceived as locators of IP addresses or other resource records of interest to the *network,* not of things that people would be interested in seeing.

As the Web made it easy to create and publish documents or other resources on the Internet, the number of Web pages began to grow even faster than the number of users. It did not take users long to discover that shorter, shallower URLs were easier to use, remember, and advertise than longer ones. The shortest URL of all, of course, was a straight, unadorned domain name. Thus, if one wanted to post a distinct set of resources on the Web or create an identity for an organization, product, or idea, it made sense to register a separate domain name for it rather than creating a new directory under a single domain name. For example, a car manufacturer like General Motors with many different brand or product names such as Buick or Oldsmobile eventually learned to just register *buick.com* and use that as the URL rather than *gm.com/cars/buick/,* even if all the information resided on a single computer. The DNS protocol made it fairly easy to point multiple domain names at the same computer, so there was not much waste of physical resources. Domain names began to refer to content resources rather than just network resources.

As more and more users began to type domain names into their browsers' URL windows, yet another fateful transformation of domain names' function occurred. Many novice users did not understand the hierarchical structure of the domain name system (DNS) and simply typed in the name of something they wanted. The Internet would interpret this simple name as an invalid domain and return an error message. As a user-friendly improvement in Web browser software, the browser manufacturers began to use *.com* as the default value for a name typed in with no top-level extension. If the user typed "cars" into the URL window, for example, instead of returning an error message the browser would automatically append *.com* to the end and *www.* to the beginning, and display to the user the Web site at *www.cars. com*. In doing so, the browser manufacturers reinforced the naive end user's tendency to treat domain names as a kind of directory of the Internet. This practice also massively increased the economic value of domain names registered under the *.com* top-level domain. For millions of impatient or naive users wary of search engines and other more complicated location methods, the default values turned the DNS into a search engine exclusively devoted to words registered under the *.com* domain.

Although it would take several years for the full economic effects to be felt, the "Webification" of domain names was the critical step in the endowment of the name space with economic value. It massively increased the demand for domain name registrations and gave common, famous, or generic terms under the *.com* space the commercially valuable property of being able to effortlessly deliver thousands if not millions of Web site "hits."

A serendipitous intersection of technologies produced human and market factors that transformed one technology's function. The transformation of domain names was driven by rational economic concerns about visibility in an emerging global marketplace. In the early days of the Web, a simple, intuitive name in the *.com* space might generate millions of viewers with very little investment. If someone else controlled "your" name in that space, your reputation or customer base might suffer. Thus, for economic and legal reasons, DNS policy has ever since been fixed upon the use of domain names as locators of Web sites. The forms of regulation and administration being imposed on DNS by ICANN are largely based on the assumption that DNS is used exclusively for that purpose.

Technologists who object that "DNS was never designed to be used this way" are correct in a narrow sense but miss the larger point. Many technologies end up being used in ways that their designers never intended or

Table 6.1
Number of InterNIC Domain Name Registrations, July 1994 and February 1996

No. of Second-Level Registrations

Top-Level Domain	July 1994	February 1996
.com	12,687	232,004
.edu	1,292	2,463
.org	1,388	17,775
.net	545	10,890
.gov	202	460
Other	–	168
Total	16,114	263,760

Sources: For 1994—Network Wizards Internet Domain Survey, <http://www.isc.org/ds/WWW-9501/second-levels.html>; for 1996—Registration Services Performance Measures for February 1996, <http://www.networksolutions.com/en_US/legal/internic/coop-stats/feb96.html>.

visualized. These unanticipated uses in turn can generate inflection points in a technology's evolution by provoking new forms of economic activity and new forms of regulation. This in turn can reward certain technological capabilities and effectively foreclose others.

6.1.3   Charging for Domain Names
The cooperative agreement between the National Science Foundation and Network Solutions (NSI) for registration services was concluded just months before the Web's sudden transformation of domain names. Neither party to the transaction had any idea of what was in store for them. Post-Web, the new registry was faced with a huge increase in the volume of registrations, and almost all of the increase was concentrated in the *.com* top-level domain. Registration applications handled by Network Solutions went from 300 per month in 1992 to 1,500 per month in mid-1994, then to over 30,000 per month in late 1995. The statistics in table 6.1 show the growth in the total number of names registered by the InterNIC (see section 5.5.2) from July 1994 to February 1996, as well as the dominant role of *.com* registrations in accounting for that growth.

NSF had no charter to support commercial registrations. A report by Jon Postel to the Internet Architecture Board in October 1994 observed that "NSF is getting tired of paying for 2,000 .com registrations per month, each one taking about four minutes of someone's time, allowing for little to no screening of the requests."[7] NSF held consultative discussions on charging for domain names, and an expert advisory panel brought in to evaluate the performance of the InterNIC contractors concluded in a December 1994 report that Network Solutions should "begin charging for .COM domain name registrations, and later charge for name registrations in all domains."[8] Shortly after the decision to charge was made, a multibillion-dollar Washington-area defense contractor, Science Applications International Corporation (SAIC), purchased Network Solutions. The transaction was concluded in March 1995. In a letter from NSF to Network Solutions dated September 13, 1995, Amendment 4 to the cooperative agreement officially authorized the registry to charge fees for domain name registrations in *.com, .net,* and *.org.*[9] Initial registration of a name would cost US$100 and last for two years; annual renewal after the two-year period would cost US$50. Thirty percent of the registration fee would go into an "intellectual infrastructure fund" at the disposal of the NSF. NSF would continue to pay for *.edu* registrations and on an interim basis for *.gov.* The charges went into effect September 14, 1995.

The Web and the commercialization of Internet access stimulated the development of a domain name market in other countries as well. In England, commercial ISPs arose in the early 1990s and formed an organization known as the London Internet Exchange (LINX). In order to meet the ISPs' demand for domain names for their customers, a registry was operated by a voluntary "naming committee" that included the designated technical contact for the *.uk* top-level domain, Dr. William Black, and volunteers from various LINX members. No charge was levied by the naming committee for domain name registration. By 1996, however, the need for a more professional, well-defined, and open service for registrations in *.uk* prompted the creation of Nominet UK, a new nonprofit corporation. Nominet was organized as a wholesaler of domain names to ISPs, with the initial fee set at 60 pence for each two-year period. In Germany the *.de* registry was run by universities until late in 1996, when a consortium of ISPs formed DENIC. Asian and developing country registries, however, tended to remain closely tied to their roots in universities and government science and technology ministries for a longer period of time. As of March 1997 registries serving 67 of the world's country code top-level domains (ccTLDs) charged fees for domain name registration.[10] None of them, however, were operating at anything near the scale of the InterNIC.

6.1.4   The Name Space as Common Pool Resource

The InterNIC's response to the Web explosion turned the generic top-level domain name space into a common pool resource. The massive increase in the volume of registrations undermined the feasibility of any administrative rationing rules except first-come/first-served.

The complete opening up of domain name registrations was not quite a deliberate policy decision, but it was the only option, given the pressures of growth and the prior commitment to accommodating the widest diffusion of the Internet. The costs created by registrations quickly exceeded the staff and budget constraints of the InterNIC cooperative agreement. Network Solutions was using funds from other projects to cover the cost of the staff, office space, phone systems, and computers needed to keep up. The InterNIC could not keep up with growth if it attempted to review and police registration applications. As a former worker put it, "In growth from 400 requests per day total—including new, modify and delete for domains, contact updates, host updates—to 25,000 and up per day, much of the focus became turn-around time and protection of data being updated via authentication. Policing was not given much priority under the technology and funding constraints. The whole registration process/budget was not designed for vanity-tagging the Internet."[11]

As the process of registering a domain name was accelerated and automated, the InterNIC abandoned previous attempts to enforce a rule of one domain name per person.[12] It also gave up any attempt to maintain distinctions between the types of registrants that were allowed to use names in *.com, .net,* and *.org.*[13] It was not possible for InterNIC to decide whether a particular applicant had a "right" to the specific name he was trying to register. Any such reviews, which would require manual handling of applications, would have slowed the execution of domain name registrations to a trickle, creating a bigger and bigger backlog.

Thus, the InterNIC's part of the name space became a common pool resource. Individuals appropriated units of the resource (they registered second-level names) using the rule of capture. There were almost no economic or legal constraints on appropriation. A user could register any name she wanted and take any number of names. Until September 1995 names could be registered at no charge (although users who relied on Internet service providers might incur registration-related service charges). Even after fees were imposed, it took months for Network Solutions to begin billing and much longer to collect effectively.[14] Once it was implemented, the fee for registration was trivial compared to the perceived economic value of many names. And the prices were the same for all names, regardless of the variations in their value. The source of the economic value, of course, was a name's ability to deliver the browser-using public to a particular Web site.

The Web set in motion a positive feedback loop that led to the overwhelming dominance of the domain name market by *.com, .net,* and *.org* for the rest of the decade. The initial flood of registrations under *.com* encouraged browser programs to make it the default. The browser defaults vested *.com* registrations with a special value. That value encouraged individuals to appropriate names in *.com,* leading to even faster growth in that domain. The large number of registrations in *.com* reinforced the expectations of the user public that most of the content on the Web would be registered under *.com,* making it more likely that users would look for sites there. That further accelerated the demand for *.com* registrations, continuing the cycle. The *.net* and *.org* domains became second-best options for those who could not get *.com* or a way of protecting the exclusivity of a *.com* registration through multiple registrations. As the number of registrations exploded, it became less and less feasible to discriminate among applications.

The global dominance of *.com* was further reinforced by the more restrictive approaches to registration taken in most other countries. While the InterNIC strained and struggled to accommodate demand, registries in many other countries imposed rigid rules on who could get a domain name and how many they could get. Whereas *.com* opened up the second level of the hierarchy to any taker, many country codes created naming conventions at the second level that users were forced to fit into. Japan and France, for example, heavily restricted eligibility for domain names and tried to fit all registrations into predetermined hierarchies.[15] The *.com, .net,* and *.org* domains also were more attractive to businesses seeking a global audience because of their generic character. Thus, by July 1995 there were two and a half times as many host computers under the Inter-NIC domains (3.92 million) as there were in the seven largest country domains combined (1.52 million in Great Britain, Japan, Germany, Australia, Canada, Netherlands and France).[16] The U.K. registry, the second largest in the world at the end of 1996, was fielding 3,000 to 4,000 registrations a month; Network Solutions was registering 75,000 to 85,000.[17] As late as 1999 more French organizations were registered under *.com* than under *.fr.* As of late 2000 barely 200,000 domains were registered under *.jp* (Japan), fewer than the *.com* domain in January 1996.

By allowing the market to evolve spontaneously as a common pool, the Americans created rights conflicts, but they also created an entirely new industry and cultivated among U.S. businesses the technical and management skills needed to achieve global leadership in it. Moreover, precisely because the uncontrolled appropriation activity pulled the government and the industry into new kinds of property rights conflicts, American stakeholders, for better or worse, would take the lead in defining the terms of the institutional innovations that would be required to resolve them.

6.1.5 Property Rights Conflicts

An inescapable feature of common pool resources is that as demand intensifies, appropriators are more likely to come into conflict with each other. As this happens, the conflicting parties may begin to articulate property claims and seek to have exclusive ownership rights created or upheld by legal and political institutions. Property rights conflicts over domain names began to achieve public visibility in 1994, fairly soon after the Web's transformation of the *.com, .net,* and *.org* domains. The conflicts became widespread in 1995 and 1996.

There were two catalysts of rights conflicts. One was the perceived clash between trademark protection, a preexisting form of property rights in names, and second-level domain name registrations. The other was a conflict over the right to top-level domain name assignments, which were valued because they might bring with them the right to sell registrations to second-level domain names. Both conflicts led inexorably to contests over control of the root, for whoever set policy at the root level would significantly affect events at the lower levels. The rest of the chapter follows the rights conflicts up the domain name hierarchy, starting with second-level domains and moving up to the root level.

6.2   Conflicts over Second-Level Domains

With the rise of the World Wide Web, second-level domain names in the guise of Web URLs began to appear frequently on television and in print, e.g., *www.dell.com*. The domain names of new online businesses, such as *amazon.com*, were taking on the characteristics of brand names. The growing perception that domain names possessed significant business value stimulated efforts to secure stronger property rights over them. Trademark litigation became the vehicle for these assertions. Section 6.2.1 outlines a taxonomy of the types of conflicts that developed.

6.2.1   Domain Name Disputes

Character String Conflicts   One type of conflict that emerged quickly during the domain name rush of 1994–1996 was contention over the same character string. Two or more organizations with the same name, or with some legitimate reason to register a domain, desired the same registration. Under pure common pool conditions, whoever registered the name first would get the assignment. The heightened economic stakes created by commerce on the Web, however, gave some market participants a strong incentive to challenge that rationing principle. The most convenient vehicle for such challenges was a trademark claim. As one lawyer involved in domain name disputes wrote, "In a substantial fraction of domain name disputes the plaintiff presents the case as if it were a traditional trademark case with goods or services being marketed in a way that allegedly gives rise to confusion, while the reality is that no goods or services are involved, let alone confusion. In such disputes it becomes clear that the complaint, reduced to its essence, is 'we wish we had registered the domain name first, and we really want to have the domain name now'" (Oppedahl 1997).

The potential for conflict over character strings was exacerbated by the unexpected way the Internet emerged as a mass medium. Hundreds of major companies were slow to recognize the commercial potential of the Internet. A report by *Wired* magazine found that in May 1994 only one-third of the Fortune 500 companies had registered domains corresponding to their corporate names, and 14 percent of them had had their names registered by someone else (Quittner 1994). The Miller Brewing Company found that *miller.com* had been registered by a computer consultant with the surname Miller. To the chagrin of Beanie Babies manufacturer Ty, Inc., its corporate name had been registered by an individual whose three-year-old son was named Ty. In some cases, the companies would simply pay the original registrant to relinquish the name, but in many others, the companies asserted trademark infringement and initiated or threatened lawsuits. The practice of using trademark litigation (or the Network Solutions dispute resolution policy; see section 6.2.2) to extract desirable domain names from legitimate prior registrants became known as "reverse domain name hijacking" (Rony and Rony 1998, 392). A study conducted in 1998 found that about half of the publicly documented cases of domain name–trademark conflict could be classified as rooted in character string contention (Mueller 1999b).

Name Speculation   Rights conflicts also developed over the practice of name speculation. Name speculation occurred when an individual registered domain names entirely for their resale value. From an economic point of view, name speculation was a predictable form of arbitrage given common pool conditions. The value of the names available, measured in terms of their predicted resale value or their ability to generate Web traffic, exceeded the cost of acquiring them. Since there were no limits on appropriating names and the registry's pricing did not discriminate between different levels of value among available names, the formation of a secondary market was inevitable. By 1997–1998 there were many organized domain name brokerages and online auction sites.

A large portion of name speculation involved registration of generic or catchy terms that the registrant thought might have value to someone later. As early as October 1994 a journalist observed that "savvy business folks are racing out and registering any domain name they can think of: their own company names, obviously, and generic names like *drugs.com* and *sex.com,* and silly names that might have some kind of speculative value one day, like *roadkill.com*" (Quittner 1994). Common pool conditions encouraged indiscriminate appropriation, pushing major corporations such as Proctor and Gamble and Kraft/General Foods to register up to 200 domain names, including *badbreath.com, underarm.com,* and *diarrhea. com.*

On the other hand, a significant number of early name speculators deliberately registered and attempted to sell famous company names or trademarked brand and product names. Typically, the speculator would register the names but not link them to any Web site, and then contact the organizations or people with an interest in the name (or wait for them to call) and offer to sell the names to them for five- or six-figure sums. One of the pioneers of this type of speculation was an Illinois individual named Dennis Toeppen, who in 1995 registered approximately 200 domain names, most of them trademarked, such as "Eddie Bauer," many of them coined or unique, such as "Panavision." When contacted by the owners, Toeppen made explicit offers of sale to the companies. These practices led to strong legal challenges to the first-come/first-served principle by outraged trademark holders. At the time, the legal status of name speculation was still unclear. Toeppen's lawyers affirmed the legitimacy of the first-come/first-served principle, and questioned whether mere registration of a domain name without any associated use capable of confusing or misleading customers could qualify as infringement or dilution. In the *Intermatic* and *Panavision* decisions, however, the U.S. federal courts came out unambiguously against speculation in trademarked names. Noting that while "mere registration, by itself" was not sufficient to infringe or dilute a mark, the court said the defendant was making commercial use of the marks by trading on their economic value as domain names.[18] Such an unauthorized commercial use qualified as dilution under federal law. An analogous case in Great Britain also found name speculators guilty of passing off.[19]

Typo-Squatting　A variant of name speculation that developed somewhat later was typo-squatting. Typo-squatters registered common misspellings of the domain names of popular Web sites or company names in order to benefit from potentially large volumes of spillover traffic generated by users who incorrectly typed in a domain name (table 6.2). Major

Table 6.2
Typosquatting on Yahoo!

All 37 names were registered by one person	
atlantayahoo.com	*yahooe.com*
ayahoo.com	*yahoof.com*
bostonyahoo.com	*yahoofr.com*
cayahoo.com	*yahoola.com*
dcyahoo.com	*yahoony.com*
dfwyahoo.com	*yahoop.com*
jahu.com	*yahoouk.com*
kyahoo.com	*yahop.com*
layahoo.com	*yahpoo.com*
nyahoo.com	*yalhoo.com*
nyyahoo.com	*yaohh.com*
pageryahoo.com	*yashoo.com*
seattleyahoo.com	*yayou.com*
wyahoo.com	*yhahoo.com*
yaghoo.com	*yhu.com*
yahjoo.com	*yiahoo.com*
yahoa.com	*youhoo.com*
yahooca.com	*yuahoo.com*
yahoode.com	

ICANN Uniform Dispute Resolution Policy
Source: (UDRP), WIPO case no. D2000-0273

Internet-related names such as "AOL" and "Yahoo" were favorite targets of typo-squatters.[20] By diverting users to their own Web sites, typo-squatters might generate thousands of "hits," which were commercially valuable as a way of getting the visitors interested in their own wares or increasing revenue from advertisers whose payments were based on "hits." The more innocuous typo-squatter sites just contained a display ad and even a link to the correctly typed site name, but in a few cases careless typists found themselves staring at porn sites.

Parody, Preemption, and Diversion   The unique ability of domain names to locate and retrieve Web sites facilitated their use for preemption or diversion of competitors' Internet traffic. By registering a competitor's name in the coveted *.com* space, one could block it from getting the name and, even better, divert people who might be seeking the competitor's site. Some surprisingly large and respectable businesses succumbed to this temptation in 1994. Telecommunication carrier Sprint briefly held the registration for *mci.com*. The college directory and test preparation service Princeton Review registered *kaplan.com*, a domain name associated with its chief competitor, Stanley Kaplan, and used it to post an unfavorable comparison of Kaplan's service with its own. An arbitrator ordered the name transferred to Kaplan.[21]

These kinds of cases involved commercial activities that fell rather easily into established definitions of unfair competition. But domain names could also be used as the labels for sites that parodied or criticized the named organization. The most famous early case of this type involved the domain name *peta.org*. PETA was an acronym commonly associated with the animal rights group People for the Ethical Treatment of Animals. In 1995 *peta.org* was registered by Michael Doughney and used to create a satirical Web site promoting a fictitious organization, People Eating Tasty Animals. Litigation commenced in 1996;[22] one product of this was the formation of the Domain Name Rights Coalition, a Washington-based activist organization funded by Doughney to lobby against the domination of the domain name space by trademark interests. The animal rights group PETA, taking a page from its critic's book, registered *ringlingbrothers.com* and used it to direct Web users to information critical of circuses' treatment of animals. An anti-abortion activist registered *plannedparenthood.com*, using it to promote his book against abortion.[23] These cases raised important questions about the definition of commercial use and the proper balance between free speech rights and intellectual property rights in the name space.

Rights of Personality   Another area in which the nature of domain name conflicts tested the application of traditional trademark rights involved the registration of other people's names. Usually the name registered was of someone famous: movie stars, singers, and other media personalities, real and invented. In some cases, the registrations seem to have been executed for speculative purposes, and in other cases, they were linked to fan sites or information about the personality in question.[24]

6.2.2 The Network Solutions Dispute Resolution Policy

One early lawsuit over a second-level domain name prompted Network Solutions to draw back from pure first-come/first-served assignment criteria. In March 1994 a Virginia business consultant, David Boone, registered the domain *knowledgenet.com* as part of his plan to build an email circle of business consultants for the exchange of referrals and leads. Less than a year earlier, a computer networking and consulting firm, KnowledgeNet, Inc., had registered a service mark and trademark (but not a domain name) for the same term. After learning of Boone's domain name registration in June 1994, it sent cease-and-desist letters to Boone and complained to Network Solutions. The registry insisted that it assigned domain names on a first-come/first-served basis and could not make any changes without the consent of Boone's company. Boone refused to give up the domain name.

KnowledgeNet sued for trademark infringement, unfair competition, and "racketeering activities" in federal court in December. The defendants included the registry Network Solutions and Boone's Internet service provider as well as Boone. Network Solutions was charged with "facilitat[ing] illegal use of the marks" by "allowing, and then refusing to reassign, the domain name."[25] The case was settled in mid-1995 when Boone found the legal expenses of defending his case too burdensome and entered into a consent decree giving the plaintiff nearly everything it had asked for. But the KnowledgeNet case had unsettled Network Solutions, at the time a small company unused to lawsuits and financially strapped by the flood of registrations. In July 1995, Network Solutions issued a "Domain Dispute Resolution Policy Statement" designed to shield itself from future trademark-related lawsuits. In its policy statement, Network Solutions declared that it "has neither the legal resources nor the legal obligation to screen requested Domain Names to determine if the use of a Domain Name by an Applicant may infringe upon the right(s) of a third party." It then set out a series of contractual conditions that would be imposed on all registrants in the InterNIC-operated domains. It required registrants to certify that they had a bona fide intention to use the name, and that the proposed name did not interfere with or infringe the trademarks or intellectual property rights of any third parties. The policy gave Network Solutions the right to withdraw a domain name from use if presented with a court order or arbitration panel decision transferring the name.

The policy's most important and controversial feature was an attempt to privilege trademark holders in disputes over names in order to protect Network Solutions from litigation. If a party could show that it had a trademark in a domain name registered by someone else, and if the registrant could not present evidence of its own trademark in the name, or show use of the name prior to the grant of the trademark, the registry would place the disputed name on hold pending resolution of the dispute. As long as a domain was suspended, the name would not resolve in DNS.[26] Only federally registered marks were recognized, leaving common law trademarks unprotected.

The opportunity to suspend disputed names was quickly seized upon by hundreds of trademark holders. Dispute resolutions under the policy numbered 166 in 1995, 745 in 1996, 905 in 1997, and 838 in 1998. But the policy was widely criticized among Internet users and the legal profession for its encouragement of reverse domain name hijacking. The policy, one legal scholar wrote, "unilaterally cuts off a domain name at the behest of a trademark holder, even in the absence of infringement or dilution, ignoring otherwise permissible concurrent use of registered and common law trademarks. This policy also encourages poaching by trademark holders who might not otherwise have a colorable claim in court" (Nathenson 1997).

By substituting a mechanical test (the presence or absence of a prior trademark registration) for the case-specific determinations needed to evaluate claims of trademark infringement, the policy routinely produced blatant injustices. Generic terms innocently registered under the *.com* domain, such as *clue, perfection, prince,* and *roadrunner,* were suspended under the policy. The policy reached its nadir in 1997, when it was invoked by the Prema Toy Company, producers of the Gumby and Pokey characters, in an attempt to take away the domain *pokey.org* from a 12-year-old child's personal Web site.[27] Moreover, the policy failed to keep Network Solutions out of litigation. Although the small businesses and individual domain name holders who were the victims of the policy lacked the resources to be as litigious as the typical trademark holder, a significant number of them challenged Network Solutions' domain name suspensions in court.[28] The policy did not satisfy many trademark holders, either, because it could not encompass misspellings or variants, just domain names that exactly matched the character string of a registered trademark. The unpopular policy went through several iterations after 1995 as the negative reaction mounted. See Ballon (2000) and Oppedahl (1996) for detailed descriptions.

6.2.3　The Liability of the Registry

Another trademark-related lawsuit sought to impose on Network Solutions an even stronger form of involvement in the policing of registrations. The defense contractor Lockheed Martin was attempting to prevent various small businesses and individuals from registering the term "skunk works" or several variants as a domain name. On May 7, 1996, Lockheed sent Network Solutions a letter advising the company that Lockheed owned the mark and demanded that the InterNIC cease registering domain names that referred to or included the trademarked terms. It also requested a list of registered domain names containing the words "skunk works" or any variations of it. When Network Solutions refused to accede, Lockheed sued, contending that the registry had a duty to screen domain name applications and that its failure to do so made it guilty of trademark infringement, dilution, and contributory infringement.

In November 1997, U.S. District Judge Dean Pregerson issued a summary judgment clearing Network Solutions of the charges.[29] The opinion is one of the most clearly stated and carefully reasoned discussions of the relationship between domain names and trademarks in U.S. law. Domain names, the judge noted, have two distinct functions: a technical one as a unique identifier of hosts on the Internet, and a trademark function that can identify an offering of goods or services on the Internet. Pulling together legal precedents involving toll-free telephone numbers, radio broadcast call letters, and other domain name cases, the opinion held that registration of a domain name by itself cannot infringe a trademark. Infringement occurs when the domain name is *used* in certain ways. Network Solutions was innocent of trademark infringement because it was not making use of the domain names to identify goods and services: "NSI's use of domain names is connected to the names' technical function on the Internet to designate computer addresses, not to the names' trademark function to distinguish goods and services." NSI was innocent of dilution because, although it profited from the sale of domain names, it was not trading on the value of domain names as trademarks but only on their value as addresses. Finally, Network Solutions was cleared of contributory infringement because its involvement with the use of a domain name was remote; the company had little if any knowledge of or control over the use of a domain name, nor was it in any position to judge the validity of a trademark claim. Network Solutions, in its capacity as registry, had "no affirmative duty to police the Internet for infringing uses" of trademarks. A similar case seeking to find the New Zealand country code registry guilty of contributory infringement also resulted in a victory for the registry, absolving it of responsibility to police trademarks at the point of registration.[30]

6.2.4   The Battle over Transaction Costs

From 1995 to 1997, the courts in the United States and in other nations gradually established precedents capable of resolving property rights conflicts over second-level domain names. Established legal tests for trademark infringement, such as consumer confusion, commercial use, unfair competition and contributory infringement, were being applied to the new fact patterns of domain name registration. The courts were consistently deciding against speculators in trademarked names and (fairly consistently) overturning attempts at reverse domain name hijacking. The courts had also established a clear precedent that domain name registries could not be vested with a duty to police the registration process on behalf of trademark owners.

And yet, major trademark holders were still highly dissatisfied with the situation. They felt victimized by rampant name speculation and did not see litigation as the answer. The cost of nuisance registrations (US$100) was extremely low; the cost of litigation to recover objectionable registrations started in the tens of thousands of dollars. The high transaction costs of litigation adversely affected innocent registrants as well as trademark holders because many ordinary registrants could not afford to contest unfair challenges. Both foreign and domestic registrants were not required to identify themselves correctly in the registration record.

In this regard, the NSI dispute resolution policy was a highly significant development in Internet governance. Although put forward by Network

Solutions with the stated objective of relieving itself of responsibility for screening registrations, it was actually the first attempt to bypass formal litigation, rooted in the law of territorial states, and to use the bottleneck power of the registry itself to police and enforce property rights in names. Similarly, the lawsuits attempting to force registries to police registrations on behalf of trademark holders, despite their lack of success, were also milestones in the struggle over name space governance. They indicated clearly that trademark holders wanted to be able to shift the transaction costs of policing marks in the name space away from themselves and onto other parties. What national courts refused to give them, applying traditional standards of law, they would achieve later via the World Intellectual Property Organization (WIPO) and ICANN.

And so, a new epistemic community was drawn into the domain name fray: the intellectual property bar. Organizations such as the International Trademark Association (INTA), the U.S. Patent and Trademark Office, and the American Intellectual Property Law Association, as well as lobbyists and intellectual property counsel for major brand-holding corporations such as IBM and AT&T, started to investigate the issue at this time.

6.3   Conflicts over Top-Level Domains

Amidst the intellectual property battles, the new policy of charging for domain names was turning domain name registration into a profitable enterprise. SAIC had infused its new acquisition with the cash needed to automate its registration operations. Network Solutions' revenues rose to US$19 million in 1996—small by current standards but triple what it had been the year before. In 1997 annual revenues leaped to US$45.3 million, and in September of that year an initial public offering of 3.3 million shares on NASDAQ generated a market value of US$350 million.

Network Solutions' success fueled demand for new top-level domain name assignments. The demand came from business people who wanted in on the bonanza, and, for very different reasons, from the Internet engineering community. But the property rights and public policy problems raised by the creation of new top-level domains proved to be even more difficult to resolve than the fights over second-level domain names. Ultimately, the technical community's organic institutions—the Internet Assigned Numbers Authority (IANA) and the Internet Architecture Board (IAB)—proved to be incapable of responding to the need for new top-level domains. Their informal chain of authority lacked sufficient legitimacy and recognition in the commercial and political world. The Internet engineering community lost control of its name space at this time.

6.3.1 Delegation Conflicts over Country Codes—RFC 1591

The growing significance of the Internet after 1991 began to make the delegation of country code top-level domains contentious. In some countries, different government agencies or organizations within the country competed among themselves for the right to be delegated the country code. IANA sometimes received letters from people purporting to be government authorities requesting a change in the delegation. Some of them did not really have the claimed authority or appropriate qualifications (Klensin 2001). Issues about which nationalities qualified for a country code began to arise.

In an attempt to clarify the basis for making TLD delegations, Postel drafted a more explicit policy, which was released as RFC 1591 in March 1994. This was just before the World Wide Web explosion and only a year and a half before Network Solutions was authorized to charge for domain names. The document enumerated the following criteria for making a delegation:

• There must be a designated manager for supervising the domain's name space, and the administrative contact must reside in the country.

• The designated manager is the trustee of the top-level domain for both the nation and the global Internet community.

• The designated manager must be equitable to all groups in the domain that request domain names.

• Significantly interested parties in the domain should agree that the designated manager is the appropriate party.

• The designated manager must do a satisfactory job of operating the DNS service for the domain.

The statement proposed to set up an "Internet DNS Names Review Board" to resolve disputes about delegations. It also explicitly distanced

IANA from the politically contentious problem of deciding what qualified as a country.

RFC 1591 has been called "one of Jon Postel's masterpieces" by one Internet veteran (Klensin 2001). From an institutional perspective, however, RFC 1591 was more like a symptom of a growing problem: the traditional Internet community's inability to cope with the commercial and political pressures closing in on top-level domain delegations. The strongest and most effective aspect of the policy was its decision to strictly adhere to the ISO-3166-1 list as the basis for ccTLDs. The list—an official standard produced by a UN agency—was a reasonably objective item that shielded IANA from political pressure to modify the list of available top-level domains. RFC 1591 also reflected Postel's wise sense that whenever possible, conflicts or competition within a country should be resolved before a delegation was made rather than thrusting IANA into a position to determine who was "right." In general, however, RFC 1591 proved ineffective or arbitrary.

RFC 1591 was an anachronism almost as soon as it was issued. The Web was transforming the Internet into a mass medium, and domain name registration was about to become a lucrative market. Yet Postel still thought of TLD administration as a "public service," and to him this meant not just nonprofit supply but service "carried out at no or minimal cost to the users (Klensin 2001). The policy was based on a "trustee" concept of delegation but specified the criteria of trusteeship in only the vaguest terms and basically gave one man (Postel) the right to determine who was a "significantly interested party" and who best qualified as a trustee. Interestingly, RFC 1591 defined ccTLD managers as trustees for *two* distinct communities: the country *and* the "global Internet community." Only a year before a cacophony of conflicting claims to names would begin to transform the institutional arrangements of the Internet, Postel offered the aphorism, "Concerns about 'rights' and 'ownership' of domains are inappropriate. It is appropriate to be concerned about 'responsibilities' and 'service' to the community." In short, RFC 1591 took the philosophy and informal practices that had worked well when the Internet was the responsibility of a relatively small, noncommercial community of engineers and tried to transmute it into a platform for allocating a globally contested resource. It didn't work.

From 1994 to 1997, following the publication of RFC 1591, the last remaining country code delegations were added to the root at an accelerating pace. The RFC served as a minor restraint on a stampede to occupy valuable territory. Administrative contacts for developing country TLDs often did not reside in the affected country.[31] Many of the country codes delegated by Postel at this time were in fact to commercial entities. Many tiny countries and dependencies, by virtue of their presence on the ISO-3166 list, could claim a TLD—a valuable right that commercial corporations in developed economies sought unsuccessfully for years. Some of the small territories utilized this windfall as a revenue-generating source, creating a new breed of ccTLD: the quasi-generic country code.[32] In a few cases, notably Haiti, Postel was dragged into domestic disputes and made arbitrary decisions.[33] The lofty notions about trusteeship for the nation and the global Internet community were soon replaced by a new rule in practice: "Follow the expressed wishes of the government of the country with regard to the domain name manager for the country code corresponding to that country."

The Names Review Board was never established. RFC 1591 failed to provide a solid procedural basis for delegating new generic top-level names. Its whole approach to the trademark problem was to propose to limit the role of the registration authority to providing "contact information to both parties." A wise policy, perhaps, but ultimately one that was honored only in the breach, as first Network Solutions and later ICANN directly involved registries in dispute resolution. In short, while RFC 1591 may have been useful as an informal set of guidelines within the Internet community, it did nothing to resolve the growing property rights conflicts taking place at the top level.

6.3.2 *newdom* and the Response to Charging

A rift was growing between Network Solutions and the Internet technical community. The community had reacted uncomfortably to the acquisition of the InterNIC registry by a multibillion-dollar defense contractor in March 1996. Many of its participants did not approve of the commercialization of domain names generally.[34] The company's dispute resolution policy was unpopular, not so much because of its substance but because it was perceived as a move made without consulting the broader community.[35] The decision by NSF to allow charging for domains was also widely perceived as something that happened without sufficient consultation.[36]

The announcement of that decision in September 1995, therefore, precipitated a strong reaction on the email lists frequented by the techies. Only two days after NSF transmitted its letter authorizing charging, Jon Postel sent an email to the Internet Society board: "I think this introduction of charging by the InterNIC for domain registrations is sufficient cause to take steps to set up a small number of alternate top-level domains managed by other registration centers. I'd like to see some competition between registration services to encourage good service at low prices."[37]

Postel's attitude was shared by many others in the technical community. Creating new top-level domains (TLDs) was a way to reassert the authority of "the community" over Internet administration. A new mailing list/ working group on new top-level domains, *newdom,* was formed on September 15, 1995.

The *newdom* list became the first great battleground of what would become a five-year struggle to authorize new top-level domains. The group's original goal had been to implement competition in domain name registration within a few months, before Network Solutions was actually able to bill anyone. The list members quickly discovered, however, that defining top-level domains, which had been controversial in 1984 when no money was at stake, raised even more complex questions in the new commercialized environment. Among the issues the list confronted were the following:

• How many new TLDs should be or could be added? If limits must be imposed, how does one decide who gets to administer a new TLD and who doesn't? Will those limits provoke lawsuits?

• If there are competing applications for the same TLD, how does one decide which applicant gets it? Will those decisions spark lawsuits?

• Should the root server administrator benefit from the addition of new TLDs, for example, by charging a fee, auctioning off the right, or demanding a percentage of revenues?

• Are delegations made in perpetuity, or for a fixed term? How can they be retracted?

• Can there be intellectual property in a TLD string? Do those rights inhere in the registrant, the registry, or the root administrator?

• Do the administrators of a TLD domain "own" the right to enter registrations under the TLD, or must they share the right to perform registrations with other companies? Do they own the zone files?

• Will the addition of new TLDs create additional headaches for trademark owners who have already registered their names in existing domains? If a successful business was established at *www.shop.com,* for example, what happens when *www.shop.web* or *www.shop.inc* becomes available?

Some of the *newdom* participants, notably Perry Metzger, Scott Bradner, John Gilmore, and Terry Poot, opposed the creation of any new top-level domains. They favored instead the development of technical solutions that would make it possible to allow competing companies (what would later be called registrars) to register names under existing top-level domains. Many others, including Simon Higgs and Karl Denninger, favored the rapid creation of new registries like Network Solutions, but with different top-level domain names. Jon Postel supported the latter view. He was not yet convinced that a feasible method of sharing a top-level domain had been defined. He proposed to go ahead with the authorization of new, exclusive top-level domains while working in parallel to define a feasible shared-registry model that could be implemented later.[38] The group followed his lead.[39]

The most important product of the *newdom* list was a draft RFC entitled "New Registries and the Delegation of International Top-Level Domains," more widely known simply as draft-postel (Postel 1996). Although it became the focal point of international debate on new top-level domains for the better part of 1996, it remained an Internet-Draft and never attained the status of an official RFC. Draft-postel had two salient features. It proposed a fairly liberal, market-driven, but controlled method of allowing the top-level name space to expand in response to demand. And it proposed to use the authorization of new top-level domains to fund Postel's IANA operation. IANA would become part of the Internet Society, which would provide it a "legal and financial umbrella."

In the first year of implementation, draft-postel proposed to charter 50 new top-level registries, each, like Network Solutions, able to offer three new top-level domain names, for a total of 150 new TLDs. After that, ten new registries would be chartered every year; as before, each would have exclusive control of three new top-level names.[40] The new registries would be chartered for five-year terms and would enjoy a presumption of renewal if they provided good service. Applicants would pay a US$1,000 application fee. Successfully chartered registries would pay US$10,000 and 1 percent of their annual revenues into a fund managed by the Internet Society.[41] The funds would be used to provide insurance against legal or operational problems caused by the collapse of a registry and to support the activities of IANA. The fees and revenue percentages, and IANA's right to impose them, were one of the greatest sources of controversy.

To be chartered, new registries would have to meet three criteria: one pertaining to registration services, the second pertaining to operational resources such as Internet connectivity and name server performance, and the third pertaining to financial capability. These criteria were minimal and technically justifiable, and they consciously avoided any attempt to assert regulatory control over most aspects of business or technology. The proposal also specified commonsense criteria and methods for revoking or refusing to renew a charter.

6.3.3 The Top Level as Common Pool?

During the development of draft-postel, a number of the individuals in the United States who had been agitating for new top-level domains established their own "experimental" registries. In April 1996, Eugene Kashpureff set up the AlterNIC registry and claimed the *.exp, .ltd, .lnx, .med, .nic,* and *.xxx* top-level domains as his intellectual property. Kashpureff ran his own root zone name server to support the new domains. Similarly, Karl Denninger, of the Chicago area ISP MCSNet, asserted a claim to the *.biz* domain, and Christopher Ambler, of Image Online Design, staked a claim to *.web.* In effect, a form of appropriation in the top-level name space was taking place in which operators sought to develop property rights through first-use, by establishing a registry providing name service for a selected top-level name. A de facto system of coordination and mutual recognition existed among some of these actors; they recognized each other's claims and pointed to each other's name servers. Sometime in the late summer of 1996, some of them began to sell registrations under their top-level domains.

Table 6.3 shows a list of top-level domain name applications submitted to IANA. The list was compiled by Postel in December 1996. Many of the proposed strings were predictable. There were six separate applications for *.www,* three applications for *.sex,* applications for *.news, .music,* and *.fun.* But some were more problematical. There were applications for *.abc* and *.cbs* by an individual who had no relationship to the American broadcast networks. There was an application for *.euro.* An applicant named Mark had applied for the top-level domain *.mark,* raising the possibility that the "vanity-tagging of the Internet" that had already ballooned the *.com* zone might move into the top level of the domain name hierarchy.

The alternative top-level domain entrepreneurs had participated in or followed the *newdom* list but had fairly critical and tense relations with the IANA group. They considered IANA to be a closed aristocracy or a maddening bureaucracy. The IANA/IETF crowd viewed many of them as crass mercenaries or "crazies." IANA was being forced to deal with a new type of stakeholder. They were not cooperative techies with roots in academic computer science, but impatient, brash, and sometimes entirely money-minded entrepreneurs. Kashpureff, for example, was a self-taught computer whiz and community college dropout who made his first big money computerizing the paperwork for a Seattle tow-truck business (Diamond 1998). Although the final proposal in draft-postel had been adjusted to meet some of their concerns, the relationship was an awkward one.

Nothing demonstrated the awkwardness better than an attempt in July to negotiate the implementation terms of draft-postel. Postel's new top-level domain scheme had proposed to create an ad hoc committee to receive and evaluate applications for top-level domains. On July 31, 1996, Bill Manning, an Information Sciences Institute (ISI) employee who worked with Postel on IANA functions, met with Chris Ambler, Simon Higgs, and another prospective registry operator to discuss the evaluation criteria. Manning's notes of the meeting indicate that the participants felt that a "good faith effort" to establish a working registration service was one criterion that should be used. The issue of fees to be paid to IANA by

Table 6.3
TLD Applications to IANA, 1995–1996

TLD Strings	Method	Time and Date	Requester
.news	Form	14 Sep 1995 00:23:26	Simon Higgs
.www	Form	15 Sep 1995 13:15:36	Chris Cain
.web	Form	15 Sep 1995 16:04:28	Scott Adams
.usa, .earth	Form	16 Sep 1995 04:22:35	John Palmer
.gvt, .npo, .isp, .uni	Form	17 Sep 1995 20:59:54	Scott Ellentuch
.plc	Form	17 Sep 1995 23:46:04	Gordon Dewis
.shop, .mall, .eat, .sex, .hot, .wow, .trash, .pub, .non, .ego, .job, .ask, .aid, .old .art, .eng, .hosp, .med, .law, .ins, .farm, .car, .air, .util, .srv, .media, .npo, .trade	Mail	19 Sep 1995 08:06:47	Jeff Weisberg
.bsn, .sbs, .ntw, .gvt, .crp, .uni, .msc, .per, .srv, .cmm, .www, .pbc, .egn, .mgf	Mail	19 Sep 1995 14:20:58	Chris Christensen
.ind	Form	20 Sep 1995 09:35:53	Marc Nicholas
.bbs, .isp	Form	22 Sep 1995 09:55:56	Gordon Dewis
.xxx, .nap	Form	22 Sep 1995 18:29	American Information Network
.carib	Form	23 Sep 1995 02:07:13	Carlo Marazzi
.biz	Form	23 Sep 1995 13:45:32	Matthew Grossman

Table 6.3
(continued)

TLD Strings	Method	Time and Date	Requester
.usa	Form	24 Sep 1995 16:57:46	Scott Ellentuch
.usa	Form	27 Sep 1995 12:51:38	Rick Mount and Chris Phillips
.www	Form	2 Oct 1995 11:41:26	David Kenzik
.biz	Form	5 Oct 1995 14:25:48	Andrew Doane
.coupons, .rebates	Form	5 Dec 1995 13:13	Simon Higgs
.web	Form	11 Feb 1996 17:06:50	Mike Lester
.alt	Form	13 Feb 1996 17:50:44	James Howard
.agr	Form	12 Mar 1996 19:21:16	Jonathan Baker
.alt	Form	20 Mar 1996 00:02:34	Gregory Massel
.dot	Mail	26 Mar 1996 20:22:22	Christian Nielsen
.eur, .euro	Mail	13 May 1996 14:32:20	Bernard de Rubinat
.inc	Mail	26 Jun 1996 14:30:10	Jace Greenman
.info, .veg	Form	26 Jun 1996 21:29:33	Das Devaraj
.alt, .live, .post	Form	27 Jun 1996 15:41:29	Michael Dillon
.biz	Form	1 Jul 1996 09:47:41	Karl Denninger
.web, .auto, .www, .car	Form	1 Jul 1996 18:47:	Chris Ambler
.corp, .music		3 Jul 1996 21:00	

(118 other TLDs) applications listed until 26 Nov 1996

the registries was also discussed. At the end of the meeting, Ambler gave Manning a check from his company for US$1,000, intended to serve as the application fee specified in the draft.[42] Later, the envelope was returned to him, unopened.[43] On August 2, Postel sent a message to the *newdom* mailing list stating, "The suggestion that the IANA is accepting money to reserve new top-level domains is completely false."[44]

6.4   Conflicts over the Root

In the DNS hierarchy, the power to add new top-level domains or to assign existing top-level names to specific applicants is held by whoever defines the root zone file. But where did the formal authority for this lie? Who owned the name and address spaces? More than a year before the big push to create new top-level domains, the privatization, commercialization, and internationalization of the Internet had prompted discussions of this question in the technical community and the U.S. government. The IAB, in its October 1994 minutes on the problems caused by the rapid growth of domain name registration, admitted that the bigger problem underlying it all was that "it is unclear who actually controls the name space and what is fair procedure."[45] The commercialization of domain names made this question more difficult to answer, by raising the stakes and bringing new interest groups into the dialogue.

Between 1994 and 1996 three distinct parties emerged to assert claims on the root: the Internet Society (ISOC), the U.S. government, and alternative root servers.

6.4.1   The Internet Society Claims the Root

As noted in chapter 5, the Internet engineering community had created its own authority structure composed of the Internet Engineering Task Force (IETF), IANA, and the Internet Architecture Board. Superimposed over this structure, rather loosely and tenuously at this point, was the Internet Society; its purpose was to provide a corporate identity, legal protection, and financial support to the other components when needed. The Internet Architecture Board already had been fully incorporated into the Internet Society. The IETF rank and file, however, did not yet identify with ISOC. The relationship between them was a "cantankerous" one, with doubts still being openly voiced about what ISOC was and whether it was of any benefit to the community.[46]

Just before the domain name wars erupted, the IAB and the Internet Society were attempting to transfer formal authority over the root into ISOC's fledgling organizational structure. In July 1994, Postel prepared a draft charter for IANA, proposing that the Internet Society's board of trustees would delegate to the IAB the right to select the IANA. Although the model for "chartering" IANA was IAB's movement under ISOC's umbrella in 1992, IANA's situation was more complicated. IANA was not an informally constituted committee but a set of functions performed pursuant to government contracts with ISI. The name and address spaces could be considered valuable resources. In effect, Postel was proposing that these functions and resources be privatized. A final draft of the proposal, circulated in February 1995, encountered resistance from parties in the Federal Networking Council (see section 6.4.2). The controversies over charging and new top-level domains intervened before those issues could be resolved.

Ownership of the root of the IPv6 address tree was also being explicitly discussed within the IAB early in 1995. Here again, the Internet Society was being put forward by the leading hierarchs as the proper institutional home for the resources.[47] The January 1995 minutes of the IAB teleconference recorded the board's preference that the IANA control the address space and allocate addresses following guidelines created by the IAB and the IETF. In order to protect IANA against disputes regarding address allocation, the IAB proposed to vest formal ownership of the v6 address space with the Internet Society.[48]

The explosion of a market for domain names later that year created intense controversy but nevertheless dovetailed neatly with the Internet Society's broad agenda of privatizing the Internet's name and address spaces. The problem of name space governance, and the legal threats faced by Postel in his capacity as IANA, proved that an organizational home was needed for the root. The Internet Society now had a reason to exist. It saw itself, a nongovernmental and international body with technical expertise, as the natural authority over the name and address spaces. A governance role in the lucrative domain name market, moreover, could solve IANA's and the Internet Society's funding problems as well. Thus, in November

1995, Internet Society president Lawrence Landweber, IAB chair Brian Carpenter, Jon Postel, and Nicholas Trio of IBM prepared an Internet-Draft proposing that "the Internet Society should take a formal role in the oversight and licensing of competitive registries for the international Internet name space, in support of the IANA and with the assistance of the IAB."[49] The draft defined that formal role as including "setting policy, providing administrative oversight, and directly managing the selection of domain name providers for non-national top-level domains."

Draft-postel, drawn up only a few months later, was shaped to a significant degree by the desire to operationalize that new role. In June 1996, at its annual meeting in Montreal, the Internet Society's board of trustees voted in principle to support the proposal. The Internet Society was now formally backing a plan to assign commercially valuable property rights in top-level domains to competing registries, collect fees from the licensees, and in the process establish itself as the manager of the DNS root—all without any formal legal or governmental authorization.

6.4.2   The U.S. Government Claim

The Internet Society's claims did not go uncontested. As soon as the Internet Society began to circulate its IANA charter early in 1995, Robert Aiken, the U.S. Energy Department's representative on the Federal Networking Council (FNC), began to ask uncomfortable questions. In a March 1995 email message that went out to the IETF, the Federal Networking Council, the Coordinating Committee on Intercontinental Research Networks, and the ISOC board, he asked, "Is ISOC claiming that it has jurisdiction and overall responsibility for the top-level address and name space? If yes, how did ISOC obtain this responsibility; if no, then who does own it?"[50]

In his reply to Aiken, Vint Cerf argued that the Internet was becoming increasingly international and public in character and that management of the name and address space needed to adjust: "[I]t seems to me as if it is possible to make some deliberate agreements now among the interested parties (among which I would include the NICs, the IANA, the various U.S. Gov't research agencies, and ISOC) as to how to proceed in the future. My bias is to try to treat all of this as a global matter and to settle the responsibility on the Internet Society as an nongovernmental agent serving the community."[51] No formal decision seems to have emerged from these exchanges. They did, however, prompt the National Science Foundation to sponsor a conference on the "coordination, privatization, and internationalization" of the Internet in November 1995.[52] The event brought together many of the key participants in Internet administration.

At that conference, Mike St. Johns, the DARPA representative on the Federal Networking Council, set out a description of authority over the name and number spaces that stood in stark contrast to the one being advanced by the Internet Society. The Defense Department, he asserted, owned the name and address spaces. It had delegated "ownership" of IPv4 addresses to the FNC "with the understanding that DOD would continue to have first call on the number space *if* they needed it, but that block and other delegations would be done by the InterNIC in consultation with the IANA" and other agencies. Policy ownership of the DNS root, St. Johns asserted, was transferred to the FNC at roughly the same time as the number space was delegated. St. Johns believed that policy control of the *.com, .org,* and *.net* domains remained with the FNC. According to St. Johns, the InterNIC and the IANA were funded by NSF and ARPA, respectively, and therefore those federal agencies "maintain both fiduciary and program responsibilities" for them.[53] Other comments reveal that both Aiken and St. Johns were critical of the Internet Society and felt that it lacked the "international standing" to take over authority for the root.

The non-U.S. participants were not pleased. Reacting from a European perspective, Daniel Karrenberg of Réseaux IP Européens (RIPE) asserted that "the IANA, not the InterNIC" owns the address space and urged everyone to "take an international perspective."[54] David Conrad, representing the newly created regional address registry for the Asia-Pacific region, voiced similar sentiments. Even within the United States, most members of the technical community, particularly Cerf and Postel, were deeply uncomfortable with assertions of national authority over Internet administration.

6.4.3 The Broadening Dialogue

The November 20, 1995, event proved to be the first of a series of conferences and workshops on Internet governance that continued throughout the year 1996. The conferences expanded the dialogue beyond the Internet engineering community to include representatives of trademark holders, legal scholars, and international organizations such as the International Telecommunication Union (ITU), the Organization for Economic Cooperation and Development (OECD), and the World Intellectual Property Organization (WIPO). This included a February 1996 conference on Internet administrative infrastructure sponsored by the Internet Society and the Commercial Internet eXchange (CIX), a June 1996 meeting sponsored by OECD in Dublin, and a September 1996 conference on "Coordination and Administration of the Internet" sponsored by the Harvard Information Infrastructure Project, the National Science Foundation, CIX, and the Internet Society.

As soon as draft-postel was put forward as a live option, the proposal encountered vocal opposition from a variety of interest groups. Attacks were made not only on the substantive policy it defined but also on the legitimacy of IANA/ISOC to set policy and to collect funds from the authorization of new top-level domains.

One of the most vehement critics of draft-postel was Robert Shaw, an ITU staff member. Shaw charged that IANA lacked the authority to "tax the root"[55] and ridiculed draft-postel's informal arrangements: "According to Postel's draft, these potentially multimillion-dollar-generating registries will be awarded by an 'ad hoc working group' [who are] for the most part engineers [with] no real legal or policy framework behind them" (Shaw 1997). A deeper agenda underlay the ITU's interest in domain name issues. As the intergovernmental organization that had presided for decades over a regime of state-owned telephone monopolies (Cowhey 1990), the ITU was uncertain of its role and status in a new, liberalized order. With the Internet on the rise, private-sector-led standards forums proliferating, and the days of traditional, circuit-switched telephone service seemingly numbered, the ITU needed to assert a role for itself in Internet governance or standards setting. The governance debates presented it with an opportunity to establish itself as an actor in that arena.

Trademark holders also objected to draft-postel's expansion of the name space, although their role was not as prominent at this juncture as it would be later. They feared that it would increase the scope for name speculation and trademark dilution, and that mark holders would feel obliged to register their names in all new domains (Maher 1996). At this time David

Maher, co-chair of a new Committee on the Internet formed by the International Trademark Association, emerged as one of the spokesmen for the trademark community on domain name issues. Maher had served as trademark counsel to McDonald's Corporation and in that capacity had facilitated the highly publicized transfer of *mcdonalds.com* from the journalist Joshua Quittner to the company.

Draft-postel even failed to win the support of the prospective domain name registration businesses, despite its plan to authorize hundreds of new registries. By late October 1996, the alternative registry operators had become completely disenchanted with the IANA-led process and had begun to voice explicit attacks on Postel and the process that had produced the draft.[56] What had begun as complaints about the fees required to enter the market, and IANA's and the Internet Society's authority to assess them, evolved into a deeper challenge to the whole IANA model of DNS administration, with a single, authoritative root zone file set by a central authority. Leading critics such as Karl Denninger argued that rights to top-level domains should be established on a first-use basis by registry operators and that the root servers supporting those registries could be coordinated on a voluntary basis: "The problem [IANA] people have with this scheme is that it undermines the control structure that some people just don't want to give up. Specifically, if you have a dozen TLD consortia, defined by the root name server "sets," then NOBODY—not IANA—not ALTERNIC—not MCSNet—not ITU—not ANYONE—can dictate to people what the fees or market forces are that cause TLDs to exist."[57]

In a widely read article, a columnist in *Communications Week* with ties to the alternative root operators attacked the "Net governance cartel" and dismissed draft-postel as an "Amway-style multilevel marketing scheme whereby IANA would essentially franchise TLDs, collecting a piece of the action from downstream distributors while maintaining authoritative control" (Frezza 1996). The *newdom* list degenerated into a shouting match between supporters and detractors of Postel/IANA. Paul Vixie, writer of the BIND code and a member of the Internet old guard, accused the alternative registries of an attempted coup: "Rather than work within the process (which would at this point mean attending some ISOC open board meetings) they are attempting a coup. I think IANA's done a fine job for a decade and that it is insulting, to say the least, for folks to try a power grab when the IANA's open/public change process is just about complete. . . . The people who want to pull [the DNS root] away from IANA are not in this for your revolution, man, they're in it for the money."[58]

By the fall of 1996 it was clear that Postel and the Internet Society lacked the legitimacy and support needed to implement their plan. But no other claimant with wider support emerged. Aware of the strong resistance from international networking entities to a U.S. government claim, the federal government took no action to advance or renege on St. Johns' statements. The Federal Networking Council seemed paralyzed; its advisory committee repeatedly sent it strongly worded messages urging it to transfer policy authority over top-level domain administration from the National Science Foundation to "some appropriate agency," but nothing happened.[59] The alternative root server confederations could not get Network Solutions or Postel to add their new top-level domains into the root, and they lacked the broad support required to provoke a coordinated migration to a new root server system.

7

The Root in Play

Postel . . . really passionately believed that he, personally, owned the root, and that neither USG [the U.S. government] nor NSI had any rights at all. But he also understood that he had to be careful how he said that, and to whom, lest he be thought of as either deranged or power-mad. (He was neither.)
—Brian Reid, August 2000

On October 31, 1996, Paul Vixie, maintainer of the BIND software used by nearly all the Internet's domain name servers at the time, sent the following warning to the main mailing list of the Internet Engineering Task Force (IETF): "I have told IANA and I have told InterNIC—now I'll tell you kind folks. If IANA's proposal [draft-postel] stagnates past January 15, 1997, without obvious progress and actual registries being licensed or in the process of being licensed, I will declare the cause lost. At that point it will be up to a consortium of Internet providers, probably through CIX [Commercial Internet eXchange] . . . to tell me what I ought to put in the "root.cache" file that I ship with BIND."

Vixie's message contained a not-so-subtle threat: If something wasn't done about the Network Solutions (NSI) monopoly, the IP addresses of alternative root servers would find their way into the default values contained in the BIND software. Inclusion of alternative root servers in the dominant name server software would have made the new, homesteaded top-level domains visible to most of the world's name servers. The traditional Internet groups' centralized control over the root would have been completely broken. Vixie was not the only one contemplating such a move; at that time two major U.S.-based Internet service providers were also considering pointing to the AlterNIC root.[1]

Vixie's action was but one of several symptoms of the institutional crisis afflicting the Internet name and address spaces from the end of 1996 to the beginning of 1998. While packets continued to move and the domain name system (DNS) continued to resolve names, there was no clear policy authority over the root.

The root was literally "in play" for a span of about 14 months, a period that witnessed a power struggle over another Internet Society–led plan to privatize the DNS root, a hijacking of the InterNIC registration site in July 1997, an antitrust suit against Network Solutions (NSI), and a redirection of the root servers in January 1998 by Postel himself. The period is punctuated by the formal intervention of the U.S. government, in the form of a Green Paper that asserted U.S. authority over the root.

7.1   IAHC and the gTLD-MoU

In October 1996 the Internet Society (ISOC) seems to have recognized that if it were to succeed in its mission to assert control of the root, it would have to break new institutional ground. Drawing on the contacts formed during the ongoing debates and conferences, the Internet Society put together what it called a "blue ribbon international panel" to develop and implement a blueprint for a global governance structure for the domain name system.[2] The 11-member group (see table 7.1) was named the International Ad Hoc Committee (IAHC).

The IAHC initiative reflected the continuing desire of the Internet Architecture Board (IAB), Postel, and the Internet Society to formalize their now-contested authority over the root and introduce a competitive alternative to Network Solutions. It included two representatives of the Internet Architecture Board, two members appointed by IANA (i.e., by Postel), and two appointed by the Internet Society. But the committee considerably expanded the definition of the relevant community. The IAHC included two representatives of trademark holders, one appointed by the International Trademark Association (INTA) and another by the World Intellectual Property Organization (WIPO). The International Telecommunication Union (ITU) was given one representative, as was the Federal Networking Council (FNC). According to the FNC minutes, the FNC sought membership on the advisory committee "in recognition of the government's historic stewardship role in this sector" (Simon 1998).

Table 7.1
The Composition of the IAHC

Name	Affiliation
Don Heath, Chair	Internet Society
Sally Abel	International Trademark Association
Albert Tramposch	World Intellectual Property Association
David Maher	Intellectual property attorney (selected by ISOC)
Jun Murai	Keio University, Japan, WIDE Project (selected by IAB)
Geoff Huston	Telstra, Australian education and research Internet (selected by IAB)
Hank Nussbacher	IBM Israel (selected by ISOC)
Robert Shaw	International Telecommunication Union
Perry Metzger	Internet Engineering Task Force (selected by IANA)
David Crocker	Internet Engineering Task Force (selected by IANA)
George Strawn	National Science Foundation (selected by FNC)

The IAHC was chaired by Don Heath, the Internet Society's new chief executive officer. Heath, a Cerf protégé, came to ISOC via MCI Telecommunications in May 1996 and was highly enthusiastic about forging a new, expanded role for ISOC.[3] But it was Internet Society president Lawrence Landweber who acted as the catalyst of the ambitious plans. Landweber insisted that the IAHC include representatives from outside the technical community and that invitations be sent to organizations acting as formal representatives rather than as individuals. He also urged Heath to chair the IAHC on behalf of the Internet Society.[4]

In political terms, the committee represented a coalition between the technical community's governing hierarchy (ISOC/IAB/IANA) and other political forces that had contested the ISOC claim on the root in the previous round: trademark owners, the ITU, and the FNC. All were incorporated into the planning process and (FNC excepted) would later be given permanent roles in the proposed governance regime. The political coalition was also notable for whom it excluded. Network Solutions was not invited to be a part of the group. Neither were any representatives of the alternative registries. There was no representative of commercial Internet service providers.[5]

Even though its membership was dominated by the technical community's governing hierarchy, the IAHC's procedures broke sharply with IETF procedures and norms. The *newdom* process had been based, roughly, on the procedures set out in RFC 1591. That process was simply ended and its results discarded. Participation in the IAHC was not open, meetings were closed, and no official minutes were kept of the deliberations. An aggressive schedule was imposed, with extra urgency added by the circulation of Vixie's threat only a few days after the group's formation. The committee's charter was released on November 11, 1996, and public comments were solicited via email. Only three months later, a final report laid out a new system of Internet governance (IAHC 1997).

The IAHC completely jettisoned Postel's series of drafts and the claims of the alternative registries. Instead, the final report started with the principle that "the Internet top-level domain (TLD) name space is a public resource and is subject to the public trust." That language had been promoted by the ITU's Shaw and reflected concepts never before used in the Internet arena but well known in the context of state-owned or state-regulated post, telephone, and telegraph companies. The language attempted to situate the Internet's name and number resources within the normative principles used by the ITU to administer regulated public telecommunication services, numbering resources, radio spectrum, and satellite slots (Rutkowski 1997).

The IAHC report also diverged sharply from draft-postel by proposing shared rather than exclusive top-level domains. It conceived of the registry database as a natural monopoly and sought to separate the "wholesale" operation of the monopoly registry database from the "retail" function of registering names for customers, billing them, and maintaining contact information. The former function was called the registry and the latter the registrar. Under the IAHC plan, a global monopoly registry would be administered on a nonprofit basis. The registry would be co-owned by multiple, competing registrars, who would all share access to the same top-level domains. The number of registrars was artificially limited to 28 companies in order to ensure that the initial group would be a manageable size for developing technical and operational details. The 28 companies would be selected by lottery, with four coming from each of seven global regions. In short, the plan created a cartel, with entry into it governed by norms of geographical equity. This was a typical outcome for an international, intergovernmental organization, but highly atypical of the Internet.

Another dramatic change was that the new system proposed by IAHC linked trademark protection procedures directly to the administration of the DNS. This important but controversial innovation was meant to eliminate the trademark owners' objections to new TLDs by giving them extraordinary power over domain name registrations. Domain names would not be operational until after a 60-day waiting period, during which they would be subject to review by "administrative challenge panels" run by WIPO. Neither the law nor the legal principles WIPO would use to resolve disputes were specified. IAHC also proposed to exclude from the domain name space all names that corresponded to or resembled "famous" trademarks. Finally, the proposal imposed an artificial limit on the number of top-level domains. Whereas Postel had originally thought in terms of hundreds of new descriptive top-level domains and annual additions of more, IAHC proposed to add only seven.[6] The final report did not make any commitments to add more. This, too, was a concession to the trademark interests. The smaller the name space, the easier their policing problem. Thus, the IAHC expanded the name space slightly but treated it as a regulated cartel.

The IAHC also established a corporate structure that straddled the boundary between the public and private sectors. The overarching framework of the governance structure was a document known as the Generic Top-Level Domain Memorandum of Understanding (gTLD-MoU). The preamble of the gTLD-MoU claimed that the agreement was made in the name of "the Internet community," an attempt by the drafters to recall the small-scale, communitarian, consensus-based regime of the ARPANET and the early IETF.

In the proposed plan, registrars would be incorporated in Geneva, Switzerland, as a nonprofit Council of Registrars (CORE). To join CORE, registrars had to pay a US$20,000 entry fee and US$2,000 per month, plus an anticipated but as yet unspecified fee to the registry for each domain name registration. The top governance authority was a committee designated as the Policy Oversight Committee (POC). POC's membership would mirror the composition of the IAHC: two members were to be appointed to it by the Internet Society, the Internet Architecture Board, IANA, and CORE; one member each was to be appointed by ITU, INTA, and WIPO. In formulating policy the POC would issue requests for comments just as a regulatory commission might. There was also a Policy Advisory Board (PAB), a consultative body that any signatory to the gTLD-MoU could join. For the Internet technical hierarchy, the structure was intended to provide a vehicle for taking possession of the Network Solutions registry after the expiration of the Cooperative Agreement in April 1998. Network Solutions would be encouraged to participate in CORE as a registrar but would no longer have any control over the *.com, .net,* and *.org* registry (Simon 1998).

ITU Secretary-General Dr. Pekka Tarjanne hailed the MoU as an embodiment of a new form of international cooperation he called "voluntary multilateralism."[7] The ITU volunteered to serve as the official repository of the MoU and took on the tasks of circulating it to public and private sector entities involved in telecommunication and information, inviting them to sign it. It also offered to "facilitate further co-operation in the implementation of this MoU."

The gTLD-MoU was signed by Heath and Postel on March 1, 1997. The Internet Society and ITU then organized an official signing ceremony in Geneva at the end of April in an attempt to assume all of the trappings of an international treaty agreement. Members of the IAHC conducted an international series of promotional meetings and press releases to win acceptance of the proposal. Yet the Internet Society and IANA still had no more formal legal authority over the root than they had had in mid-1996.

7.2   Political Reaction to the gTLD-MoU

The gTLD-MoU was a turning point in the evolution of Internet governance. Control of the root ceased to be a subject of discourse in conferences, mailing lists, and memos, and became the object of an outright power struggle played out in an international arena. The policy agendas of the actors, both pro and con, became more sharply defined; where there were conflicts of interest, lines were drawn and factions formed. Contention among these factions then drew into the fray governmental actors with higher levels of policymaking authority.

"The MoUvement," as its proponents came to call the gTLD-MoU, marked a sharp break with the governance arrangements of the academic Internet—the Internet of DARPA, the IETF, and the National Science

Foundation. This was true for several reasons. The initiative formally involved actors and organizations new to Internet administration, such as the intellectual property interests and international organizations. But the technical community itself was altered in important ways. Established IETF procedures had been abandoned. The technical community's leadership—IAB, IANA, and ISOC—had thrust themselves directly into a highly politicized arena, moving away from their past focus on technical standards setting and embracing a new role as policymakers and regulators. The political, personal, and economic alliances that went into the complicated MoU compromised their neutrality, making them into partisan defenders of a particular view of the domain name registration industry. The close ties between the Internet Society and CORE, the consortium of commercial registrars that would financially support the new governance arrangement and replace Network Solutions as the operational home of the root, set ISOC and its allies on a collision course with Network Solutions. The MoUvement's alliance with intergovernmental organizations and its insistence on its right to assume control of the root on its own initiative set it on a collision course with the U.S. government.

By asserting such a bold and unequivocal claim to the root and forming an international coalition to back it up, the IAHC advanced and polarized the governance debate. Other key actors were forced to clarify their positions, put forward their own claims, and seek support for them.

7.2.1 Network Solutions

Network Solutions was the obvious target of the gTLD-MoU. Publicly, Network Solutions reacted to the draft IAHC proposal in a cautious, noncommittal way, stressing its willingness to work with the committee to achieve consensus.[8] Similarly, MoUvement spokespeople publicly encouraged NSI to sign on as a registrar and publicized their expectation that it eventually would. But no one was fooled. The gTLD-MoU was fundamentally inimical to Network Solutions' economic interests. As events progressed, the company began to use its lobbying muscle within the United States to undermine and defeat the agreement.

Early in 1997, Network Solutions was preparing for an initial public offering of stock that would bring in hundreds of millions of dollars. Its increasingly profitable control of the *.com* domain was the engine of its stock market value. The prospect of losing control of the *.com* registry to a Geneva-based corporation run by avowed enemies and of competing on price with dozens of new registrars in the *.com* space could not have been an attractive one. Network Solutions' preferred outcome was a permanent property right in the *.com, .net* and *.org* top-level domains, with competition taking the form of new registries with exclusive control of new top-level names, as proposed in draft-postel. Thus, a Network Solutions spokesman told the press in April 1997, "It is not our intention to share .com or the other [top-level domains] we register. Those would obviously [be] assets that we've developed . . . much as Microsoft wouldn't share DOS [disk operating system]."[9] In its initial public offering documents, Network Solutions repeatedly referred to *.com* as its "brand" and also asserted property rights over "a database of information relating to customers in its registration business."[10]

Network Solutions at this point came to explicitly support the claim of the U.S. government to authoritative control over the root. NSI was *persona non grata* within the ISOC-dominated technical community. It was also perceived with hostility by foreign governments and businesses, as a symbol of U.S. dominance of the Internet and the cause of the domain name turmoil. In contrast, the company was well positioned in Washington D.C. Backed by the lobbying and financial resources of its parent company, SAIC, and as a longstanding government contractor, it found a U.S.-centered institutional framework more predictable and more amenable to its interests.

7.2.2   The Alternative Registries

The (mostly North American) entrepreneurs who had been positioning themselves to occupy top-level domains under the framework created by draft-postel were outraged by the results of the IAHC. Their business model had been explicitly precluded by the proposed regime. Adding injury to insult, the IAHC proposed to occupy two of the top-level domain names staked out by entrepreneurs (*.web* and *.arts*). The alternative registries questioned the fairness and openness of the IAHC's procedures as well as its substantive policy decisions.[11] Their previous attacks on the legitimacy of IANA and the process that had produced draft-postel notwithstanding, they characterized the IAHC as an illegitimate power grab. One alternative registry tried to fight the MoUvement with litigation. In February 1997, Chris Ambler, prospective proprietor of the *.web* top-level domain, sued IANA in California for violating his prior-use and intellectual property claims in *.web*. The complaint was withdrawn without prejudice before a final ruling could be issued, but the judge appeared to be unsympathetic to his case.[12]

In March 1997 a group of six small Internet service providers and three other businesses met in Atlanta in an attempt to organize to revive the fortunes of the alternative root movement. Calling themselves Enhanced Domain Name Service (eDNS), they attempted to set up an alternative root server network that would support many new TLDs as well as the established ones.

Opposition to the gTLD-MoU began to bring some members of the *alt.root* community into a tactical alliance with Network Solutions at this point. Both interests were proposing a similar economic model for the top-level domain name registries, and both believed that resolving the policy issues within the legal and institutional framework of the United States was more likely to produce results to their liking.

7.2.3 American Civil Society Groups

By now the domain name wars were reaching groups and interests outside the immediate purview of Internet infrastructure. The broad societal reaction was mixed, with most actors viewing the gTLD-MoU as unrepresentative and preemptive even though they supported competition and some kind of institutional change.

The gTLD-MoU aroused the opposition of U.S.-based civil liberties organizations concerned about their lack of representation and the power that the proposals gave to trademark interests and international organizations. Free-speech advocates, already mobilized by abuses of Network Solutions' dispute resolution policy, now believed that even more sweeping rights were being given to intellectual property holders. Kathy Kleiman, the general counsel for the Domain Names Rights Coalition, claimed that "the committee has . . . no representation of small business, individuals, or attorneys who support limits on trademark law. The draft favors large trademark owners who can stop others from using even common names on the Internet. The underlying premise is that a domain name is a trademark, and that premise is fundamentally flawed."[13] Other public interest organizations, such as Computer Professionals for Social Responsibility, accused the IAHC process of being "closed, rushed, and unbalanced" and asked for more time for input from consumers and the public.[14] While these civil society groups were usually critical of Network Solutions and looked forward to competition in the domain name industry, they did not see the gTLD-MoU as an acceptable solution. Being based in the United States, they, too, tended to support resolving the controversies within a U.S.-based institutional framework, often invoking the First Amendment and other rights derived from the U.S. Constitution.

7.2.4   European Commission

Reflecting the lower level of Internet penetration in Europe at that time, European governments and civil society groups were mostly unaware of the emerging governance wars, except for policy specialists and organizations directly involved in domain name registration and internetworking. The European Union was monitoring domain name issues through its Directorate General 13, the branch in charge of telecommunication policy. Following the release of the gTLD-MoU proposal, the DG-13 official Christopher Wilkinson wrote to the Internet Society's Don Heath on January 17, 1997, expressing dissatisfaction with the lack of European participation and the inadequate amount of time provided for consultation. Wilkinson then convened a meeting of European Internet community members.[15] The meeting was attended by representatives of nine top-level domain administrators of member states, Daniel Karrenberg of RIPE-NCC, and a few commercial Internet service providers. The attendees reached a consensus that they should not sign the gTLD-MoU.

Drawing on the results of this meeting, the European Commission DG-13 sent comments to the U.S. State Department and other federal agencies expressing dissatisfaction with the IAHC proposal.[16] The commission called for "further public debate" and direct European participation. Although specific criticisms were made of the dominance of English words in the new top-level names, the selection of registrars by lottery, and issues related to the sharing of top-level domains, the main underlying concern seems to have been that the process was moving too fast and was driven primarily by U.S.-based organizations and interests.

7.2.5 Business Community

Reaction in the international business community was not uniform. Because of the leading role of the ITU, the gTLD-MoU attracted significant support from telephone companies outside the United States. Eventually, France Telecom, Deutsche Telekom, Telecom Italia, Sweden's Telia AB, Japan's KDD, Bell Canada, and Australia's Telstra became signatories. MCI was an early supporter because of the influence of Vint Cerf within that organization; moreover, MCI used its leverage as a major purchaser of Digital Equipment Corporation products to get Digital to sign, too. Indeed, it was the participation of the ITU and the support of old-line telephone companies that unnerved many of the gTLD-MoU's opponents; it appeared as if the Internet were being taken over by the old guard. Another significant source of business support for the plan, however, came from small Internet service providers (ISPs) and prospective domain name registration firms in Europe and Asia, which saw a chance to make inroads into a business dominated by U.S. companies. Companies like Melbourne IT, an Australian ISP, and NetNames, an international domain name consultancy, joined forces with the MoUvement early on.

On the other hand, major multinationals such as IBM, British Telecom, Bell Atlantic, and AT&T opposed the MoU or refused to lend their support. These companies had little or no interest in the business opportunities presented by an expanded name space. They were primarily concerned about the effect of new top-level domains on trademark protection. In later comments, for example, AT&T criticized the gTLD-MoU proposal as being insufficiently protective of trademarks in the domain name space, and the proposed governance structure as having "insufficient representation" of trademark holders.[17]

7.3 Challenges to Network Solutions

Although the gTLD-MoU was unpopular, many stakeholders and policymakers still viewed the Network Solutions monopoly as the fundamental problem. The stalemate over draft-postel and the unappetizing alternative posed by the gTLD-MoU created a mounting sense of frustration, leading to more aggressive tactics.

7.3.1   Antitrust Challenge

One registry entrepreneur chose to challenge Network Solutions using antitrust law. Unlike the other alternative registries, Paul Garrin, the proprietor of Name.Space, believed that all top-level domains should be shared. In January 1996, Garrin established an alternative root that allowed customers to create a new top-level domain name on request. Garrin conceived of the registry as a "publisher" of names proposed by customers, and exerted only "editorial" control over the top-level names inserted into the DNS. By mid-1997, Name.Space was supporting approximately 530 new generic words as top-level domain names, such as *.zone, .art, .music,* and *.space.* In principle, any other company could register second-level names under the TLDs supported by Name.Space, but in order to do so it would have to make heavy investments in software development in order to interoperate with Garrin's system. In that respect Garrin was, like the gTLD-MoU, attempting to establish a new DNS root more or less under his control.

In March 1997, unable to attain critical mass for his alternative root system, Garrin formally asked Network Solutions to amend the root zone file to include Name.Space's top-level domains. Adding the Name.Space top-level domains to the Network Solutions–operated root zone would have transformed the commercial environment of the DNS. As the only established registry for hundreds of new domains, Name.Space would have been quickly elevated to the status of a peer of Network Solutions. On the other hand, a refusal to add them might be construed as anticompetitive, bringing NSI into conflict with the antitrust laws.

Aware of the legal trap that was being set, Network Solutions deferred Garrin's request, replying that it had an unwritten agreement to refer all such requests to IANA. When the request was passed on to IANA, however, Postel refused to assert or accept any formal legal responsibility. A letter from a University of Southern California lawyer replied, "We are aware of no contract or other agreement that gives IANA authority over [Network Solutions'] operations. The IANA has no authority to establish a generic top-level domain without an Internet community consensus arrived at through committee review and ample opportunity for public input."

With IANA deferring to an amorphous "Internet community consensus," Network Solutions turned to the National Science Foundation for guidance, sending a formal request to the program officer supervising its cooperative agreement to add new top-level domains. In the meantime, Name.Space filed an antitrust lawsuit in federal district court.[18]

In its June 25, 1997, response to Network Solutions, the National Science Foundation rejected the request. The response cited ongoing discussions among the National Science Foundation and several other federal agencies of the "governance and authority issues raised in your letter." Because these discussions were not complete, the NSF requested that "NSI take NO action to create additional TLDs or to add any other new TLDs to the Internet root zone file until NSF, in consultation with other U.S. government agencies, has completed its deliberations in this area and is able to provide further guidance."[19]

In order to strengthen its legal position, in August the NSF issued a clarification that the June 25 letter was intended to be a directive under the 1993 NSI Cooperative Agreement. On September 17, 1997, Name.Space amended its complaint and named both Network Solutions and the National Science Foundation as defendants in its antitrust suit.[20] The amended complaint also accused NSF of violating free-speech rights guaranteed under the First Amendment by arbitrarily restricting the list of available domain names.

Although Name.Space later lost on all counts, the threat of antitrust liability forced the actors to clarify the formal sources and relations of authority. In response to the lawsuit, Network Solutions denied having any policy authority over the root, looking first to IANA and then to the U.S. government for responsibility. IANA, too, disclaimed authority over Network Solutions, and asserted only "an equivocal authority over the root, the ability to act on the basis of consensus" (Froomkin 2000). The National Science Foundation, on the other hand, was forced to assume responsibility over Network Solutions through its Cooperative Agreement contract. And the federal government was pushed into arguing that its registry contractor was a government instrumentality.

7.3.2   The Kashpureff Hack

AlterNIC's Eugene Kashpureff took even more radical action. Frustrated with Network Solutions' unwillingness to add new names to the root and the lack of new competition, he exploited a security hole in DNS implementation that allowed him to substitute the IP address of his own computer for the address of the Network Solutions server, and insert that false mapping into the authoritative name server for the InterNIC site. As a result, for a few days in July 1997 most users trying to register names at the Network Solutions–operated InterNIC were redirected to Kashpureff's AlterNIC site, where they encountered a protest message[21] and a link to the real InterNIC site. "If they think they own the entire domain name space," Kashpureff told reporters, "I've got news for them. Over the weekend, I possessed their name."[22]

Kashpureff's domain guerilla warfare was perceived by some as a heroic act of civil disobedience, by others as dangerous and antisocial if not criminal. Either way, he had concretized the vulnerability of the DNS. Network Solutions filed a civil suit against him, which was settled when he paid a token fee and issued a public apology. The U.S. Federal Bureau of Investigation, however, later pursued him on criminal charges of wire fraud (Diamond 1998).

7.4   The U.S. Government Intervenes

Up to this point the most powerful potential claimant of the root, the U.S. government, had not taken any initiative. The gTLD-MoU and other developments, however, made it impossible to continue doing nothing. The controversies generated by the gTLD-MoU, the Name.Space litigation, and the impending expirations of IANA's funding and the Network Solutions Cooperative Agreement forced the federal government to either yield or assert responsibility.

7.4.1   The National Science Foundation Exits

The National Science Foundation decided to let go. Both Network Solutions and the Internet technical hierarchy had strong ties to the agency, and NSF seemed to have been immobilized by the bitter feud developing between them. By early 1997 the agency wanted only to extract itself from the whole controversy.[23]

In April 1997 the NSF brushed aside a report from its own Inspector General's Office calling for continued federal oversight of Internet names and numbers.[24] The report had argued for the imposition of fees on names and addresses to "supplement the government's investment in the Internet." The NSF response noted that regulation and taxation of Internet addresses was "not an appropriate function" for the agency. Instead, it pointed to the IAHC proposals to privatize DNS as one of several "next-step solutions that are being implemented" and spoke glowingly of the Internet Society as an "an international organization whose members reflect the breadth of the entire Internet community."[25] The statement announced that NSF had "no plans to renew or to recompete [the NSI] Cooperative Agreement."[26]

In fact, a few months before, NSF and Network Solutions had agreed in principle to terminate the 1993 Cooperative Agreement a year early, on April 1, 1997. Early termination of the agreement would have given Network Solutions de facto property rights in the *.com, .net,* and *.org* registry. Depending on the conditions of the termination, it could have left unresolved the question of whether NSI had property rights in the database of domain name registrants. And it would have further clouded the issue of who had the authority to add new top-level domains to the root. NSF and Network Solutions were also making plans to spin off the IP address registry functions from Network Solutions to an independent American Registry for Internet Numbers (ARIN).[27] One Internet veteran wrote that "it's my feeling the NSF is acting to simply walk away from the situation, leaving it among the contestants, NSI being the strongest, to duke it out."[28]

NSF's exit strategy, however, was interrupted by the intervention of a White House–led Interagency Working Group (see section 7.4.2). Members of the interagency group wanted more time to consider the issues and the implications of various options before any decisive action was taken. NSF was not allowed to terminate the Network Solutions contract early. Other steps taken at this time seem to have been designed to ensure that the federal government would continue to have direct leverage over the outcome. When Jon Postel's DARPA funding ended in April 1997, for example, he appealed to the private sector IP address registries for support.

The U.S. government suddenly came up with funds from the Energy Department and NASA to continue funding Postel.[29]

7.4.2   The White House and the Commerce Department Enter

With the NSF no longer able to set policy, responsibility for formulating U.S. government policy was assumed by the presidential policy adviser Ira Magaziner. Magaziner headed an Interagency Task Force created in December 1995 to develop policy on Global Electronic Commerce on the Internet. As the e-commerce guru for the Clinton administration, Magaziner had made "private sector leadership" the key principle guiding administration policy.[30] The emphasis on private sector solutions and industry self-regulation was strongly supported by major industry actors such as MCI Telecommunications, IBM, PSINet, and AT&T.

Domain name issues did not attract Magaziner's attention until December 1996, when the U.S. Patent and Trademark Office, with the backing of the U.S. Department of Commerce, moved to initiate a Notice of Inquiry on trademarks and domain names. According to Magaziner, "I heard them raising a concern that was backed up by a number of business people that if you ignored trademarks in the issuance of domain names, it could have a negative commercial impact."[31] Magaziner had also become aware of NSF's attempt to terminate the Network Solutions contract early, and learned that IANA's DARPA contract was also set to expire in April. Ironically, Magaziner's concept of private sector leadership did not countenance simply walking away. Some voices within the administration and in the corporate world believed that the stability of the Internet would be threatened unless the government created formal arrangements to replace IANA and InterNIC. Magaziner responded by forming a separate Interagency Working Group on domain names in March 1997.

The Interagency Working Group was chaired by Brian Kahin of the White House Office of Science and Technology Policy. Kahin's eventual cochair was J. Beckwith Burr, a lawyer from the Federal Trade Commission who later moved to the Commerce Department when it became the lead agency for the U.S. policy intervention.[32] Representatives from the National Science Foundation, the Defense Department, the Federal Communications Commission, the Justice Department, the Patent and Trademark Office, and the State Department all participated.

Initially, the U.S. government reacted negatively to the IAHC proposals. The leading role of the ITU in particular seems to have generated antipathy. The Working Group was only a few weeks old when the ITU issued its invitation to the gTLD-MoU's meeting of signatories and "potential signatories," scheduled for May 1. A sharply worded reply cable from Secretary of State Madeline Albright to the U.S. mission in Geneva questioned the ITU's authority to call a full meeting of member states without the authorization of national governments. Albright noted that "the USG has not yet developed a position on any of the proposals to reform the Internet domain name system, including the gLTD-MoU [sic], nor on the appropriate role, if any, of the ITU, WIPO, or other international organizations in the administration of the Internet."[33] On May 2, the U.S. press reported that the Interagency Working Group would *not* support the gTLD-MoU. An unidentified member of the group was quoted as saying, "We are concerned about the possibility that [international] organizations will have too great a role in the process and we won't have a private sector–driven process. There are also some concerns," the unnamed official said, "about addressing an Internet-related issue in a forum that has traditionally done telecommunications regulation, like the ITU."

The working group spent the rest of the spring preparing for a formal public proceeding to solicit input on how to handle the transition. The Commerce Department was chosen to replace the National Science Foundation as the lead agency, and Burr was transferred there. Within the Commerce Department, responsibility for handling the proceeding was assigned to what many considered to be a "weak, understaffed"[34] branch, the National Telecommunications and Information Administration (NTIA). On July 1, 1997, a Presidential Executive Order authorized the Secretary of Commerce to "support efforts to make the governance of the domain name system private and competitive and to create a contractually based self-regulatory regime that deals with potential conflicts between domain name usage and trademark laws on a global basis."[35] On the next day, the NTIA opened a proceeding asking for public comment on DNS policy issues.[36] "The government has not endorsed any plan at this time," the document stated, "but believes that it is very important to reach consensus on these policy issues as soon as possible." It asked for comment on the appropriate principles to use to guide the transition and on the proper organizational framework, and for suggestions on specific issues such as new TLD creation, shared vs. exclusive top-level domains, and trademark protection. By mid-August, over 430 parties had filed comments in the proceeding (Mathiason and Kuhlman 1998).

7.4.3   Fait Accompli?

The gTLD-MoU partisans had committed themselves to a position from which it was difficult to back down. They had asserted that the root was theirs to dispose of. They believed that their process had been open and legitimate, and had produced a workable consensus of the Internet community. While they were willing to tweak the most unpopular elements of the proposal, they refused to make any concessions regarding their authority, for that would mean prolonging Network Solutions' monopoly and dissipating their first-mover's power to define the agenda and control the new institutions. Thus, as the negative signals from the State Department and the Interagency Working Group came out in the middle of 1997, the IAHC leadership responded by openly challenging the U.S. government's authority. As a contemporary news article reported, "The ad hoc committee has said it doesn't need the U.S. government's approval to go ahead with its plan. Appointed by the Internet Society, the committee says it has direct control of the computers that run the Net's addressing system through the Internet Assigned Numbers Authority (IANA). The government has 'no choice' but to go along with its plans, IAHC chair and ISOC president Don Heath has said."[37]

Indeed, the IAHC members began to execute their plan as if their authority to do so were still unquestioned, in the hope that they would win by default. An interim Policy Oversight Committee was constituted in August 1997 and began to accept money from registrar applicants. Eventually, 88 companies paid in, creating a fund of nearly US$1 million. Software development contracts for the shared registry system were initiated, and an implementation schedule was released. January 1998 was set as the starting date for new registrations.

But the IAHC's authority to get their new names into the root was still in doubt. Postel's IANA could plausibly claim policy authority over the root, but Network Solutions actually operated the authoritative A root server, so nothing could be done without its acquiescence. And as a byproduct of the Name.Space litigation, Network Solutions had explicit instructions from the National Science Foundation not to add any new top-level domains to the root. A confrontation was looming. As an IAHC member, David Crocker, noted in the fall of 1997: "We are fast approaching a critical moment. . . . The moment is the request by IANA for addition of the new generic TLDs (gTLDs) to the root DNS servers. The request will be issued when the gTLD-MoU's CORE project plans require it for testing, prior to live registration operation of these gTLDs. Nearly 90 companies have committed significant funds and effort to this activity, so it's rather more than a theoretical exercise."[38]

The U.S. government's intention to make policy through Magaziner's working group and the NTIA proceeding represented a clear threat to these plans. To counter what it viewed as unwarranted intervention by the U.S. government, the IAHC began to seek political support from foreign governments. Thirty-five of the registrars authorized by the interim POC were European companies, and several others were Asian, giving non-U.S. interests a stake in the proposed regime. In a November 13, 1997, email from Crocker to a private CORE email list, acquired and leaked by reporter Gordon Cook, the strategy was stated explicitly: "It appears that the folks at the U.S. government continue to miss the point that the rest of the world and its governments think that the Internet is a global resource, rather than strictly being an entity belonging to the U.S. Other governments need to communicate their interests in this effort to open up control of Internet infrastructure. It would be very helpful for contingents from non-U.S. countries to band together and lobby their own governments to communicate to the U.S. folks."[39]

The situation became even more polarized when U.S. congressional hearings were held on September 30 and October 2, 1997. The hearings were dominated by gTLD-MoU opponents, some of whom played on nationalistic sentiments.[40]

7.5   The Green Paper and Its Aftermath

The NTIA was supposed to issue a policy statement based on the public comments in early November. That date was repeatedly postponed because of the intense lobbying and the extensive stakeholder consultations of Magaziner, Kahin, and Burr. The MoU forces were adding signatories, trying to build momentum, and urging the Interagency Working Group to accede to the addition of its new gTLDs to the root. Its opponents, including Network Solutions and the alternative registries, wanted the NTIA proceeding to start from a clean slate. Finally, on January 28, 1998, the NTIA published online a Notice of Proposed Rulemaking. The document, known as the Green Paper because of its status as a discussion draft seeking an additional round of comments, was a tremendous blow to the Internet Society and its backers.

In the Green Paper, the U.S. government asserted its authority over the name and address root but also indicated its intention to relinquish that authority in a way that involved Internet stakeholders internationally. Much to the chagrin of the MoUvement, the document did not recognize IANA's relations with the Internet Society and did not even mention the IAHC process that had produced the gTLD-MoU and CORE.

Instead, the Green Paper was a relatively straightforward privatization proposal, putting forward some basic principles to guide the federal government in transferring the IANA functions to a private not-for-profit corporation.[41] The proposal repeatedly recognized that international "stakeholders want a larger voice in Internet coordination," and pledged that the new governance arrangements would "ensure international input in decision making" but nevertheless asserted that the U.S. government had to direct the transition because of its responsibility for the contractors in control of the root and the need for stability. As a governance structure, the Green Paper proposed a 14-member board of directors drawn in a balanced fashion from various stakeholder groups.[42]

To open up the domain name market to competition, the Green Paper offered several key policy decisions. It proposed to authorize five new registries, each assigned one new top-level domain name. The low number was characterized as a cautious compromise between those who wanted no new TLDs at all and those who wanted many more; the new domains would serve as an experiment in the effects of registry-level competition. Competition within top-level domains would be fostered by shared access to registries. Both the new domains and the existing *.com, .net,* and *.org* domains would be opened up to competing registrars, and Network Solutions would be required to separate its registry and registrar businesses.

On trademark questions, the Green Paper specifically rejected waiting periods and a moratorium on new top-level domains as acceptable policy alternatives, and questioned the need for a uniform dispute resolution policy. Instead, it proposed that gTLD registries be required to select their own dispute resolution processes that met some minimum criteria specified in the Paper.[43]

Prior to the release of the Green Paper, on December 10, 1997, Magaziner had met with Jon Postel in Washington. Magaziner related what he called good news and bad news to Postel. The good news was that he had found funding for IANA that would last until September 30, 1998, the date when the new corporation envisioned in the Green Paper would be up and running. The bad news was that it would be the U.S. government, not Postel or IANA, that would decide whether and when new TLDs would be added to the root.[44]

Magaziner's warning made it clear to Postel, more than a month before the release of the Green Paper, that the U.S. government was not going to stand aside while the Internet Society, CORE, and POC took control of the root. Apparently concerned about the direction U.S. policy was taking, Postel on January 28 arranged for a challenge to U.S. authority that rivaled the gTLD-MoU in boldness. Postel organized a redirection of the root— what he later referred to as a test and others called a hijacking of the root.

The authoritative root zone file was hosted on the A root server operated by Network Solutions. NSI's operational control of the root was, of course, the chief impediment to the gTLD-MoU's ability to implement its plan. On that date in January, only two days before the public release of the Green Paper, Postel sent an email message to all the secondary root servers calling for a coordinated shift to IANA as the source of the authoritative root zone file. "At some point down the road," Postel wrote, "it will be appropriate for the root domain to be edited and published directly by the IANA. As a small step in this direction we would like to have the secondaries for the root domain pull the root zone (by zone transfer) directly from IANA's own name server." Based on these instructions from Postel, eight of the twelve root servers were modified to take their authoritative zone files from Postel's name server. Root servers B, C, D, F, I, K, L, and M—all of the servers at universities and research institutes, including RIPE and Nordunet in Europe—participated in Postel's "test." Servers E,

G, H, and J—the ones at NASA, the U.S. military network, the Ballistics Research Lab, and NSI—did not. The claim to authoritative root server status was in play.

Although Postel later downplayed the significance of the event, there can be little doubt that the redirection was a direct challenge to U.S. government authority. Paul Vixie, who operated the K root server that participated in the redirection, conjectured that "he was firing a shot across the bow, saying [to NSI] you may have COM, but I've got the dot."[45] Vixie himself asked a friend the night before it happened to watch over his family if he went to jail.[46]

The implications of a coordinated redirection of the root were not lost on anyone. Although he did not do so, Postel *could have* added to the root server system the new gTLDs proposed by the gTLD-MoU. Had he done so, however, the result would have been two different Internet roots, possibly fragmenting Internet connectivity.[47] Magaziner and Burr learned of the redirection as they were putting the finishing touches on the Green Paper. Postel was ordered to return the root servers' configuration to their original state, and he complied. Magaziner later publicly stated that any attempt to manipulate the root without the U.S. government's permission would be prosecuted as a criminal offense.

8

Institutionalizing the Root: The Formation of ICANN

Don Heath: IANA's method of working has always been, in fact, to assess what the community, the community . . . the broad Internet stakeholders wanted, and [IANA] would never do anything on its own unless it was acceptable generally. . . . Jon knows, Postel and IANA know, that they cannot function unless they are meeting the will of the Internet community at large.

Anthony Rutkowski: The notion that there is any Internet community is a myth. In fact it's rather the converse. [Laughter] You've got probably a dozen or fifteen different, fairly insular communities that all have to dovetail into that. . . .

—Transcript of public hearing on the Green Paper, February 23, 1998

Institutionalization occurs when the parties involved in the exploitation of a resource adopt group rules and customs regarding its allocation and use. The process of contracting for property rights, however, can only take place when the parties are in communication with each other and have established mutually acceptable methods and arenas for bargaining and negotiation. It took some time for the struggle to control the Internet's name and address space to reach the stage where formal collective action was possible.

The exchange that begins this chapter, between Don Heath, president and chief executive officer of the Internet Society (ISOC) at the time, and Anthony Rutkowski, Heath's predecessor who had become a harsh critic of ISOC, poignantly illustrates one reason why the road to effective collection action was so rocky. Traditional notions of an Internet community were derived from the halcyon days of the 1980s, when a small cadre of computer scientists facilitated the emergence of an informally organized standards community (the Internet Engineering Task Force—IETF) and there was an interconnection among research and education networks worldwide. Respected authority figures such as Jon Postel could determine informally "the will" of such a community. But the Internet of the late 1990s was a very different place. In addition to the opinions of a tightly knit epistemic community of technologists, decisions had to take into account the interests and ambitions of businesses of all shapes and sizes, consumers, politicians from different parts of the world, and all the opportunities for legal conflict among producers and consumers. The number of bargaining parties was now much larger, and their interests were heterogeneous.

Table 8.1 lists key stakeholder groups and describes their interests. By 1998 each of those groups was activated around Internet governance issues. Each had formed some concept of what was at stake and was capable of promoting policy alternatives that reflected their interests. Each group's relationship to other groups, whether one of alliance or opposition, was becoming known.

Between the release of the Green Paper in late January 1998 and the issuance of the final White Paper in June 1998, a subset of the groups listed in table 8.1 formed a "dominant coalition" capable of driving the institutionalization process to conclusion. This chapter analyzes the origins and composition of the "dominant coalition" and its capture of ICANN in its formative stages. Chapter 9 details the enactment of its agenda in the two-and-a-half years following the release of the White Paper.

8.1 From Green Paper to White Paper

The release of the Green Paper quickly polarized the governance debate around the issue of the U.S. government's role.[1] Under the Green Paper, domain name system (DNS) privatization would have taken place in a U.S. legal and institutional framework, possibly as rule-making subject to the U.S. Administrative Procedures Act.[2] Most participants in the United States welcomed the procedural solidity that the U.S. Commerce Department proceeding brought to what had been a chaotic process, even if they wanted to modify specific aspects of the policy.[3]

The groups that opposed the Green Paper, on the other hand, reviled it as U.S. coup d'état that took no heed of the international character of the Internet. Opponents saw it as a form of intrusive government intervention in the affairs of what had been a self-governing community. These included, of course, the U.S.-based Internet Society and other members of the Generic Top-Level Domain Memorandum of Understanding (gTLD-MoU) coalition, which rejected the authority of the U.S. government. Indeed, the Green Paper ended up firmly uniting the European Commission (EC) and policymakers in the few involved national governments with supporters of the gTLD-MoU, despite their earlier rejection of the initiative as "too U.S.-centric."[4]

8.1.1   Fighting the Green Paper

The gTLD-MoU had been formed around an international network composed of members of the technical community, prospective registrars, and intergovernmental organizations. That network was now leveraged to arouse significant opposition to the U.S. government's proposal. The Council of Registrars (CORE) utilized the US$1 million in registrar application fees it had collected to hire a public relations firm and a lobbyist.[5] The Internet Society and CORE organized a campaign to file comments in the National Telecommunications and Information Administration (NTIA) proceeding, rousing their membership with emailed calls to action and setting up Web sites with ready-made messages to file in the proceeding. Ironically, given the MoU's cartel-like structure and alliances with intergovernmental organizations, the campaign relied heavily on libertarian rhetoric. The "self-governance" and "private sector leadership" of the gTLD-MoU were contrasted with the "governmental meddling" proposed by Magaziner and NTIA. The plan for competing, for-profit registries was decried as monopolistic. The campaign paid off, as NTIA received a flood of ISOC- or CORE-inspired responses.[6]

Key CORE executive committee members and prospective registrars were located in Australia and Europe.[7] As representatives of business interests seeking entry to a U.S.-dominated market, their efforts aroused interest and support from their domestic governments. The CORE interests were particularly successful at turning the European Commission and the government of Australia against the Green Paper. The EC's harshly critical response to the Green Paper charged that "The U.S. Green paper proposals appear not to recognise the need to implement an international approach. The current U.S. proposals could, in the name of the globalisation

Table 8.1
Stakeholders List in Internet Governance

---

1. U.S. Government
A highly complex organization subject to multiple points of access and pressure, the U.S. government acted, or rather reacted, as an intermediary for diverse and often conflicting interests. Because the constituencies to which it responded were deeply divided, its main objective was to get rid of the problem without creating serious political liabilities or yielding too much control to foreign interests.

2. Network Solutions, Inc.
A profit-making firm controlling 70 percent of the global market for domain name registration, it wanted to establish a stable property right over its generic top-level domains or, barring that, to prolong its special market position as long as possible.

3. Internet Technical Community
Encompasses the original ARPANET elite, the IANA, the Internet Architecture Board, and other leading hierarchs of the IETF, and the founders and staff of RIPE-NCC and AP-NIC. The technical community wanted to maintain its historical control over the Internet's name and address spaces. It also developed an economic interest in DNS management as a source of support for its activities. Overlaps with (4) and (6).

4. Research and Education Networking Organizations
Administrators and engineers of government-subsidized research and education networks. Organized nationally around organizations like EDUCAUSE in the United States or science and technology and education ministries outside the United States. Overlaps with the technical community through the Internet Society and the National Science Foundation, and had a similar interest in maintaining the status quo in administrative control of the Internet.

5. Trademark and Intellectual Property Interests
Major trademark holders opposed expansion of the name space and demanded more effective and inexpensive ways to monitor domain name assignments and enforce their claims of exclusive rights over specific names. Representative groups were INTA, FICPI, MPAA, AIM, and WIPO.

6. Large Telecommunications and e-Commerce Corporations
Organized around GIP, ITAA, WITSA, and the International Chamber of Commerce, these companies were primarily interested in fostering stable, predictable administration of the Internet while retaining private sector control. Many were also major trademark holders and placed high priority on the intellectual property protection agenda. Included IBM, MCI, AT&T, AOL, France Telecom, and Deutsche Telekom.

Table 8.1
(continued)

7. Prospective Market Entrants
Businesses seeking entry into the domain name market. This grouping was split into two distinct and opposing stakeholders: *CORE registrars*—smaller, mostly non-U.S. businesses seeking entry into the commercial market for *.com, .net,* and *.org* registrations as registrars and as co-owners of a global, shared registry, allied with the Internet Society and against Network Solutions. *Claimants to new TLD strings*—small entrepreneurs and maverick technical people who created their own top-level domains and registries, and attempted to support them in non-IANA root server confederations. Both groups wanted competitive entry into the market, but promoted different ideological and policy agendas.

8. Local and Regional Internet Service Providers
Smaller-scale ISPs and their trade associations, including CIX and ISP/C in the United States, Euro-ISPA, APIA. As consumers of IP addresses lower on the chain than the larger infrastructure providers in (6), this group had an interest in a stable, accountable assignment authority and was concerned with getting a seat at the table for its constituents.

9. Country Code Registries
A highly diverse group encompassing large-scale, private sector nonprofit consortiums in Germany and England, quasi-commercial TLDs in island territories, and registries run by government science and technology ministries. All held de facto property rights to TLD strings and had incentives similar to Network Solutions', except that there was no hostility or rivalry between them and the technical community. Included Domainz (NZ), CENTR, APTLD, IATLD.

10. Civil Society and Civil Liberties Organizations
Organized public interest groups saw in the domain name wars threats to freedom of expression and a dangerous expansion of intellectual property rights. Included DNRC, EFF, CPSR, ACM, ACLU.

11. Intergovernmental Organizations and National Governments
ITU and WIPO responded to organizational imperatives to incorporate Internet governance functions into their mission. The European Commission and a few key national governments, notably France and Australia, similarly wanted to secure for themselves a seat at the decision-making table, but were also concerned with countering U.S. economic and political dominance of the Internet, and with asserting rights over specific names and registries.

and privatisation of the Internet, consolidate permanent U.S. jurisdiction over the Internet as a whole, including dispute resolution and trademarks used on the Internet."[8]

The government of Australia intervened through its National Office for the Information Economy, directed by Paul Twomey, a protégé of Senator Richard Alston. It criticized the Green Paper for its "unduly dominant role for U.S. jurisdiction and interests," for failing to describe how the governing body would be accountable to national interests, and for its two-year reservation of U.S. government "policy oversight" over the root.[9] Whereas U.S. commentators tended to support the Green Paper's call for quick decisions on new domains, European and Asian interests urged NTIA to defer all such decisions so that a new, internationally representative organization could make them.

Opposition to the Green Paper had more to do with who would be in control of the transition than the actual policies that would be adopted. Both the Green Paper and the gTLD-MoU would have created a handful of new top-level domains, instituted shared registries, and pushed toward some form of linkage between registries and dispute resolution.[10] Moving forward under U.S. government auspices, however, would have weakened the influence of the gTLD-MoU framers and the international organizations that had been assigned powerful positions within its framework. The European Commission and other national governments would be reduced to the status of commentators and observers.

8.1.2   Assembling the Dominant Coalition

At some time between the January release of the Green Paper and the June release of the final policy statement, organized business lobbying groups spearheaded the formation of a dominant coalition. Political leadership came from the Internet divisions of IBM and MCI.

The key vehicle for organizing business interests was the Global Internet Project (GIP). GIP was formed in 1996 by high-level executives of 16 Internet, telecommunications, and e-commerce firms.[11] Its objective, which had taken shape during the controversies over encryption and content regulation in the mid-1990s, was to resist "unnecessary international regulations and national laws that impede or inhibit [the Internet's] growth." Ironically, one could hear from the corporate backers of a process that would lead to the institutionalization and regulation of the Internet faint echoes of the libertarian rhetoric of John Perry Barlow. The group's mission statement claimed, "Old, outdated, national regulatory models should not be applied to the Internet. Instead, new international and non-governmental approaches to policy must be developed, that will be flexible enough to keep pace with the rapid evolution of technology and the marketplace. Often these approaches will rely upon market mechanisms for self-regulation, rather than government regulation."[12]

IBM's vice president for Internet technology, John Patrick, took over leadership of the group early in 1998. Shortly thereafter, GIP began to focus on Internet governance. While its small core of executives set strategy for the group, plans were executed by the Information Technology Association of America (ITAA), a Washington-based business lobby claiming 10,000 members in 1998. ITAA in turn was the central secretariat of a consortium of information technology industry associations from 41 nations known as the World Information Technology and Services Alliance (WITSA).

The business leaders behind GIP were, naturally enough, deeply involved in the Clinton administration's attempt to develop a global framework for electronic commerce, and encouraged Magaziner's policy of private sector leadership. At the release of the Clinton administration's e-commerce framework in July 1997, IBM president Lou Gertsner spoke on an equal status with the President and Vice President. The relationship to the White House was solidified in December 1997, when Patrick hired Mike Nelson into IBM's government affairs office and put him to work promoting GIP's agenda. Nelson, an influential member of the White House Office of Science and Technology Policy, had supervised many of the Clinton administration's National Information Infrastructure initiatives. Before that, he had drafted the High Performance Computing Act as Senator Albert Gore's staff member. At about the same time it hired Nelson, IBM recruited Brian Carpenter, the CERN scientist who chaired the Internet Architecture Board (IAB). MCI-Worldcom, which was emerging as the world's dominant Internet backbone provider, was also an active, founding member of GIP. Sometime in the middle of 1998, Vint Cerf, a vice president at MCI, began to work directly with GIP on its Internet governance initiatives. MCI had other strategic ties to the technical community as well: John Klensin, an IAB member since 1996, was an MCI employee.

Later, IBM's Internet division would play a highly visible role in the selection of ICANN's initial board. With MCI, it would later engineer fundraising and public relations support for the new organization and even come to its financial rescue at a critical time in its evolution.[13] In 1999, ITAA and WITSA would play a decisive role in defining a representational structure for the new Domain Name Supporting Organization that made business and trademark interests dominant. IBM's involvement in Internet governance was motivated both by its concerns about trademark dilution and more fundamentally by its strategy of developing a robust e-commerce industry over the Internet. The latter required creating a stable, predictable institutional framework for root administration. A stable administration would not rock the boat by permitting, willy-nilly, the entry of hundreds of new registries and would take strong measures to preserve brand identities.

In many respects, the coalition's core members bore a striking resemblance to the IBM, MCI, and University of Michigan consortium that had operated the National Science Foundation's Internet backbone from 1987 to 1995. In the course of developing the NSFNET backbone, IBM, MCI, a few key university network administrators, and the Internet technical hierarchy all cultivated close working relationships with federal agencies to gain access to funding. Professional linkages among the members of these organizations were maintained through organizations such as the Federal Networking Council Advisory Committee, Educom, and the Internet Society.

But the NSFNET backbone group was a *domestic* coalition and thus could work within an established framework of national laws, regulations, and policies. Internet governance was irretrievably international, and most key players were united in the premise that they did not want to work through established international institutions such as the International Telecommunication Union (ITU). Nor did they want the problem to be solved via new treaties or new forms of collective action among nation-states. What then did they want? Prior to the White Paper, the constituents of what would become the dominant coalition were divided or uncoordinated on that question.

The gTLD-MoU had pioneered an international alliance but lacked the unified support of two critical constituents: the U.S. government and big business. The U.S. government was uncomfortable with the prominent role of the ITU, and at odds with the Internet Assigned Numbers Authority (IANA) and the Internet Society over their attempts to privatize the root on their own initiative. Though MCI had been a strong supporter of gTLD-MoU, IBM and AT&T had withheld their support because of trademark concerns. IBM executives also had been alienated by the "arrogance" of some of the International Ad Hoc Committee (IAHC) members.[14]

During the development of the White Paper, Magaziner and GIP would play a key role in unifying the technical hierarchy, trademark holders, and larger telecommunication and information technology companies around a common agenda. Magaziner, who had been in close communication with Postel and other IAB members during the preparation of the Green Paper,[15] came to agree that the new governance organization should be a continuation of the existing IANA.[16] The governance entity should be incorporated in the United States, not in Europe as the gTLD-MoU had proposed, but the board should be internationally representative. There would be no new top-level domains until the concerns of trademark holders were taken care of.

The emerging political linkages among these groups were illuminated by a related development. On February 11, 1998, Jon Postel and Brian Carpenter, an IBM Internet division employee and chair of the Internet Architecture Board, jointly announced the creation of an IANA Transition Advisory Group (ITAG). ITAG was a six-member committee composed of senior members of the Internet technical hierarchy: Carpenter, Randy Bush of Verio, Inc. (an Internet service provider), David Farber of the University of Pennsylvania, Geoff Huston of Telstra (the dominant Australian telecommunication provider), John Klensin of MCI, and Steve Wolff, former director of the National Science Foundation's Computer and Information Sciences and Engineering Division, who now worked for Cisco. All were technical people long associated with IETF inner circles.

The purpose of ITAG was to advise Postel on how to handle the transition from a U.S.-government-funded set of functions to a new international nonprofit corporation with a formal board of directors. The news release claimed that the group would pay "particular attention to its open, international governance." The formation of the group shortly after the release of the Green Paper and Postel's root redirection debacle signaled recognition by the technical hierarchy that it had to come to terms with the ongoing U.S.-government proceeding.

Winning the support of Postel and the technical community would bring into the fold an international network of stakeholders with control of important resources. This included the regional address registries in Asia and Europe, root server operators in London, Norway, and Japan, and many operators of country code top-level domains (ccTLDs). Most ccTLD operators were affiliated with universities or government research networks that had received their delegations directly from Postel.

The U.S. government in turn served as the bridge between the U.S. corporate and technical groups and other national governments and international organizations. Almost by default, it became the accepted intermediary for resolving the institutional problem. But as it learned from the reaction to the Green Paper, it had to stay in the background rather than the foreground. Thus, it would impose some basic principles and constraints on the process and serve as a guarantor of the emerging institution's stability, but defer key policy decisions to the new entity. The U.S. government also came to defer to European pressure to allow an international organization, WIPO, to take the lead in resolving the trademark problem.[17] While non-U.S. parties succeeded in extracting important concessions from the U.S.-centered interests, they stood at the periphery rather than the core of the "dominant coalition." In the progression from gTLD-MoU to the White Paper, ITU in particular lost status and influence.

Stakeholders ignored, excluded, or marginalized by the dominant coalition included Network Solutions (NSI), the alternative registries, smaller Internet service providers and their trade associations, civil society and civil liberties organizations, and the governments of developing countries. As the following discussion shows, the policy agendas of these interests were too far removed from those of the coalition to be accommodated. Network Solutions still had significant bargaining power, and its exclusion would pose severe problems for the new institution. Most of the other interests, however, having no viable claim on or control of strategic resources, lacked the bargaining strength to challenge the dominant coalition. Figure 8.1 shows the composition of the coalition.

8.1.3 The White Paper

The Clinton administration released its final plan, the so-called White Paper, on June 3, 1998 (NTIA 1998b). The White Paper surprised everyone

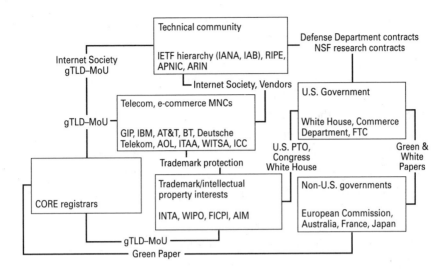

Figure 8.1
The dominant coalition, 1998

who was not privy to the behind-the-scenes negotiations that created it. It took the form of a nonbinding "statement of policy" rather than a rule-making document, and it abandoned direct action by the U.S. government. No new TLDs would be authorized. No competing registries would be recognized. No binding decisions about the structure or composition of the new corporation's board would be made. Instead, the Commerce Department merely announced its intention "to recognize, by entering into agreement with, and to seek international support for," a new not-for-profit corporation to administer policy for the Internet name and address system. The department would simply wait for "private sector stakeholders" to form a corporation suitable for its recognition. It asked that the private sector be ready with a "consensus-based" proposal in time for the expiration of the Network Solutions contract on September 30, 1998. Ostensibly, it was now up to the warring factions of the Internet to settle the issues.[18]

Although it allowed the private sector to create what it called NewCo and define its board and structure, the White Paper did prescribe its characteristics in some detail. It should be headquartered in the United States. Its board of directors should be "internationally representative" and balanced to equitably represent various "stakeholders." These were identified as IP address registries, domain name registries and registrars, the technical community, Internet service providers, and users including commercial entities, noncommercial users, and individuals. Government officials should not be allowed on the board. The White Paper contemplated the appointment of an interim board to jump-start the new corporation. In general, the corporation should be governed on the basis of open and transparent decision-making processes.

The White Paper also described in some detail the policies it thought NewCo should adopt. The Commerce Department pledged that it would revise its agreements with Network Solutions to "take actions to promote competition," which meant opening up the generic top-level domains to competing registrars. The globally dominant registry would also be required to "recognize the role of the new corporation to establish and implement DNS policy." Regarding domain name disputes and trademark protection, the statement abandoned the Green Paper's registry-centered approach and came out in support of a uniform dispute resolution policy. Moreover, it deferred to WIPO, asking it to initiate a global consultative process to develop recommendations for a uniform dispute resolution system and policies to protect famous trademarks in new top-level domains. It also called for an independent study to evaluate the effects of new top-level domains on trademark holders. The work of the IAHC was explicitly recognized.

To those who drafted it, the policy statement outlined a bargain capable of satisfying a coalition of some of the most powerful claimants: the U.S. government; IANA, the Internet Society, and the IAB; the major industry players orchestrated by GIP; the trademark interests; and the European Commission and other involved national governments. Behind the scenes, these groups had made a tenuous peace. The new organization would be "built around the existing IANA."[19] This won the enthusiastic support of the Internet Society and the gTLD-MoU parties,[20] and the GIP members, who had strong ties to, or directly employed, many of the leading technical people. Business interests also favored the concept of private sector leadership and a reduced role for government action. And, like the other trademark interests, they were relieved about the delay in new top-level domains and the promise of a dispute resolution system designed by WIPO. The European Commission, which had been given advance drafts of the document, approved of the fact that the U.S. government was leaving specific policy decisions to a new organization that would be internationally representative.[21] Foreign governments were also happy that Network Solutions' gTLDs would be opened to CORE registrars and that an international organization, WIPO, had been given an important role in resolving the trademark problem.

8.2   The International Forum on the White Paper

But the White Paper had broadcast a profoundly mixed message. Read from a viewpoint less cognizant of the insiders' bargain, the White Paper seemed to embody a sincere commitment to self-governance and a willingness to accept whatever the broader Internet community decided to do. Many people involved in Internet governance took the call for a private sector–led consensus at face value and welcomed the challenge. They interpreted the White Paper as an opportunity to come together on neutral territory and forge an unconstrained consensus on what would be the new corporation's structure, powers, initial board members, and management. The U.S. government actively encouraged that perception. It "repeatedly and publicly encouraged all Internet stakeholders . . . to participate in an open, consensus-driven process."[22] That optimistic spirit led to the series of truly self-organized meetings known as the International Forum on the White Paper.

8.2.1   Bringing the Parties Together

The first to respond to the White Paper's call for private initiative were Anthony Rutkowski, who had become a consultant for Network Solutions, and Kathryn Kleiman of the Domain Name Rights Coalition (DNRC). Both represented interests outside the dominant coalition. They proposed a Global Incorporation Alliance Workshop in Reston, Virginia.[23] Tamar Frankel, someone with experience in mediating corporate governance and industry self-regulation negotiations, was tapped to lead the workshop. Members of the Internet Society and CORE initially balked at participating in the event. The concept of an open process that brought all the contending parties together, however, gained support and momentum. In mid-June, trade associations of ISPs publicly came out in favor of the workshop and proposed to expand it to a series of face-to-face meetings around the world.[24] The incorporation workshop was renamed the International Forum on the White Paper (IFWP). A steering committee for the IFWP was organized that, rather remarkably, managed to seat representatives of nearly all the warring parties.[25] In July the European Commission organized a European consultative meeting to prepare for the IFWP meetings, resulting in the establishment of the EC Panel of Participants, a group of stakeholder representatives to advise the commission and develop a common position in the IFWP process. By the second meeting in Geneva, the Harvard University Law School's Berkman Center was helping to moderate meetings and archive its activities. In Latin America, a new Internet association was formed partly in response to the Buenos Aires IFWP meeting. Country code top-level domain name administrators also began to organize in its wake.

In parallel with the IFWP process, however, IANA and ISOC pursued their own agenda. Following the advice of his IANA Transition Advisory Group, Postel had acquired the services of a lawyer, the prominent Washington antitrust counsel Joe Sims of Jones, Day, Reavis and Pogue. Sims worked with Postel to draft articles of incorporation and bylaws for the new corporation. Sims proposed a closed corporation dominated by the technical community. It would incorporate under California law as a nonprofit public benefit corporation, a structure typically used for educational and charitable organizations. Half of the board would be self-selected by the initial board members. The other half would be appointed by functional constituencies called Supporting Organizations. Two of the three Supporting Organizations (addresses and protocols) would be controlled by the technical community. The composition of the third Supporting Organization, devoted to domain names, was not specified, but presumably was intended to represent business and user stakeholders in line with the criteria of the White Paper.

Sims attended most of the IFWP meetings, and Postel himself appeared briefly at the Geneva meeting, which overlapped with the Internet Society's annual convention. It gradually became evident, however, that the interests lined up behind IANA did not consider the IFWP process to be the real arena for arriving at a decision. Instead, Postel and Sims made it clear that they intended to use their own draft articles and bylaws as the basis for incorporation and would decide unilaterally whether to amend them or not based on comments submitted to the IANA Web site and informal consultations among their acquaintances in the dominant coalition. Postel's refusal to fully participate in IFWP began to grate on the groups and individuals involved, who believed that IFWP incorporated the consensual process called for in the White Paper. Frustration with IANA's refusal to modify its draft led to the drafting of an alternative proposal in August.

As the IFWP meetings progressed, it became clear that the open process was producing consensus around an organizational model sharply different from the one proposed by Sims and Postel. The public benefit corporation proposed by Sims vested significant power in the board and management, and gave the board sweeping powers to unilaterally change its structure by amending the bylaws. Accountability to a community of stakeholders was minimal. As Tamar Frankel (1998) observed,

A public benefit organization does not insure a balance of power among the different stakeholders. In fact, it negates the existence of stakeholders, and the need for a balance of power among them. . . . It is assumed that the board and the president . . . know what is good for all these groups and for the [community] as a whole. Further, the corporation by definition negates the need for protection against capture. Captured altruism and idealism are welcome. In short, this type of organization vests in its board virtually unrestricted powers to manage, structure, and restructure the corporation. Whether the corporation will fulfill its declared and future mission depends on . . . the good will and trustworthiness of the members of the board, not on the constitutional documents that vest power in the board. (2)

The IFWP process, in contrast, proposed a nonprofit, membership-based organization managed and controlled by an elected board representing various interest groups. This model was based on the assumption that the participants in the new organization would serve not because they were altruistic, but in order to advance their business, professional, or personal interests; hence, the organization was set up like a business corporation that substituted members for shareholders.

8.2.2 The Process Breaks Down

Tensions between these two parallel processes—the open, democratic proceedings of the IFWP and the private, informal networking of IANA—steadily mounted during the summer of 1998. The growing gap between the technical community's loyalty to Postel and the legal and political concerns of the IFWP was dramatized at the Forty-Second IETF meeting in Chicago on August 26. Postel and the IFWP's Frankel were both present at the plenary session. With IAB chair and IBM employee Brian Carpenter in control of the agenda, an emotional endorsement of the Postel-Sims draft was orchestrated. Carpenter read a "draft declaration of IAB support and IAB endorsement" for the Postel-Sims draft and asked the meeting for a "rough consensus" endorsement of it. A member of the audience stood up and asked the attendees to give Jon Postel a standing ovation "for all his good work over the last 20 years and his work on his latest 'new IANA' draft." Postel's efforts were endorsed by acclamation, with a few notable exceptions.[26] Nearly all of those present had never read either proposal.[27]

Matters came to a head in late August, when the supporters of the IFWP tried to finalize their process. Two additional meetings were proposed: a restricted session that would bring the key stakeholders together in a closed negotiating session to finalize a constitution and interim board for the new corporation, and a public ratification meeting that would review those decisions and assess community input on them. There was also talk of an online voting process among IFWP participants to elect the initial board and to extend the ratification process to those who could not attend the meeting. Harvard's Berkman Center offered to host and mediate the meetings in Boston. The negotiating session was scheduled for September 12–13, and the ratification meeting was set for September 19.

Most stakeholders, including Network Solutions, had indicated their willingness to participate in the negotiating session. But IANA refused. Although most IFWP participants were unaware of it, their attempts to make IFWP into an authoritative arena for collective action posed a serious threat to the expectations and plans of the dominant coalition. It was one thing for the IFWP meetings to formulate resolutions and consensus points about broad issues. If IFWP hosted a real "constitutional convention," however, it threatened the hegemony of IANA and GIP over the incorporation process. As one participant in the negotiations recalled, "[Joe] Sims resisted the idea of a [final] meeting; he wanted to bypass IFWP completely."[28] To subject Sims's and Postel's incorporation proposals and interim board selections to approval and modification by an open, international forum that included many opponents and critics would be to risk losing control over the results.

As a loosely organized, informal group, the IFWP steering committee was in no position to resist centrifugal pressures. The committee contained several supporters of the IANA faction who obstructed attempts to push the IFWP process forward to authoritative decisions. In late August, prodded by Sims, the pro-IANA members of the steering committee withdrew their support for IFWP in order to allow IANA to take charge of the incorporation process. Mike Roberts of EDUCAUSE was particularly adamant about closing down the IFWP.[29] Only later did it become known that Roberts had already been tapped to serve as the first president of ICANN. Lacking sufficient backing and participation, Harvard and the IFWP steering committee canceled the final meetings, and the IFWP itself fell into disarray. From this point on, IANA became the undisputed focal point of the incorporation process. With control secure, the Global Internet Project held a press conference a few days after the IFWP had been disposed of, announcing its plans to raise start-up funding for the new nonprofit organization.[30]

The breakdown of the IFWP process concerned Magaziner and Burr. They urged IANA and Network Solutions to resolve their outstanding differences in some other way. The two parties' legal teams entered into private negotiations, and on September 17 released draft articles of incorporation and bylaws for an Internet Corporation for Assigned Names and Numbers (ICANN). The Internet's "constitutional convention" had been reduced to two government contractors—each a holder of de facto property rights over critical parts of the Internet's name and number space—negotiating in private. Even the IANA–Network Solutions agreement did not prove to be stable, however. The draft contained two clauses intended to protect Network Solutions against expropriation.[31] That made the proposal unpopular with many key backers of the dominant coalition, notably gTLD-MoU members and technical organizations outside the United States. IANA quickly backed away from the deal and on September 30 submitted to the Department of Commerce a fifth version of its proposed corporate documents with those clauses removed, and a list of interim board members (see section 8.2.3).

In the meantime, a small band of diehard IFWP-process supporters refused to accept the cancellation of the September 19 ratification meeting. They met on that date in Boston anyway to draft an alternative to the Postel-Sims proposal.[32] The resulting Boston Working Group (BWG) draft, as it came to be known, made the new corporation accountable to a membership that would elect the nine at-large board members. The group criticized the IANA draft for its "vague lines of accountability, limited, if any, means for individual participation, . . . a high degree of susceptibility to capture by companies and organizations, and [the absence of] a membership structure."[33] Another proposal was submitted under the banner of an alternative root server system called the Open Root Server Confederation (ORSC).[34] ORSC also proposed a membership corporation, but one composed primarily of organizations. Two other widely circulated documents proposed modifications of their own.[35] All these proposals claimed support from significant, but by no means dominant, segments of the "Internet community."

8.2.3 Captured from the Start

Perhaps the most serious blow to the White Paper's goal of building the new corporation upon a consensual foundation came with the appointment of ICANN's initial board and management. Almost everyone outside the IANA-GIP inner circles expected the initial board and management to be selected through some open, iterative process. Magaziner himself had told an interviewer on September 21 that he had expected "broad public discussion" of the names of proposed board members.[36] On October 5, however, Postel and Sims released a complete list of their nine interim board selections and made it clear that it was not subject to modification.

The interim board selections were the product of private negotiations and consultations among core members of the dominant coalition: Postel and Sims, Postel's friends at ISOC and IAB, IBM and other GIP members, the European Commission, and the Australian government. The IBM lobbyist Roger Cochetti, who began to assemble a list of names the first week in August, played a particularly active role and recruited the future board chair Esther Dyson.[37] The EC's Wilkinson directly nominated and "insisted upon" certain candidates to Sims in line with a tacit agreement with Magaziner and Burr that Europe would be given three seats on the board.[38] The Australian government also advanced a name and later pronounced itself satisfied with the results.

During the summer, Postel had stated that he intended to deliberately avoid selecting initial board members who were actively involved in DNS issues or associated with any particular faction. While this was true of most (not all) of the selections, the board members' lack of familiarity with the issues and the absence of any strong ties to involved constituencies meant that the board could not serve as an effective check upon policy directions set by the management.

And it was the core group's total control over the management of the new corporation, not the board selections per se, that proved most significant in the long run. Sims was in control of legal policy. Postel was predesignated as chief technical officer. At the same time as they selected the initial board, Sims and Postel designated EDUCAUSE's Mike Roberts as president; his ratification by the board October 25 was a mere formality. Roberts was no "neutral." He was a charter member of the Internet Society, a supporter of gTLD-MoU, a strong opponent of Network Solutions, and the man many viewed as directly responsible for sabotaging the IFWP. Real operational control of the corporation, therefore, was entirely in the hands of one faction. A neophyte, unpaid board selected by the management itself would be in no position to countermand it.

The dominant role of management became even more problematical when Postel died suddenly of complications from a heart attack, on October 18, 1998. One of the architects of the Internet's name and address spaces, and a man who commanded deep respect among the technical community, Postel had been the new corporation's most valuable asset. His death robbed the organization of its moral center, a good part of its institutional memory, and most of what remained of its legitimacy.

8.2.4   Network Solutions and Amendment 11

Network Solutions was excluded by the dominant coalition; indeed to many coalition members its market power was the focal point of the process. To the technical community it represented an unwelcome and threatening intrusion of commercial and proprietary interests into the core of Internet administration. To prospective entrants it represented a highly skewed distribution of wealth, which is unlikely to survive most collective action processes. To trademark owners its willingness to profit from an open, first-come/first-served domain name market was a major irritant.

Nevertheless, Network Solutions had significant bargaining power. It knew how to lobby in Washington and had the financial resources to do so. It controlled the gigantic *.com* zone and the authoritative root server.

A refusal by Network Solutions to participate in any new regime might result in the de facto privatization of the root in its hands.

Network Solutions' Cooperative Agreement with the U.S. government, which authorized it to operate the A root server and serve as the registry for the generic top-level domains, was set to expire September 30, 1998, the same date as Magaziner's deadline for forming the new corporation. But the possibility of terminating the contract did not give the U.S. government significant leverage over the company. Network Solutions claimed to have intellectual property rights in the database of *.com, .net,* and *.org* registrants; thus, it recognized no obligation to turn over the crucial zone files and registrant data to the U.S. government or to any new contractor when the Cooperative Agreement terminated. It claimed to own the zone files and therefore could continue to resolve names using them, with or without a contract. If its intellectual property claim was not upheld, the company had a fallback position: it would provide the government with a copy of the zone files when its contract expired, but it had a legal right to retain a copy for itself and continue operating a *.com, .net,* and *.org* registry on its own.

In either case, simple termination of the agreement would leave NSI in unsupervised or unregulated control of nearly three-fourths of the global domain name market. Most of the world's name servers already pointed at NSI for authoritative information about *.com, .net, .org,* and *.edu* domains. If Network Solutions continued to operate its own gTLD registries, sheer inertia would ensure that most of the world's name servers would continue to point at them. Network Solutions could even use its leverage over the dominant TLDs to create the critical mass needed to establish a viable alternative root under its own control. This was *real* privatization of DNS, and when confronted with the prospect of it, the U.S. government blanched. The government faced an unappetizing choice between contesting NSI's property claims in court, leading to prolonged uncertainty, or trying to move the root to another contractor to operate in competition with an unreconstructed NSI, risking fragmentation of the Internet.

At this juncture neither side seemed eager for a confrontation. On October 6, 1998, the Commerce Department and Network Solutions came to an agreement that would pave the way for the White Paper transition while leaving the hardest issues to be resolved at a later time. In Amendment 11 to the NSI Cooperative Agreement, Network Solutions agreed to design a shared registry system that would allow competing registrars to market domain name registrations in *.com, .net,* and *.org.* The company would separate its registrar (retail) operations from its (wholesale) registry functions into separate divisions. The Commerce Department fixed the price of NSI's wholesale registry at US$9 per name-year. The U.S. government would get a copy of the second-level domain name registration data controlled by Network Solutions. Moreover, NSI promised to make no changes to the root without written authorization from the U.S. government. Finally, Commerce extracted from Network Solutions a promise to recognize and enter into a contract with the new corporation contemplated by the White Paper.

8.2.5   The Failure of Consensus
The White Paper's attempt to facilitate open, private sector collective action had failed. Magaziner had called for a single proposal representing a broad consensus of the extended "Internet community." What the Commerce Department got by September 30 was four or five different proposals with important substantive differences about membership, the nature of the Supporting Organizations, protection of freedom of expression, and the composition of the interim board. Key bargaining parties had not even come to agreement on a common negotiating arena (IFWP vs. IANA). Although U.S. government officials, particularly Magaziner, were genuinely committed to an inclusive process, their decision to remove themselves from the incorporation process (and the tight time line they imposed) made it difficult to rectify the situation. The only card the U.S. government could play was to recognize or refuse to recognize a corporation. And its contract renewal deadlines had put itself in a position where it had to recognize *some* corporation very soon.

A final round of public comments on the multiple proposals put before the Commerce Department confirmed the divisions among the participants and the tenuous support for the ICANN proposal.[39] ICANN won praise from predictable sources—the Internet Society, CORE, IAB, the European Commission, and the GIP-led business interests. But only 28 of the 70-odd comments submitted provided an endorsement. The majority of the comments voiced complaints about the composition of the interim board and its method of selection, or favored letting IANA/ICANN lead the incorporation process but demanded membership and accountability provisions similar to the alternative proposals. Nearly 20 of the comments endorsed the BWG or ORSC proposals, or flatly rejected the ICANN proposal. On October 30, Frankel released a detailed "analysis of the proposed structures for the new corporation" claiming that the ICANN proposal "flaunts the principles established in the White Paper [and] the open IFWP process" and "makes a mockery of the trust people put in the process" (Frankel 1998, 3).

After reviewing the comments, the U.S. government announced that it intended to move forward with the ICANN proposal, but Magaziner and Burr made it clear that they agreed with many of the criticisms. They asked Sims and the newly anointed interim board to enter into negotiations with the Boston Working Group and the Open Root Server Confederation.[40] These negotiations, carried out in late October, resulted in a significant concession: the bylaws were amended to make it clear that the board had an "unconditional mandate" to create a membership structure that would directly elect the nine at-large directors.[41] ICANN agreed to establish an advisory committee on membership to pave the way for the creation of a global membership structure. It also was required to improve the transparency of its operations.

The Commerce Department entered into a memorandum of understanding with ICANN on November 25, 1998. ICANN agreed to "jointly design, develop, and test the mechanisms, methods and procedures" needed to transfer management of the root to a private sector, not-for-profit entity.[42] A few months later, ICANN entered into an agreement with the University of Southern California, the institutional home of the Information Sciences Institute (ISI), to take over the IANA functions. The Commerce Department officially recognized ICANN as the White Paper's private sector, not-for-profit entity on February 26, 1999.

Only a few months later the new chairman of the board, Esther Dyson, was able to declare without a trace of irony, "ICANN is nothing more than the reflection of [Internet] community consensus."[43]

9

The New Regime

ICANN is nothing but the gTLD-MoU in slow motion.
—Richard Sexton, October 1999

In its first two-and-a-half years of operation, ICANN worked with the U.S. Department of Commerce to transform administration of the DNS root into the platform for contract-based governance of the Internet. The new regime defined and distributed property rights in the domain name space and imposed economic regulation on the domain name industry. The property system that ICANN created was a highly regulated and conservative one, analogous in many respects to broadcast licensing in the United States. Its essential features can be summarized as follows:

• Network Solutions' monopoly profits were redistributed to a broader class of claimants by regulating its wholesale rates and transforming *.com*, *.net*, and *.org* into shared domains.

• The administration of the domain name space was linked directly to intellectual property protection. Trademark protection became one of the major determinants of the contractual features of registering a domain name, of policies regarding access to information about domain name registrants, and of policies governing the creation of new top-level domains.

• End users were stripped of most of their property rights in domain names and deliberately deprived of most opportunities for representation in ICANN's processes.

• Artificial scarcity in top-level domains was maintained. Just as in broadcast licensing, artificial scarcity fostered a regime of merit assignment and weak property rights for licensees.

• Network Solutions succeeded in retaining a long-term property right over the *.com* registry. The Generic Top-Level Domain Memorandum of Understanding (gTLD-MoU) faction's attempt to require all registries to be nonprofit was unsuccessful.

• National governments and intergovernmental organizations won a limited role within ICANN's structure and used it to assert rights over the delegation and assignment of country codes, names of geographic and urban places, and names for international organizations (so far with only partial success).

• The U.S. government retained residual authority over the DNS root. Instead of giving up that authority after two years, as originally contemplated, the government has held on to it indefinitely.

As noted in chapter 4, the initial formation of property rights always creates conflicts over the distribution of wealth. These conflicts were resolved in ways that favored members of the "dominant coalition" or those whose de facto control of important resources gave them significant bargaining power. Figure 9.1 shows the organizational structure of ICANN.

9.1   Redistributing the Riches of *.com:* Registrar Accreditation

Dealing with the dominance of Network Solutions was the top priority of the new regime. Competition was claimed as its objective, rhetorically, but there was little support in the dominant coalition for new competing registries. The trademark interests and the Global Internet Project (GIP) activists opposed authorizing new registries able to offer new top-level domain names. (Even among those who supported new top-level domains, there were differences of opinion about how to do it.) Instead, the dominant interest groups coalesced around a policy of regulating Network Solutions and redistributing its monopoly profits to a broader class of industry participants. ICANN and the Commerce Department acted quickly to achieve this objective.[1] A registrar accreditation regime was proposed and implemented in a few months, and it all happened before ICANN's Domain Name Supporting Organization (DNSO), supposedly the primary source of policy recommendations regarding domain names, was constituted.

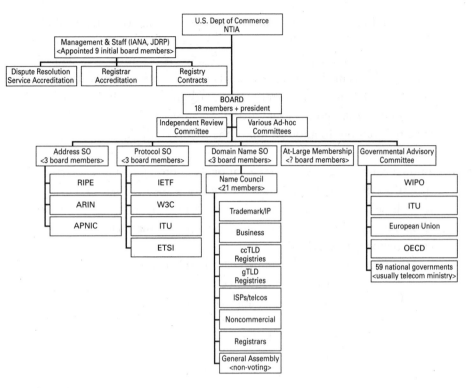

Figure 9.1
ICANN Organization Chart

Network Solutions (NSI) and the Department of Commerce had already agreed to create a shared registration system (SRS) that would allow multiple, competing registrars to sell names in *.com, .net,* and *.org* on a retail basis. In Amendment 11, NSI had agreed to provide approved registrars with equal access to its registry services if they licensed Network Solutions' shared registration system software. ICANN and the Commerce Department, however, came to support a stronger and more active role for the root administrator. Instead of just contracting with registries and allowing registries to contract with registrars, they came to believe that creating a level playing field in the registrar market required ICANN, rather than Network Solutions, to establish its own accreditation requirements and apply them directly to registrars in the generic TLDs (gTLDs). That decision strengthened the centralized and regulatory character of the emerging regime.

Thus, in March 1999, ICANN issued a set of regulations that would be used to accredit any company that wanted to register domain names in the Network Solutions top-level domains. These "registration accreditation guidelines" specified numerous financial and business qualifications for companies entering the registrar market, including paying ICANN a fixed fee of US$5,000, and a variable fee of US$1 per year for every domain name registration. In anticipation of the results of the World Intellectual Property Organization (WIPO) process (see section 9.2), the accreditation contract contained a variety of regulations to protect trademark interests.[2] In April 1999, ICANN accredited five registrars to participate in the "testbed" phase of the shared registry. The choice of initial registrars rewarded dominant coalition members, particularly those that had contributed start-up money to ICANN.[3]

In the same month, the Commerce Department amended the Network Solutions Cooperative Agreement once again to regulate its economic relations with the accredited registrars.[4] The wholesale price for registration was fixed at US$9 per name-year. In essence, Commerce treated the NSI registry as a regulated utility, declaring that "the price to be paid by registrars for each domain name registration . . . should reflect demonstrated costs and a reasonable rate of return."[5] But Networks Solutions' bargaining power was evident. It retained exclusive control of the gTLD registry, and registrars had to pay a one-time fee of US$10,000 to Network Solutions to be equipped with the SRS software. NSI itself also was allowed to continue selling domain names in the retail market, making it the only "registrar" that did not need to be accredited by ICANN.

After starting the registrar testbed in April 1999, ICANN and the Commerce Department boasted that competition had been introduced into the domain name business.[6] But in reality the Commerce Department was simply regulating NSI's wholesale rates and offering the price discounts achieved via regulation to a special class of businesses that paid ICANN for the privilege of accreditation and NSI for proprietary software. Later, after the new regime was fully implemented (see section 9.3), registrar competition did indeed bid down the price of domain name registration. The more significant institutional effect, however, was to put authority over almost all retail domain name registration in ICANN's hands and to reinforce the dominance of the *.com* registry in the global market. Once

end users were forced to go through ICANN-accredited registrars to get
.com, .net, and *.org* domain names, ICANN could impose economic and
trademark-related regulations on registrars as a condition of accreditation. This gave it regulatory control over 70 percent of the market (country code TLDs were not included in these arrangements). The arrangement
also permitted ICANN to exploit its government-created gateway into the
generic top-level domain name market as a funding source to sustain its
own activities. With over two million domain names being registered each
quarter and the number of total registrations doubling every year, ICANN
was anticipating an annual budget of US$8–30 million over the next three
years.

The shared registration system also greatly reinforced the market dominance of the *.com* domain. It decreased the price of many *.com* registrations and created an expanded sales force (accredited registrars) for the
output of the Network Solutions registry. From the middle of 1999 to
the middle of 2000, the number of domains registered in *.com* tripled. The
first quarter of 2000 "saw astounding acceleration in *.com, .net,* and *.org*
registrations worldwide," according to an NSI quarterly report.[7] An especially noteworthy aspect of the growth was a massive increase in *.com*
registrations from organizations outside the English-speaking world. International registrations increased 241 percent year-on-year,[8] and the
gTLDs' share of global domain name registrations began to increase relative to registrations in country codes. The high switching costs associated
with changing a domain name, and ICANN's refusal to create new top-
level domains for two more years (see section 9.6), gave *.com* towering
dominance.

ICANN's plans for a US$1 per domain name fee were thwarted, how-
ever. Assailed as "the domain name tax" by ICANN's opponents, including a still-recalcitrant Network Solutions, the fee attracted the attention of
the U.S. Congress.[9] Under pressure from Congress, the Commerce Department forced ICANN to abandon the fee. The result was a financial crisis for ICANN that was not resolved until November 1999, when
Network Solutions was fully assimilated into the regime (see section 9.3).

Accredited registrars are now assessed quarterly fees based on the share
of the ICANN budget assigned to gTLD registrars; the fees vary in accord
with the number of names they have registered. Translated into a per-name

basis, fees assessed according to this method are closer to US$0.10 per name than US$1 per name. As of early 2001, approximately 80 accredited registrars were listed by ICANN.

9.2   Branding the Name Space: WHOIS and UDRP

At least since the gTLD-MoU, intellectual property interests had insisted on directly linking management of the DNS root with trademark protection functions in order to reduce their transaction costs. They hoped to reengineer the contractual regime of domain name registration to facilitate centralized policing and enforcement of their rights. Some even wanted to use DNS to expand the scope of their property rights, for example, by obtaining global exclusion of a mark from the domain name space regardless of how the mark was used. If implemented, these policies would dramatically reduce the transaction costs of trademark protection in the domain name space. But those reductions would be achieved at the expense of other, less powerful interests. The costs of supplying registrar service would increase; the costs of the institutional overhead (for ICANN) supported by the Internet industry would increase; barriers to entry into the registry and registrar market would increase; possession of a domain name by individuals would become riskier. In short, the intellectual property holders' agenda for the DNS would require shifting transaction costs away from themselves and on to others.

That agenda could not be executed unless the Internet root was administered by an organization that transcended national jurisdiction and was fully committed to the subordination of the domain name system to the protection of incumbent intellectual property in names. The Department of Commerce fully supported the trademark lobby's wishes. The White Paper made trademark domain name dispute resolution a critical part of ICANN's mandate. It authorized WIPO, an entity entirely beholden to intellectual property owners, to create a set of policy recommendations for handling the disputes.

WIPO responded by initiating, only one month after the release of the White Paper, an extensive global consultation procedure. At the conclusion of its first round of consultations in December 1998, it issued an interim report with specific proposals (WIPO 1998). The report revealed that WIPO and the major multinational intellectual property holders were fully aware of the tremendous opportunity ICANN presented for a favorable redistribution of wealth. The database of domain name registrations not only offered a point of automated and centralized surveillance of registration records, it also offered administrators the leverage for effective and inexpensive enforcement: the withdrawal of a domain name. The December interim report strained for the strongest intellectual property regime imaginable. It proposed the following:

• Secure complete and accurate contact information from all domain name registrants, and make the use of false, misleading, or inaccurate registration information grounds for forfeiting a domain name, even without any intellectual property violation.

• Make the databases (known as the WHOIS database) containing the contact information of domain name registrants cheaply and easily available, regardless of privacy considerations, so that intellectual property rights holders could use it to identify potential violations and issue effective legal challenges to any domain name registration in the world.

• Create a new system of global dispute resolution to protect intellectual property on the Internet. All domain name registrants would be contractually bound to submit to an arbitration process when they registered a name. (By positioning itself as the sole dispute resolution service provider, WIPO also stood to benefit economically from the proposal.)

• Extend WIPO's proposed adjudication procedures to every type of intellectual property dispute involving the Internet, including rights of personality and copyright as well as trademark. WIPO ceased using the word *trademark* to describe the object of the proceeding and used *intellectual property* instead.

• Define procedures to allow WIPO to recognize and protect "famous" trademarks by excluding them from the DNS database in all top-level domains. Famous mark holders would only have to pay a one-time fee reflecting administrative costs to obtain these exclusion rights in perpetuity.

WIPO's overreaching in the interim report generated a powerful backlash. Its comments site was deluged with negative reactions from domain name registries, organizations representing the Internet technical community, civil liberties groups, and many individual domain name holders

(Froomkin 1999). WIPO was forced to modify significantly its final report, but the earlier report is valuable as an indication of the specific distribution of wealth hoped for by the intellectual property interests.

In its final report (WIPO 1999), issued April 30, WIPO retracted the focus of its compulsory dispute resolution process to "abusive" domain name registrations and confined its focus to trademark concerns rather than intellectual property in general. It grudgingly recognized the existence of reverse domain name hijacking. The revised proposals still sought to give intellectual property owners access to complete and accurate contact information about domain name registrants, and a uniform and mandatory dispute resolution procedure. Arbitrators were instructed to apply national laws whenever possible. The final report also retained recommendations that "a mechanism be established before the introduction of any new open gTLDs whereby exclusions can be obtained and enforced for marks that are famous or well-known across a widespread geographical area and across different classes of goods and services."

To ICANN and the Commerce Department, protecting trademark holders was the second-highest priority after introducing competition in the *.com* space. After the conclusion of the WIPO process, ICANN leveraged its centralized, exclusive control of the domain name root to implement a trademark dispute resolution regime. It defined a Uniform Dispute Resolution Policy (UDRP) and bound all registrars of domain names under *.com*, *.net*, and *.org* to it as a condition of accreditation.[10] Through their contracts with registrars, all registrants of domain names under the generic TLDs are contractually bound to submit to arbitration under the UDRP.

The UDRP procedure allows any person, anywhere in the world, who believes that a domain name registration infringes his trademark right, to challenge a registration. Independent arbitrators make a decision quickly and (relative to courts) inexpensively. ICANN does not handle disputes itself but rather accredits independent dispute resolution service providers (RSPs). The RSPs assemble their own stable of arbitrators and compete for the business of resolving domain name disputes. To successfully challenge a name, a trademark holder must prove three things: that the domain name is identical or confusingly similar to a mark in which the complainant has rights; that the registrant has no rights or legitimate interests in the domain name; and that the domain name has been registered and is being used in bad faith.

The UDRP is arguably ICANN's most significant accomplishment. It handled over 2,500 cases involving nearly 4,000 domain names in its first year. Procedurally, the UDRP is heavily biased in favor of complainants. It allows the trademark holder to select the dispute provider, thereby encouraging dispute resolution service providers to compete for the allegiance of trademark holders. The resultant forum shopping ensures that no defendant-friendly service provider can survive (Mueller 2000). It provides little time for respondents to react or prepare (Froomkin 2000). Moreover, once a name has been taken away through the UDRP, it is unclear, at least in the United States, whether the original registrant can get it back from the courts.[11]

ICANN's attempts to safeguard intellectual property interests in the domain name space also shaped its policies toward the introduction of new top-level domains (see section 9.5). New TLDs were given a low priority relative to other objectives. Movement toward that goal was extremely slow. When new ones were introduced, the number was small and the approval process encouraged registries to employ practices that would privilege trademark holders in the initial assignment of names. So-called "sunrise" or "daybreak" procedures, for example, allow all the world's trademark holders the privilege of preregistering their names in a new top-level domain before the domain is opened up to anyone else. Both techniques offer preemptive forms of protection that simply do not exist in traditional trademark law.

In this policy arena, too, ICANN's allegedly bottom-up consensual procedures did not work according to plan. A major revolt by Internet users was required to prevent ICANN's board from endorsing the WIPO report in its entirety at its May 1999 meeting in Berlin, before its DNSO had even been formed.[12] A DNSO working group on the UDRP was created in the late summer but failed to produce a concrete proposal. Most of the actual negotiating and definition of the policy was performed by an ad hoc committee assembled and led by ICANN's staff (Froomkin 1999; Weinberg 2000). Although a working group on famous trademarks made it clear that there was no consensus within ICANN's DNSO for creating a list of famous marks or any kind of "sunrise" proposal,[13] the impact of those decisions was undercut by the decisions of management and staff to encourage applicants for new top-level domains to include "sunrise" provisions and name exclusions in their proposals.

9.3   The Assimilation of Network Solutions

ICANN's registrar accreditation contracts were designed to put it in control of the terms and conditions offered to all domain name registrants in the generic TLDs. It was also evident that key members of the dominant coalition intended to extend the regime to the entire name space, including the country codes, as soon as practicable.[14] By the middle of 1999, however, there was still a gaping hole in the Commerce Department's nascent regime: Network Solutions. Network Solutions controlled almost all of the retail registration business under *.com* but was not itself an accredited registrar. It could offer domain name registrations to the public outside of the accreditation regime and also subcontract with other firms to resell access to its registry. Its registry contract was still with the Commerce Department, not with ICANN.

ICANN and the Commerce Department hoped that Network Solutions would recognize ICANN's authority to step into the shoes of the Commerce Department and establish the terms and conditions governing its operation of the *.com, .net,* and *.org* registry. After that, it was expected to sign one of ICANN's registrar accreditation contracts and become "just another registrar." Network Solutions, however, resisted recognition of ICANN. To do so would be to cede control over the asset upon which its entire business had been built; moreover, as soon as it did, most of its bargaining power over the transition process would disappear. Since ICANN at this point consisted of nothing more than nine self-appointed people, many of whom had a long history of hostility to NSI, it was only rational for the company to strenuously resist being incorporated into the regime. During the summer of 1999, ICANN's board and management reinforced these fears by stripping NSI of most of its voting rights in the DNSO and refusing to recognize constituencies that might dilute the control of the dominant coalition over the DNSO's policymaking council.

ICANN itself had no bargaining power in this struggle. The real battle was between Network Solutions and the Commerce Department. The basis of contention was the same as in October 1998: whether upon termination of the Cooperative Agreement, Network Solutions could continue to register names under the gTLDs. The absence of an agreement with ICANN did no harm to NSI; the company could continue to register names in *.com*, *.net*, and *.org* and possibly even set up an alternative root server system, completely out of the government's control. To enhance the company's bargaining power, NSI lobbyists went on the offensive against ICANN in the U.S. Congress. ICANN critics hammered away at the US$1 per name "tax" and began to embarrass the Clinton administration politically. Rep. Bliley of Virginia held hearings on the theme "Is ICANN out of control?"[15] The registrar testbed period, which could not be brought to a close until Network Solutions officially recognized ICANN, was extended several times. With no source of financial support, ICANN went deeply into debt. At that time the core of ICANN's support was clearly revealed. MCI's Vinton Cerf and IBM's John Patrick frantically appealed to the industry for loans and donations. Patrick delivered US$100,000 from IBM, and Cerf delivered a loan of US$500,000 from MCI.[16] ICANN's management leveraged connections in the White House, Congress, and the Federal Trade Commission to bring Network Solutions to heel.[17]

Finally, in late September 1999, a series of agreements were made between the Commerce Department, Network Solutions, and ICANN that represented a settlement acceptable to the three parties.[18] These agreements are the fundamental bargain upon which the new regime was founded, and their implementation starting in November 1999 was the real beginning of the new system's operation. In essence, Network Solutions agreed to enter into a registry contract and a registrar accreditation contract with ICANN and to provide the new governance regime with US$1.5 million in financial support. In exchange, it got to extend its property right over the legacy gTLD registry and got the Department of Commerce to assume various kinds of authority over ICANN. The main points of the agreements are as follows.

Network Solutions recognized ICANN and agreed to operate the *.com*, *.net*, and *.org* registry in accordance with the provisions of a "registry agreement" with ICANN. ICANN agreed to license NSI as the generic TLD registry for four years. If NSI fully divested its registry from the registrar functions within 18 months of the agreement, the registry contract would be extended for another four years. This gave Network Solutions an extended property right over the coveted *.com* registry, but at the price of divesting its registrar business. As NSI was a for-profit entity, this solution ended the debate, which had been inaugurated by the gTLD-MoU, over whether all registries should be nonprofit.

The new contracts regulated Network Solutions' rates more tightly. The wholesale registry price was reduced to US$6 per name-year from US$9 per name-year beginning January 15, 2000. NSI's retail registrar prices were deregulated (the US$35 per name-year price had been fixed by its Cooperative Agreement). NSI promised to prepay registrar fees to ICANN of US$1.25 million.

To lock the new regime into place, NSI agreed to accept domain name registrations only from ICANN-accredited registrars and not to deploy an alternative DNS root server system. It also continued to operate the authoritative root server system in accordance with the directions of the Commerce Department.

The new agreements also clarified ICANN's obligations. ICANN was required to comply with specific procedural limitations on the exercise of its authority. Many of its decisions were required to gain a two-thirds majority of the supporting organization councils. ICANN's policy authority over the Network Solutions registry can be terminated if it does not succeed in bringing other registries into its centralized contractual regime and Network Solutions is competitively disadvantaged as a result. This provision, which was directed at country code registries and particularly the quasi-generics competing with NSI, made it clear that the ICANN regime's scope must become global and uniform. The fees ICANN imposes on registrars must be "equitably apportioned" and approved by the registrars that pay two-thirds of the fees, a provision that gave Network Solutions considerable leverage over ICANN's taxing policies. The amount of registrar fees NSI must pay to ICANN was capped at US$2 million.

A revision of the registry agreement in 2001 further strengthened Network Solutions' property right over the *.com* domain and ICANN's status as the regulator of the name space. Network Solutions (which had been sold to Verisign, Inc.) agreed to pay more fees to ICANN and give up control of the *.org* registry (which accounted for 8 percent of its registrations) in exchange for a "presumptive renewal right" over the *.com* registry and an elimination of the requirement to divest its registrar business.[19]

9.4   U.S. Government Policy Authority over the Root

In a very important part of the three-way ICANN–Network Solutions–Commerce Department agreement, the Commerce Department quietly and without fanfare backed away from yielding ultimate authority over the root to ICANN or its successor. The agreement noted, "The Department of Commerce expects to receive a technical proposal from ICANN for management of the authoritative root and this management responsibility may be transferred to ICANN at some point in the future. The Department of Commerce has no plans to transfer to any entity its policy authority to direct the authoritative root server."[20]

Later, a report by the General Accounting Office raised doubts about whether under U.S. law the Commerce Department has the authority to transfer control of the root server to ICANN (GAO 2000, 25–26). The report noted that it is "unclear whether such a transition will involve a transfer of government property to a private entity." If so, such a transfer would require specific legislation. Thus, the new regime emerged as one with a special place for U.S. government authority—ironic, in view of the fact that the Green Paper, reviled as a U.S. "coup," had explicitly stated that authority would be turned over in two years. The Green Paper was also opposed because it would create new, for-profit registries. Yet now the ICANN regime had exactly one (regulated) for-profit registry with more than two-thirds of the market.

9.5   Representation: Barriers to Entry

While the new regime was busy defining, expanding, or securing the property rights of registrars, trademark holders, and registries, the rights and interests of end users went unrepresented. It is widely recognized in social theory that the interests of large numbers of people with a small stake in a resource tend to lose out in collective action processes to small, well-organized stakeholder groups with a concentrated economic interest (Olson 1971). Yet, in ICANN's case, the perspectives of end users and individuals were minimized not because of a lack of participation or interest but because decisions about the design of the institution deliberately blocked their entrée into the process. ICANN's structure was supposed to provide two avenues for broad representation: the constituencies of the

DNSO and the membership structure that would elect the nine at-large board members. Both channels were totally or partially closed off to ordinary Internet users in ICANN's first two years.

9.5.1   Representation in the DNSO

The DNSO was supposed to be representative of domain name stakeholder communities. The Green Paper, White Paper, and the IFWP deliberations all considered the general population of Internet users to be a constituency worthy of representation.[21] The final DNSO constituency structure, however, emerged from a series of meetings controlled by leaders of the dominant coalition: the Information Technology Association of America (ITAA) and its international sister organization, the World Information Technology and Services Alliance (WITSA), the Internet Society, the International Trademark Association (INTA), and the Policy Oversight Committee of the gTLD-MoU.[22] The constituency structure proposed by these groups, and accepted by ICANN's board with minor modification, was manipulated to magnify the voting power of business, trademark, and registrar groups, and to minimize or eliminate the influence of civil society organizations, noncommercial groups, and individuals.

Five of the seven DNSO constituencies (Internet service and connectivity providers, business and commercial, registrars, trademark constituencies, and TLD registries) represented business interests. Noncommercial interests were given one residual constituency that had to embrace an extremely diverse and ill-defined set of interests. No constituency for individuals was created; the leaders of a group that wanted to represent individual domain name holders were perceived as hostile to the dominant coalition and denied recognition.[23] In short, the DNSO constituency structure gave the members of the dominant coalition an unbreakable majority of the Names Council. The election of board members by the Names Council could not, therefore, act as a check upon management, which was selected by the same set of interest groups. Nor did it broaden representation on the board.

9.5.2   At-Large Membership

The debate over organizational models for ICANN sparked by the International Forum on the White Paper (IFWP) was never really resolved; instead, ICANN emerged as an uncomfortable compromise. Fundamentally, it was a public benefit corporation able to modify its bylaws at will, as Postel's lawyer had intended. But a membership requirement had been tacked onto its bylaws because of pressure from activists and the U.S. government.[24] Despite promising beginnings, ICANN's management repeatedly delayed or obstructed the election of at-large board members, and once they were chosen, the impact of membership was minimized as much as possible.

Admittedly, the problem of membership was a challenging one. The scope of the organization had to be global, like the Internet name and address spaces. The fledgling organization had to define workable criteria for a kind of global Internet citizenship and in the process confront questions of regional representation and linguistic and economic diversity. Without appropriate structures and safeguards, democratic voting methods are no less susceptible to capture and manipulation than other forms of decision making.

ICANN's original Membership Advisory Committee took the challenge quite seriously. Harvard's Berkman Center, Boston Working Group member Diane Cabell, Izumi Aizu of Japan, and board member Greg Crew constituted the core of the group. By May 1999 the Committee had delivered a comprehensive membership proposal to the ICANN board, a highly democratic model accompanied by a convincing rationale for having an at-large membership.[25] It proposed a one-person/one-vote election, in which individuals rather than organizations would be the voting unit. Members would have to renew annually, but there would be no membership fee. The at-large members would elect five board members on a regional basis and four on a global basis. A critical mass of 5,000 members would have to be registered before the elections would go into effect.

ICANN's management, however, dragged its feet in implementing the proposal. A May 27, 1999, board resolution observed that the elections are "likely to be both administratively complex and expensive" and called for the cost of implementation to be borne by the membership. Management then discovered what it considered to be an even more serious problem. California law automatically gives specific rights and powers to any member of a nonprofit corporation. Statutory members can bring derivative actions against the corporation, and inspect accounts and records. A "member" is defined by the law as "any person who, pursuant to a specific provision of a corporation's articles or bylaws, has the right to vote for the election of a director or directors or . . . has the right to vote on changes to the articles or bylaws." Thus, by creating an election for its at-large board members, ICANN would be creating statutory members.[26]

ICANN's management responded to this problem by using a legal technicality to ensure that at-large members would not really be members within the meaning of the statutory nonprofit corporations law and therefore could not claim the rights granted by the law.[27] Management attempted to avoid the problem of creating statutory members by adopting the election plan as a board resolution instead of "pursuant to a specific provision of a corporation's articles or bylaws."

A few months later, ICANN's management abandoned the recommendations of the Membership Advisory Committee. There would be no direct election of at-large board members by individuals. Instead, individual members would choose members of an at-large council, who would in turn elect board members. Faced with a rebellion at its Cairo meeting, the board backed down and promised that in the fall of 2000 individual ICANN members would directly elect one board member in each of five world geographic regions. The five elected at-large directors would sit for two years alongside four holdover directors from the initial board. A grant from the Markle Foundation funded the election process and made it possible to avoid charging membership fees.

The results of the at-large election (October 11, 2000) were stunning (table 9.1). In North America and Europe, the two world regions where the elections had been widely publicized and discussed, all of the candidates nominated by ICANN's nominating committee were defeated. The winners—and even the second and third-ranked candidates—were opponents of ICANN's policies and practices. Karl Auerbach, the victor in the North American seat, was closely affiliated with the Boston Working Group. Andy Mueller-Maguhn was described by the press as an "anarchist hacker."[28] The "Internet community consensus" that ICANN had been claiming since its inception seemed not to exist.

Following its decisive defeat in the elections, the ICANN management and board acted to contain the elected board members and minimize their impact. The bylaws were altered to keep the newly elected directors out of

Table 9.1
At-Large Election Results

Candidate	View on ICANN	Nominated by	Votes
North America			
Karl Auerbach	Very critical	Members	1,074
Barbara Simons	Critical	Members	771
Lawrence Lessig	Critical	ICANN	725
Emerson Tiller	Critical	Members	490
Harris Miller	Supporter	ICANN	179
Lyman Chapin	Supporter	ICANN	127
Don Langenberg	Supporter	ICANN	83
Europe			
Andy Mueller-Maguhn	Very critical	Members	5,948
Jeannette Hofmann	Critical	Members	2,295
Winfried Schuller	Critical of U.S. Department of Commerce	ICANN	990
Alf Hansen	Supporter	ICANN	629
Olivier Muron	Supporter	ICANN	544
Maria Livanos Cattaui	Supporter	ICANN	514
Oliver Popov	Supporter	ICANN	389

the selection process for new TLDs. A new executive committee of the board was formed that excluded the maverick members. The board pulled back yet again from the prospect of a member-elected at-large board of directors. It decided to commission a lengthy "study" of the future role of the at-large members. The study became known as the "clean sheet" study because it was based on the assumption that the very existence of the at-large membership was up for examination.

9.6   New Top-Level Domains

Since the start in 1995 of charging for domain names, most of the policy debates and proposals for institutional change were motivated by attempts to create new top-level domains. The *newdom* email list, draft-postel, the gTLD-MoU, AlterNIC, Name.Space, and other alternative root server systems all attempted to provide an alternative to *.com* and to let new registries into the market. Not surprisingly, given the political coalition that had created ICANN, that objective was considered significantly less urgent than the problem of regulating the existing generic top-level domains to protect trademarks and create business opportunities for registrars. It took ICANN nearly three years to authorize new top-level domains and make them operational. When it did finally create them, it fostered an environment of artificial scarcity designed to maximize barriers to entry and enable close regulation of the new registries. Moreover, its choices of new registries overtly rewarded incumbent stakeholders and supporters of ICANN.

The authorization of new top-level domains was the only major policy decision in the initial regime formation period that actually followed the bottom-up procedures originally envisioned for ICANN. An open working group (WG-C) devoted to new top-level domains was created in July 1999, shortly after the formation of the DNSO. During seven months of fractious debate on the group's email list, the intellectual property and business interests advocated creating only one or two new domains in the first round, whereas others called for up to 500. The working group reported its "consensus position" to the Names Council in March 2000: ICANN should begin with an initial rollout of six to ten new gTLDs, followed by an evaluation period. The group also suggested that the new TLD strings should be defined by prospective registries rather than selected by ICANN and assigned to operators. A month later, the DNSO's Names Council forwarded a resolution to the ICANN board recommending the introduction of new TLDs "in a measured and responsible manner."[29] The ICANN board agreed to create new top-level domains at its July 2000 meeting in Yokohama, Japan, and called upon its staff to define an application process and criteria.

The severe political constraints operating on ICANN inexorably pushed it into a form of merit assignment, a "beauty contest" that selects for applicants who are well-connected, large, well-established, familiar, and unthreatening. The guidelines called for a "thoroughly formulated plan" requiring the assistance of "technical experts, financial and management consultants, and lawyers."[30] Applicants had to pay a US$50,000 non-refundable fee to be considered. The application process was framed as an experiment or "proof of concept," as if adding a new top-level domain to the root (something that had happened routinely during the evolution of the DNS) was a step into unknown territory. The staff-prepared guidelines also contained numerous criteria that bordered on policy decisions. They barred from consideration any applicant involved with an alternative root system. Applications had to explain at length the procedures that would be used to protect trademark rights. Despite these hurdles, ICANN received 47 applications requesting nearly 200 new TLD strings by the October 2 deadline. The application fees alone totaled US$2.5 million, enlarging ICANN's total budget by 50 percent.

The ICANN board selected seven winners on November 16, 2000 (table 9.2). Prodded by its management and staff, the corporation amended its bylaws in order to exclude the five newly elected at-large board members from being able to participate in the selections. The winners were all established, politically connected insiders. Of the seven new top-level domains awarded by ICANN, the four most commercially desirable assignments—*.biz, .info, .pro,* and *.name*—were backed by companies that either had already established dominant positions in the ICANN-created marketplace for *.com, .net* and *.org* registrars, or were major figures in the political coalition that had created ICANN. The Afilias Group, which was awarded the *.info* domain, was an international consortium of 18 leading ICANN-accredited registrars assembled by Network Solutions, the Internet Council of Registrars (CORE), and Register.com. Collectively, Afilias members already controlled over three-fourths of the registrar market. CORE was also selected as the registry operator for the *.museum* top-level domain. The winner of the *.name* top-level domain for personal registrations was a British firm (Nameplanet.com) that had entered into a "strategic technical partnership" with IBM Corporation for its system infrastructure. The *.biz* domain was awarded to a joint venture of Melbourne IT and Neustar, the North American Numbering Plan administrator.

In making these selections, the ICANN board came into direct contact with two significant policy problems that will likely persist in the new regime. First, it refused to select any of the numerous proposals for TLDs devoted to sex (*.sex, .xxx*) or children (*.kids*). There was, in fact, a great deal of popular interest in those domains, and even some demands from politicians to mandate their creation in order to make it easier to segregate

Table 9.2
New ICANN Top-Level Domains

Domain Name	Operator(s)	Link to ICANN
.biz	Neustar (*US*), Melbourne IT (*AU*)	Melbourne IT one of the first five accredited registrars, donated start-up money to ICANN, and had strong political ties to GAC and its chair Paul Twomey.
.info	Afilias consortium	Major partners include Network Solutions, CORE, Register.com, Tucows. Partners together account for over 80% of registrar market share.
.pro	Register.com (*US*)	Register.com was one of the first five accredited registrars and second-largest registrar after NSI.
.name	Global Name Registry, Ltd. (*UK*)	
.aero	Societe de Int'l Telecommunications Aeronautiques (*FR*)	Rosa del Gado, SITA's advocate for the *.aero* domain, was a longtime Board member of the Internet Society and gTLD-MoU supporter
.coop	National Cooperative Bus. Assn (*US, UK*)	
.museum	International Council of Museums (*CH*)	Uses CORE as registry. Cary Karp, head of Museum Domain Mgmt Assn, was a participant in gTLD-MoU

Web site content on the Net. ICANN's refusal to recognize the new domains came not so much from the merit of the applicants per se but from the board's fear that licensing such top-level domains would bring it uncomfortably close to the business of content regulation. For example, ICANN did not want to take responsibility, by awarding a *.kids* top-level domain, for certifying that the content and operators of Web sites in that domain would post child-appropriate material.

Second, ICANN was forced to confront its relationship with the alternative root server systems. The board consciously avoided the longstanding conflict over *.web,* turning down Imagine Online Design's request for it but also refusing to award the coveted string to the Afilias consortium, which had requested it. The award of .*biz* also ran afoul of longstanding claims in the alternative root server community. The .*biz* top-level domain had first been created and operated by Karl Denninger, a *newdom* participant and one of the early leaders of the alternative root movement. When Denninger withdrew from the business, the top-level domain was claimed in May 2000 by a businesswoman named Leah Gallegos, who managed to gather about 3,000 registrations. The decision to authorize another .*biz* would either destroy her business or, if it managed to coexist, create name collisions.[31]

The establishment of new TLDs was the most significant test of the new institutional regime's capabilities and processes. ICANN's registry contracts are similar in function and intent to broadcasting licenses in the United States, with the exception that the regulation takes place via contract rather than public law.

9.7 Country Codes and National Governments

Governments also used ICANN to impose boundaries upon and assert rights in the Internet's name space. Using ICANN's Governmental Advisory Committee (GAC) as a platform, they attempted to project their jurisdictional authority onto what once had been an open, common pool resource. Just as the physical world was divided up into mutually exclusive territories controlled by sovereign governments, so could the name space be. Country codes were the most direct and obvious point of entry for this kind of thinking. If national governments could gain control over the assignment of their own country code, they could translate their geographic jurisdictions into cyberspace and gain a significant role for themselves in Internet governance.

Nominally, ICANN was a private corporation. The White Paper had stated that "neither national governments acting as sovereigns nor intergovernmental organizations acting as representatives of governments should participate in management of Internet names and addresses." The founding documents explicitly prevented government officials from sitting on the board. In order to assuage the demands of the European Commission and other intergovernmental organizations, however, the White Paper did leave room for governments to participate in a "non-voting, advisory capacity."[32] That concession led to the recognition by ICANN of the GAC as a permanent part of its structure. The GAC was constituted March 2, 1999, with Australia's Paul Twomey as its chair.[33]

The Americans who dominated ICANN's management and interim board initially viewed GAC as a prophylactic that did as much to keep governments out of ICANN's affairs as it did to bring them in. The GAC, however, quickly became an important player in ICANN's policymaking processes, functioning as a fourth Supporting Organization (SO) in all respects except for the election of board members.

At its first meeting, the GAC declared the Internet name space a "public resource." From then on, its leading participants mounted a persistent campaign to redefine the legal delegation procedure and practical relationship between ICANN, governments, and country code top-level domain (ccTLD) administrators. The changes were designed to give national governments direct control over ccTLD delegation and redelegation decisions. The GAC also fought to make name space references to countries exclusive and grounded in the existing political order. It demanded, for example, that ICANN abstain from assigning any top-level domain names that referred to countries, regions, languages, or peoples without the approval of the relevant government or public authority. This would rule out, for example, top-level domains for internal nationalities such as *.tibet, .wales,* and *.kashmir,* or for regions such as *.asia.*

Australia, France, and the U.K. in particular were concerned about gaining direct control over the administration of the top-level domains of their external or dependent territories. Under the ISO-3166 coding standard, many small islands and territories had their own country code, and in Jon Postel's informal delegation regime many of them had been assigned to people or organizations over which the governments had no control.

A series of communiqués issued throughout 1999 affirmed the GAC's concerns about gaining control of country code delegations.[34] In February 2000, GAC released a detailed document describing what it hoped would become the model for institutionalizing the relationship between ICANN, ccTLD delegations, and the relevant national governments or public authorities (GAC 2000). The old system of bilateral delegations should be replaced, GAC proposed, with a three-way "communication-based regime" that placed governments at the apex of the triangle. Governments, as representatives of the public interest, would designate which organization would receive the delegation of a country code, and could demand redelegation if in its opinion an existing holder lacked public support or failed to serve the public interest. ICANN would be limited to a subordinate technical and administrative role, ensuring that the ccTLD registry maintained the proper DNS functions. The delegatee was seen as a public trustee, dependent on its own government for the delegation and with no right to subcontract, sublicense, or otherwise trade the ccTLD delegation, and no intellectual property rights in the TLD string or the registry data.

The proposed GAC principles constituted a major step toward incorporating top-level domain delegations into a traditional, nation-state based framework. Neither ICANN nor the incumbent ccTLD operators, however, were eager to embrace it. Country code managers saw the "local Internet community" as the source of their authority, and while the concept of the local Internet community included local governments, it was not limited to or dominated by them.[35] ICANN initially resisted what it saw as governmental encroachment on management of the name space, fearing that ccTLD delegations could become political footballs that changed hands with every change in a state's politics.

The issue was particularly sensitive because the relationship between ccTLD registries and ICANN was still a point of friction in the emerging regime. By virtue of inheriting from the U.S. government the Network Solutions Cooperative Agreement, ICANN had clear authority over the management and policy of generic top-level domains. But its authority over country code managers was ambiguous. ICANN considered them to be one of seven DNSO constituencies and as such a fully incorporated part of its new regime. The country code managers, on the other hand, viewed themselves as outside the regime until and unless acceptable contractual agreements specifying each other's mutual obligations and responsibilities were negotiated. ICANN refused to enter negotiations, insisting that it was a policy formation organization, not a service provider. The clash in perception came to a head in 1999, when ICANN's Task Force on Funding proposed to impose on the ccTLDs an obligation to provide 35 percent of the ICANN budget.[36] The country code constituency refused to pay the full amount, offering instead a smaller sum representing what it called "interim donations" pending contractual negotiations with ICANN defining the services that would be provided.

At present, the relationship between ICANN, ccTLD managers, and national governments is not settled. The country code managers have prepared a draft contractual agreement between ICANN and ccTLD managers. The GAC continues to pursue its model of governmental control over country code delegations and has succeeded in pushing ICANN one step along that path. At the Yokohama meeting in July 2000, GAC asked ICANN "to write to the relevant governments and public authorities" to find out whether they were satisfied with the current delegations for the ccTLDs corresponding to their jurisdictions. ICANN staff prepared a draft letter, and solicited comment about its content and about whether to send it out. The GAC communiqué also took sides in the funding controversy, supporting ICANN's funding request from ccTLD operators. At some point it seems likely that a GAC-ICANN coalition will succeed in bringing the ccTLD operators into the regime.

III

Issues and Themes

10

ICANN as Global Regulatory Regime

ICANN is in many ways a completely new institutional animal.
—*The Economist* June 10, 2000

One byproduct of ICANN's less-than-immaculate conception is a rhetorical cloud around the organization that expresses the confusion and uncertainty many people feel about its identity. Is it a standards organization or a regulator? a technical coordination body or a policymaker? private or governmental?

The U.S. Department of Commerce repeatedly refers to ICANN as the result of a policy of "privatizing" the domain name system (DNS). Privatization normally means that the supply of a product or service has been transferred from the government to a private sector company. What the Commerce Department has turned over to ICANN, however, is not ownership of a service or asset but the authority to develop policies and to legislate binding rules for the domain name registration industry. Froomkin (2000) argues persuasively that it is nothing less than an illegal delegation of governmental powers. That very same Commerce Department, moreover, has reserved to itself ultimate "policy authority" over the root. The General Accounting Office (GAO 2000) says that the agency does not have the authority to transfer the name and address spaces to a private firm without congressional legislation. The concept of "privatization," therefore, does not take us very far.

ICANN's initial board and the White Paper stressed that the new organization would be a "technical coordinator," not a system of "Internet governance." But that rhetorical gloss faded rapidly. The organization's basic function as a regulator of the domain name system has become evident, including to the U.S. Congress.[1] ICANN's management now explicitly acknowledges its role as a policymaker, albeit reluctantly and *sotto voce*. On a slide in a standard presentation by ICANN's chief policy officer, Andrew McLaughlin, the headline asks "Does ICANN regulate?" On the first line below, in large type, it says, "NO: ICANN Coordinates!" A second line, in much smaller type, adds: "But: technical coordination of unique values sometimes requires accounting for non-technical policy interests." Among the "non-technical policy interests" listed are intellectual property, privacy, and competition policy, the three central public policy problems of the information age. At the ICANN Stockholm meeting in June 2001, the former board chair Esther Dyson went even further, claiming that ICANN was primarily an "antitrust authority."

So what is ICANN? This chapter argues that it is a nascent international regime, defined in chapter 4 as the organizations and rules established by states to handle governance or regulatory problems that span national boundaries. But before elaborating on that revelation, we must examine in greater detail the basis of ICANN's claim that it is something new.

10.1   What ICANN Is Not

Ultimately, ICANN's primary claim to legitimacy and uniqueness rests on its assertion that it is the Internet community's vehicle for bottom-up consensus development or self-governance. Both concepts—the idea of an Internet community and of bottom-up consensus as the basis of self-governance—reflect the legacy of the Internet Engineering Task Force (IETF) and the Internet Society. The attempt to transmute the technical community's methods into a new type of international organization can be explained in part by the important role the technical community—notably Postel, Cerf, and other members of the Internet Society inner circle—played in the formation of ICANN. But it is also true that a significant measure of the technical community's power in that process was derived from widespread acceptance of the idea that the IETF governance model was unique and worthy of emulation. As one theorist has written, "The engineers who gave us the Net (hardly a noncontentious group) also gave us the first inkling of a better way to evolve policy in a global online space" (Johnson and Crawford 2000). Key politicians such as Ira Magaziner were deeply impressed with the methods of the technical community. Even the World Intellectual Property Organization (WIPO) appropriated the technical community's nomenclature for WIPO domain name processes, labeling documents RFCs (Requests for Comments).

10.1.1 The Theory: Federalism and Consensus-Based Self-Governance

An explicit theoretical justification for modeling Internet governance on the IETF has been developed by David Johnson, with Susan Crawford (2000; 2001). As counsel to Network Solutions during the formative stages of ICANN's development, Johnson was an influential participant in the Internet governance process. His ideas directly influenced Magaziner, Burr, and ICANN's first board chair, Esther Dyson.

Johnson's thinking about ICANN is rooted in his earlier work with the legal scholar David Post on jurisdiction in cyberspace (Johnson and Post 1996; 1997; 1998). Johnson and Post recognized that the fundamental problem of Internet law and governance is that existing institutions—the democratic nation-state and the international treaty organizations—are based on the control of physical territory. Cyberspace, in contrast, creates an arena for human interaction in which location doesn't matter much.

A single global government is an unattractive solution to this problem, for reasons too numerous to recount here. So Johnson and Post sought solutions in adapting the concept of federalism. A federalist structure breaks down the collective action problem into smaller units but maintains some coordination among the parts. Post and Johnson approve of the idea of varying, even competing, sets of rules. Additionally, they contend that federalism works best when congruence—the degree to which the effects of an individual's actions are confined to the governance unit to which the individual belongs—is high but *not* perfect and complete (Johnson and Post 1998, 10). Effects and rule-making authority need to be closely related, but the optimum is somewhere below 100 percent. The virtue of an interdependent federalist structure is that local experiments create spillover effects that provoke reactions and adjustments by other decision-making units. This chain of mutual adjustments can push the social system as a whole to higher levels of welfare. A single, integrated jurisdiction, or a collection of isolated governance units, on the other hand, is more likely to get stuck in a suboptimal equilibrium. The analysis is supported by the results of modeling work by Stuart Kauffman (1993).

If one accepts the federalist premise, the next question is, What should be the collective action unit in cyberspace? Territorial governments are out, of course, because geography is mostly irrelevant to the Internet's virtual spaces. Johnson and Post propose the principle that decision-making authority over parts of the online world should be allocated to people who are "most affected" by the decisions. To implement this principle, they suggest that a federalist structure could be based on the "natural electronic boundaries" of the Internet: the "territories" or interfaces of the many private and local network systems it connects. In short, private property rights over network access and facilities provide the units of their decentralized governance structure. In Johnson's view, participation in the Internet is fundamentally voluntary in nature. And under a federalist structure, a local decision-making unit, once it has decided to join, can make its own decisions about how open or closed it will be to the rest of the Internet.

So far, so good. But the DNS and IP address roots still need a central point of coordination at the top. Where does it come from, and how is it governed? David Post emphatically recognizes the danger that such a central authority will become a Leviathan, exploiting its administration of resources to control users or the industry (Post 1998). Johnson, on the other hand, believes that the IETF governance model provides a solution to the dilemma. Participation in IETF, he notes, is voluntary and open. It is a private sector organization[2] that operates, allegedly, on the basis of working groups that allow initiatives to start at the bottom and move up through the hierarchy if and when consensus for the action develops. And so, the new regime, like the IETF, should be private rather than governmental. It should be open and consensual in nature. Ideally, the root administrator should implement only those policies that reflect the broadest consensus among affected stakeholders. Consensus exists, Johnson and Crawford (2000) write, when "opposition to a particular policy is limited in scope and intensity (or is unreasoned) and opposition does not stem from those specially impacted by the policy" (3).

This line of reasoning leads Johnson and Crawford to an explicit rejection of democratic (one-person/one-vote) methods of governance. There would be an extremely low level of congruence between a global electorate and the Internet stakeholders "most affected" by its decisions.[3] Moreover, voting presumes that ICANN is some kind of sovereign authority, which they deny. "The principle of one-person one-vote provides a basis for delegating a people's sovereignty to a government. It does not provide legitimacy for a system that seeks voluntary compliance with policies that have the support or acquiescence of all groups particularly impacted by those policies" (Johnson and Crawford 2001, 2). Their argument against democracy is more than just fear of public irrationality. They recognize that a surrender of sovereignty to an institution empowers the institution, making it easier for it to assert control over more and more aspects of life because it can credibly claim to be "acting on behalf of the people."

10.1.2   Critique of the Theory

There are two problems with the Johnson-Crawford theses. First, as demonstrated in chapter 9, neither "federalism" nor "bottom-up consensus" describes how ICANN actually operates. ICANN's management and professional staff control its agenda and frequently define policy unilaterally in the course of drafting contracts with registries and registrars. The supporting organizations have never developed the tradition or culture of independent working groups that are formed from the bottom and pass proposals up a consensus development hierarchy.

Second, the political bargains that created ICANN were struck by parties unsympathetic, if not hostile, to both federalist decentralization based on private property rights and bottom-up processes. The second problem explains the first. With a single point of control (the root) and competition for the political and economic benefits that can be derived from it, it was inevitable that political strength, not a communitarian commitment to rough consensus, would drive decisions. And because ICANN was created and captured by a political coalition that wanted to impose uniform, global regulations upon the Internet, a federalist model was deliberately avoided in favor of a broad consolidation of authority over all aspects of the name space. Johnson and Crawford write, "Participation in [the Internet] doesn't subject the participants to rules made by a global governing body." They seem to have missed the point. The purpose of ICANN is to change that. And it is succeeding, its uniform dispute resolution policy being the earliest and most obvious example.

There is a fundamental difference between ICANN and the IETF. In the end, the IETF produces only technical standards documents. Their actual adoption and implementation is entirely voluntary. The losers in the process are free to promote acceptance of other standards; there are many other places to go to get standards defined and agreed upon. Thus, one of the fundamental prerequisites of consensus-based decision making exists in IETF: it is normally in everyone's interest, from the working group level on up, to gain the assent and participation of as many relevant players as possible. There is a whole layer—one of market acceptance—interposed between the IETF and the society.

ICANN is in a completely different situation. It has monopoly control of an essential resource—the root. Control of the DNS root gives it substantial power over all top-level domain name registries, and through them it can control the domain name industry as a whole. Through its control of the identifiers it can also regulate various aspects of end user behavior. Johnson and Crawford's analysis does not devote much attention to the powerful network externalities that keep Internet service providers "voluntarily" pointing at the ICANN root, and to whether this gives the central authority quasi-coercive powers. It is not necessarily a "voluntary" regime simply because it is based on "contracts." Short of starting another root, a costly and risky prospect, there is no one else for registries to contract with.

ICANN consistently deviates from the bottom-up consensus model because of the type of decisions it has to make. The underlying subject of ICANN policies is the distribution of wealth among various industry players and consumers. Thus, if any actor or coalition of actors can gain more influence over the process and exploit it to gain a larger share of the pie, they will do so. ICANN's domain name policies are driven by power politics and economic conflicts of interest, not consensus.

There are also practical reasons why the concept of bottom-up consensus cannot work within ICANN. As soon as one concedes that one can move forward on the basis of "rough consensus" rather than unanimity, one has eliminated what is supposed to be the prime virtue of consensus-based processes: the need to persuade, rather than overrule or ignore, minorities. Unanimity is a stringent check on the abuse of power. "Rough consensus," on the other hand, is informal and cannot be precisely defined and measured. It must be "recognized" or "declared." Indeed, Johnson and Crawford's specific definition of consensus requires discerning judgments not only about *how much* opposition there is to a policy but also *from whom* the opposition comes and whether those specific parties are *substantially impacted* by the policy. Herein lies the most serious problem with the practicality of their consensus model. In large, impersonal institutions, recognition of consensus is complex and subjective, and hence easily abused. The whole problem of identifying a legitimate exercise of authority simply reverts back to debates about whether a consensus really exists.

Johnson and Crawford recognize this. "The process of consensus-building is not easy and will be subject to subversion," they write. "The presence of a consensus can be suggested when nothing of the kind can be achieved." They believe, however, that this problem has been addressed in the ICANN context by contracts that require ICANN to produce carefully documented "demonstrations of consensus support." But demonstrated to whom? Who enforces the requirement? Other than the Department of Commerce, which is a partner in the regime and at any rate claims to be promoting "self-governance," there is no formal oversight body, independent of ICANN, to review its declarations. And because it is a private, contractual regime, the legal standing of anyone who would challenge its actions in the courts is unclear.

10.2   What ICANN Is

To understand ICANN one must first move beyond the hopeful notion that the Internet is intrinsically voluntary and cannot be institutionalized or controlled. ICANN is here to change that. ICANN must be understood as a new international regime formed around a global shared resource.[4] Its purpose is to define property rights in Internet identifiers and to regulate their consumption and supply. Traditional regime theory is centered on the actions of states and holds that they come into existence to overcome collective goods problems by coordinating the behaviors of individual states. The emerging Internet governance regime is the product of an *informal* political agreement among national governments, and the agreement includes a much more extensive role for private sector actors. That fact does make ICANN different from other international regimes (see section 10.2.4), but it does not change its basic nature. It is much more accurate and analytically fruitful to define ICANN as a variant of a standard international regime than it is to think of it as something *sui generis.*

ICANN is not primarily concerned with technical coordination, nor is it a standards-setting organization. Rather, it is an institution that ties the need for technical coordination to regulation of the industry built around the resources it manages. That is why I refer to it as a global regulatory regime. The closest analogue is radio frequency administration at the national level.[5] Nominally, the assignment of radio frequencies in a given location must be coordinated to prevent electromagnetic interference among users. As any student of broadcasting and telecommunication policy knows, however, national governments don't simply *coordinate* frequency use; they *regulate* wireless industries by attaching conditions and standards to the assignment of frequencies. Sometimes the regulatory intent of the conditions is overt, as when broadcast licensees are required to fulfill specific public interest obligations or when broadcast content is regulated or censored as a condition of using a broadcast channel. The industry can also be regulated in less direct but equally important ways, through the imposition of uniform technical standards, by controlling the number of entrants into the market, or by approving or rejecting corporate mergers. The common element is that *the regime has exclusive control of a critical input into an industry and uses the leverage it has over access to that resource to regulate the industry.* In radio spectrum management, control is exercised through licenses issued by government regulatory agencies. In ICANN's case, regulation of conduct and market structure is imposed on registries and registrars via contracts with the root administrator.

ICANN's control of the root is used to make and enforce policy in three broad areas: defining and enforcing rights to names; regulation of the domain name supply industry; and the linkage of online identity to law enforcement.

10.2.1 Rights to Names

ICANN defines and enforces property rights in names. This function involves the recognition and protection of various kinds of intellectual property claims on domain name assignments, and the resolution of disputes based on those claims. Name rights are defined and enforced via the Uniform Dispute Resolution Policy (UDRP), registrar accreditation contracts that commit consumers to binding arbitration via the UDRP, and registry contracts that exclude specific names from the DNS database or impose preferential procedures for the initial assignment of names. ICANN's role in the creation of global rights to names is analyzed in greater depth in chapter 11.

10.2.2 Regulation of Domain Name Supply Industry

The second policy area is economic regulation of the supply industry for domain names. ICANN uses its control of the root to regulate the supply of top-level domains, and to regulate the price, performance, and market structure of the domain name registration industry. It (along with the Department of Commerce) imposes price controls on registries and enforces a vertical separation between registry and registrar aspects of the business. In the future, it may be required to take on additional regulatory functions pertaining to the relationship between registrars and registries, consumer complaints against registrars, and the merger of registries. ICANN's position as gateway to the root may also allow it to play an important role in the standardization of internationalized domain names (see section 10.3.3).

10.2.3 Surveillance and Law Enforcement

The third policy area involves the exploitation of the data generated by Internet identifiers to facilitate surveillance and control of Internet users by law enforcement agencies. This function is now primarily concerned with the exploitation of WHOIS data for intellectual property protection (see chapter 11). But if the ICANN regime survives, this aspect of policymaking will probably play a much larger role in the future. Paul Twomey, the Australian government official and first chair of the Governmental Advisory Committee (GAC), observed in January 1999 that a "centralized registry functioning as a monopoly" was necessary to support "consumer protection," "the resolution of intellectual property disputes," and "a capacity for indirect taxation of e-commerce."[6] The prospect of linking the surveillance capabilities enabled by the DNS databases to e-commerce taxation makes as much sense as linking it to copyright protection, so Twomey's statement cannot be dismissed as the dream of a power-hungry politician. The use of a centralized identification mechanism that gives authorities both the ability to identify private actors and some control over their access to cyberspace will probably prove to be too tempting to pass up.

10.2.4   The Informal Regime

In short, ICANN is not pioneering a radically new and better form of global policymaking. It is simply a resource-based international regulatory regime. The only remarkable and unique thing about it is that its creators have succeeded in building a rough facsimile of an international treaty organization without a treaty. The agreements were forged outside the typical international negotiating arenas, and the leading state actor, the United States, disavowed direct participation and instead delegated authority to a private corporation. However, ICANN is fundamentally a U.S. government contractor, and the White Paper process was just a less formal mechanism for gaining input from other states (as well as many private sector parties) to produce a policy document that the major parties could agree upon. There is some precedent in the formation of Comsat and Intelsat in the 1960s and 1970s (Kinsley 1976; Oslund 1977).

It is the *informality* of ICANN's arrangements, and their origins in semi-private initiatives such as the gTLD-MoU or the IANA–GIP–Internet Society alliance that is new. The instruments on which the regime is founded, such as the White Paper, the Internet Request for Comments series, and the WIPO processes, all share a fuzzy legal status, standing somewhere between formal governmental rule making and private sector arrangements. More important than the documents themselves are the informal political deals between governmental and private actors that generated them. ICANN is the product of a somewhat precarious bargain between the Internet technical hierarchy, a few major e-commerce and telecommunication firms, intellectual property interests (including WIPO), the European Union, the Department of Commerce, and one or two other national governments, notably Australia. Chapter 8 analyzed the formation of this "dominant coalition" at some length. Should any one of these major players decide to abandon or actively oppose ICANN, the edifice will crumble or require major adjustments in policy and structure. This is the *only* sense in which ICANN is based on consensus.

A clear-eyed analysis of the institutionalization of the root must conclude that, contrary to the Johnson-Crawford theory, ICANN is linked to, and shares many of the characteristics of, state sovereign power. The network externalities that support convergence on a single root provide something close to the coercive effect of law. True, there is the possibility of competing roots, but ICANN's registry contracts, and those imposed on

Network Solutions by the Department of Commerce, explicitly exclude dealings with other roots by participants in ICANN's regime. This is not the behavior of a system based on voluntary cooperation and consensus; it is an overt attempt to foreclose alternatives in order to preserve the regulatory capabilities of the regime. Furthermore, much of ICANN's agenda has been and is being driven by governments and international treaty organizations. European and Asian governments played an overt role in the selection of ICANN's initial board. An international intergovernmental organization, WIPO, took the lead in creating ICANN's approach to trademark protection and is moving to recognize new rights to names (see chapter 11). The GAC has exerted persistent pressure on the delegation and regulation of country code top-level domains. The European Union has requested and will receive a special delegation of an *.eu* top-level domain. The Commerce Department took the lead in imposing regulation on Network Solutions, and was urged on by the European Commission. And of course, the Department of Commerce still holds ultimate authority over the root.

National governments intent on regulating the Internet are beginning to discover how essential to their efforts the leverage of the root can be; recall the statement by Twomey quoted in section 10.2.3. Only in the United States, where the prestige of the IETF and the accompanying ideology of privatization and self-governance prevail, are people less attuned to this reality. In Europe, ICANN is viewed unsentimentally for what it is: a nascent Internet governance regime (Bertelsmann Foundation 2001).

10.3 Forces Affecting ICANN's Future

The new regime's place in the international order is more stable than it was in 1999, but it is not necessarily secure. In subsequent sections, I briefly discuss the issues and forces that can change or alter the new international regime. The discussions are deliberately sketchy because they address issues that are changing rapidly.

10.3.1 Membership and Global Collective Action

The fight over at-large membership, set in motion during the International Forum on the White Paper process and carried forward throughout ICANN's first three years, is one of the most important arenas of potential change. How that division is resolved will do much to define the nature of the new institution. The issue looms large because it is a battle over competing conceptions of ICANN's identity. The concept of an open, at-large membership was the only truly innovative aspect of the White Paper process. If implemented, ICANN would be the only international regime to incorporate such a high level of public participation.

To accept the need for broad-based public representation is to come fully to grips with the fact that the new organization's purpose is not just technical coordination but the development of economic and regulatory policies. It would constitute recognition that the new institution's legitimacy requires popular accountability, not claims of an insider community's consensus. Those are hard concessions for some stakeholders to make. The technical community would have to relinquish its privileged place in the regime, and the power of business stakeholders would be diminished relative to that of users. But the legitimacy of the organization as a whole would be greatly enhanced.

On the other hand, an active at-large membership capable of electing half the board might set in motion longer-term political and organizational dynamics. Johnson and Crawford are right that global membership and elections tend to bring with them assumptions about the delegation to ICANN of quasi-governmental powers. We have almost no experience with the behavior of a global electorate. We do know, however, that ICANN's first invocation of a global public vote during the fall 2000 elections set in motion competition among national blocs within regions.

Unfortunately the Johnson-Crawford theory does not provide much guidance here. There is a direct contradiction between their belief that the ICANN regime is voluntary and lacks sovereignty, and their fear that an Internet public able to elect a significant number of board members will lead to wealth-redistributing legislatures and majority-rule threats to Internet stakeholders' rights and interests. Either ICANN as an institution has the power to do evil, or it does not. If it does, doesn't the broader public have a right to some direct representation in its governance? The public's rights and interests also can be harmed. If it does not, then what is there to fear from public representation? In a voluntary regime, the major stakeholders would simply opt out if things went awry.

10.3.2   Imperfectly Articulated Relationship to Nation-States

The informal way ICANN was created may have helped it to come into being faster and may have given its backers more flexibility. But by skipping a step or two in the formation of the regime, the process created fundamental ambiguities and tensions about ICANN's legal standing and its relationship to the international order, which is still primarily composed of nation-states and their treaty organizations.

In the past, international regulatory regimes have been formed by treaties among governments. One can expect, therefore, that there will be long-term pressures from governments and other parts of society to formalize and clarify ICANN's relationship to governments. Governments, by virtue of their apparatus of representation, consider themselves to be the legitimate representatives of the general public interest. Evidence of a tension between this self-conception and ICANN's role has already surfaced in the GAC's attempt to insert itself into the country code delegation process.

The Commerce Department's reservation of ultimate policy authority over the root is a ticking time bomb that must either be defused carefully or allowed to explode unexpectedly at some point in the future. The political obstacles within the United States to relinquishing policy authority are legion. To do so would require bringing the entire ICANN and DNS can of worms before the U.S. Congress and possibly refighting the domain name wars in that arena. Nationalistic forces within the United States could easily intimidate proponents of yielding control by accusing them of "giving away the Internet." Even non-nationalists who have been close observers of ICANN's behavior in its first three years are not enthusiastic supporters of removing it from the last remaining form of public oversight. And yet, the Commerce Department reservation contradicts almost everything ICANN was supposed to be: private, internationalized, self-governing.

The relationship to nation-states will be strongly affected by the resolution of the at-large membership issues. If ICANN manages to avoid fulfilling its promise to create an at-large membership with direct input into the board, then it would be easier for politicians dissatisfied with its policies to claim that it is little more than a cartel of the domain name supply industry. And if that happens, it will be difficult for ICANN to resist attempts by governments to seek more direct and formal oversight capabilities over its actions. On the other hand, if ICANN does develop its own organic capabilities to represent the broad public interest, its resistance to interference from governments will increase. But this would be achieved at the price of becoming more governmental itself.

10.3.3   Internationalized Domain Names

Internationalizing domain names—more precisely, using non-Roman scripts as labels in the DNS—would completely transform the domain name registration industry. Multilingual domain names are extremely popular with the large majority of the world's Internet users who are not native English readers. Implementing a capability to resolve non-Roman scripts could require major changes in the DNS protocol. An IETF working group is over a year behind schedule as it confronts the complexity of human languages and problems with intellectual property rights over certain techniques.[7] Some methods of internationalization (known as server-side approaches) would redesign the entire DNS to fully accommodate new scripts, and would probably take a decade to be fully implemented. Less radical changes in DNS, implemented at the client side as software plug-ins into users' browsers, would lead to faster implementation but pose other problems.

As is the case with any change in a technical standard, universal interoperability is at risk as transition and migration take place. Uncertainty in the marketplace can encourage competing vendors supporting different standards to seek market share that may enhance their leverage over the process. Implementation of internationalized domain names could lead to a multiplicity of new roots. Because linguistic differences often come bundled with differing political and economic interests, the implications of internationalizing DNS are not to be taken lightly.[8]

Multilingual domain names may also put pressure on ICANN to expand its mission. During ICANN's creation, key members of the IETF hierarchy adamantly insisted that standards development was IETF's turf and ICANN had no place in it. Now, however, Internet Architecture Board members who are fearful of competing internationalized domain name standards have suggested that ICANN exploit its ability to regulate registries and domain names to promote a specific standard.[9] In the revision of the Verisign contracts, ICANN's legal counsel, Joe Sims, also made it clear that ICANN would like the contracts to explicitly acknowledge ICANN's authority to impose standards on registries pertaining to internationalized domain names.[10] Thus, ICANN seems poised to exploit its position at the root to regulate standards adoption, just as the Federal Communications Commission and other national regulatory authorities leverage their control of the spectrum to impose technical standards on wireless industry players.

10.3.4 WIPO 2 and New Rights to Names

A second WIPO process, initiated only a year after the first one concluded, proposes to create sweeping new rights in names and to use the domain name system to enforce them. If the new WIPO proposals are accepted, the domain name system will take another major step toward becoming a highly regulated arena, and the types of rights recognized will expand from trademark to a host of others. This issue is covered in detail in chapter 11.

10.3.5 Country Code Top-Level Domains

Country codes top-level domains (ccTLDs) are in some ways the most conservative element of the new regime, mirroring as they do the political geography of the existing international system. In another sense, they are the most disruptive, autonomous, and decentralizing force. Country code registries owe little to ICANN. Although most of their delegations originally came from Jon Postel, the new organization lacks any clear authority to withdraw them. Indeed, because of the tenuous and sometimes wholly artificial aura of "national sovereignty" surrounding them, ICANN must tread lightly in its treatment of the country codes. The protection and support of national governments serves as an effective check on the power of the U.S. "public benefit" corporation.

The ccTLDs represent a hole in the regime, just as Network Solutions did during most of 1999. Currently, ICANN has no contractual relationship with the ccTLD registries. Its ability to tax them to support the regime is contested, as noted in chapter 9. This means that over 200 registries, representing about 20 percent of the world's domain name registrations, really do have an almost entirely voluntary relationship with ICANN. They are free to adopt their own naming conventions, to adopt their own dispute resolution policies, to fund ICANN or not, as they see fit.

WIPO is systematically wooing the ccTLD registries, offering to bring them into ICANN's Uniform Dispute Resolution Policy or to help them develop their own policy. ICANN's management is investing heavily in staff resources to repair relations and rope the recalcitrant ccTLD managers into the new regime. Both ICANN and the country code constituency within the Domain Name Supporting Organization (DNSO) are working on the terms and conditions of a model contract. The ccTLD registries have already proposed to withdraw from the DNSO and form a new Supporting Organization with a guaranteed number of board seats. How this relationship is defined will do much to define the character of the regime.

10.3.6   IPv6 and the Scalability of Routing

A less immediate issue is the migration of the Internet Protocol to version 6, with its vastly expanded, 128-bit address space. Interestingly, the policies defined by the address registries for allocating and assigning the v6 address space differ little from those currently used for the IPv4 space.[11] The Address Supporting Organization plans to allocate IPv6 address blocks hierarchically through its established structure of regional address registries. Assigned users of IPv6 addresses will be considered custodians, not owners, of the addresses. The registries will still use administrative rationing methods and attempt to avoid stockpiling of addresses by requiring demonstrations of need. Most important, IPv6 does not eliminate the most important scarcity affecting the growth of the Internet: the expansion of routing tables, which imposes a need to assign addresses in a way that permits aggregation of routes. The need for route aggregation is now the major constraint on address assignment, and perhaps also the most important constraint on the growth of the Internet (Huston 2001).

The more interesting question about address allocation is, What will happen if IPv6 does *not* gain acceptance? Pressures to ration more efficiently the extremely scarce IPv4 address space may lead to calls for a greater role for market forces. A market for addresses could introduce some of the pressures for institutional change that have already affected the domain name system. A failure to transition to IPv6 could also pave the way for the entry of more radical technological alternatives that would be completely outside the control of ICANN.

11
Global Rights to Names

'Tis but thy name that is my enemy.
—Shakespeare, *Romeo and Juliet*

In Shakespeare's play *Romeo and Juliet* two clans, the Montagues and the Capulets, are locked in a blood feud. Romeo, a Montague, falls in love with a woman of the Capulet family. His predicament causes him to muse on the significance of names—"'tis but thy name that is my enemy"—and he utters the famous lines, "What's in a name? That which we call a rose by any other name would smell as sweet." But Shakespeare knew well what was in a name. Although the names themselves are arbitrary, they are markers of powerful social boundaries. Whether you were tagged Montague or Capulet was a matter of life and death. In the end, the names won and the lovers lost.

Intrinsically, not much is in domain names. Their value as locators, identifiers, and navigation aids is very much overrated. After being the focal point of global institutional change for more than six years, however, they are being made into territorial markers of great commercial and geopolitical significance. One of the most aggressive players in this drama is the World Intellectual Property Organization (WIPO). The once-obscure organization is trying to enter into a symbiotic relationship with ICANN, wherein WIPO provides the policy initiative for minting new rights in names and ICANN provides the control points for implementing and enforcing them. The dirty little secret of the whole affair is that domain names are not nearly as valuable or as important as the new institutional regime would like to pretend they are. Domain name policy is really a proxy war. Extraordinary claims over the control of words and names are being advanced in the arena of Internet domain assignment because it is hoped (or feared) that it will set precedents for the treatment of the entire online economy. For WIPO and the intellectual property interests, the domain name space has become the site for this proxy war, not because of its intrinsic importance but because it is turf that can actually be controlled, because of the centralized nature of the root.

That all this weight is being placed on a system of computer identifiers that is distributed, hierarchically organized, and asks of names only that they be unique is one of the key weaknesses in the emerging regime. Never before has so much regulatory firepower been concentrated on a resource so ill-suited for the task. The attempt to vest the humble domain name with an increasingly regulated, official status would be comical if it were not so dangerous and costly. Nevertheless, this anomaly tells us something important about institutionalization processes. Institutions, once ensconced, can redefine technical systems to suit their own purposes, foreclosing technical possibilities and lines of business development that are inconsistent with maintaining the regime.

This chapter has two objectives. The first is to demonstrate that control of the DNS root is being used to create new and expanded rights to names. In the institutional response to the domain name–trademark interface, a common refrain is that the goal is only to preserve existing rights. But the property rights in names that are being created by the new global regime are often stronger than, and always quite different from, traditional legal rights in names.

The second objective of the analysis is to demonstrate how ill-suited domain names are as a vehicle for advancing an expansive property rights agenda. Highly unrealistic assumptions must be made about the use and interpretation of domain names on the Internet in order to justify the new rights and the regulatory regime needed to enforce them.

11.1 A Web Site by Any Other Name . . .

On a computer network, identifiers are cheap, plentiful, and often playful. Names can map anything to anything. The costs of creating them and changing the mappings are low. The tradition of playful naming goes back to the Internet's origins in academia. Hosts were named after mythological figures (Thor, Zeus, Athena), characters from fantasy stories (Frodo, Gandalf, Rodan, Godzilla), or whatever else struck the fancy of the system administrators. Aside from the initial freedom to assign names, the anonymous interaction fostered by computer networks encouraged play in the adoption of user identities. The familiar joke, "on the Internet, no one knows you're a dog" encapsulates that reality. It is reinforced daily by experiences in chat rooms, public bulletin boards, and virtual worlds, where users can deliberately adopt and explore identities of their own creation (Turkle 1995; Lessig 1999). Certainly there is a dark side to the ability to conceal or change one's identity in cyberspace. Sexual predators can use it to stalk children, and securities hucksters can use it to unload stocks. Identity theft, spoofing, and spamming are common problems. But the same technology that allows one to define and alter the identity one presents to the online public also leaves behind so many trails and fingerprints that law enforcement still comes out ahead, except for a few skilled and professional culprits.

America Online, the most mainstream and commercialized of the big Internet service providers, understands the role of names in cyberspace. AOL provides each of its customer accounts with up to six screen names. The names are entirely user-selected, subject only to a uniqueness constraint and some limits on obscenity. With the exception of a primary name, the identities can be altered, adopted, or deleted at will. Random searches of AOL's member list inevitably pulls up fun names: SexxyBone, Goofyrulzz, SugarMama84, Goofy4Ever, GretaGarbo18. (If someone else has already adopted the same name, numbers must be appended to it to make it unique; apparently, there are a lot of SugarMama and Greta Garbo wannabes on AOL.)

In the AOL name space, references to cartoon characters, movie stars, novelists, TV programs, and other icons of popular culture are abundant. Not all are complimentary. In his user profile, AOL member Fecking Goofy lists his location as "the planet Pluto" and his hobby as "shagging Minnie." In open and free name spaces, as in real human interactions in conversation and physical space, people readily appropriate and incorporate into their own distinctive cultures references to "owned" names and characters. These conversations are more a reflection and reinforcement of the popularity and value of cultural icons than a dilution of them. To regulate such activity would destroy the point of it.

Usenet newsgroups are another example of a relatively free name space. Usenet is a way of organizing text-based discussion or file exchange groups around specific topics, and distributing them to users.[1] There is a group devoted to the collectors of Pez candy containers, for example, named *alt.collecting.pez.* The naming of Usenet groups is more like domain name assignment than like the adoption of AOL user names. The names are hierarchical and point to content rather than to individuals. Unlike AOL screen names, they are part of a public name space, and new ones can be assigned only after some form of collective action.[2]

Like AOL screen names and user profiles, the Usenet name space commonly incorporates trademarked names. There is a newsgroup for people who hate Barney, the purple dinosaur character on children's television, named *alt.dinosaur.barney.die.die.die.* There is a *rec.arts.disney.parks,* a group not endorsed or operated by Disney, and a *rec.arts.tv.soaps.abc.* There is a *comp.os.ms-windows* newsgroup that is not operated or licensed by the Microsoft Corporation. Within the Usenet name space, it is commonly understood that names can refer to entities without pretending to be official, authorized versions of them.

In the domain name space, on the other hand, users are not allowed to claim that their name is Mickey Mouse and that they come from Disneyland. If anyone had tried to register *barney.com* or *barney.org* to run a Web site for derogatory comments about the dinosaur character, the trademark lawyers would have pounced. Thus, an interesting and fundamental discrepancy exists between the world of domain names and other computer naming systems. Why? It is *not* because the function of domain names is fundamentally different or more important than these other kinds of names. The differences stem from a combination of history and hysteria.

Chapter 6 described the explosion of domain name registrations under *.com* in 1995 and 1996, and the ensuing collision between domain name registrations and trademark rights. During that brief period, owning a simple domain name in the *.com* space was the equivalent of possessing a global (English) keyword. Many business people and intellectual property lawyers became convinced that domain names possessed a remarkable power to attract users and establish a global identity in cyberspace. This in turn provoked a concerted effort by intellectual property interests to make domain names a controlled vocabulary, and the data generated by a registration—known as WHOIS data—into an official record that can be used by intellectual property holders to identify and track down the registrant.

11.2 Expanding Trademark Rights

Throughout the domain name controversies, almost all sides of the dispute have reiterated the principle that new laws or policies should neither expand nor diminish traditional intellectual property rights. The Commerce Department White Paper claimed that its proposals "were designed to provide trademark holders with the same rights they have in the physical world" (NTIA 1998b, sec. 8). WIPO (2001) also made a point of emphasizing this claim: "[T]he goal of the first WIPO process was not to create new rights in intellectual property, nor to accord greater protection to intellectual property in cyberspace than that which existed elsewhere. Rather, the goal was to give proper and adequate expression to the existing, multilaterally agreed standards of intellectual property protection in the context of the multi-jurisdictional medium of the Internet" (para. 18).

The notion that we are simply translating traditional rights into a new medium is easily exposed as fiction, however. The only way to do this would be to apply trademark concepts to domain name disputes on a case-by-case basis, using traditional legal standards and institutional methods. Instead, ICANN and its backers have directly inserted trademark protection criteria into the administration of the technical system. This is inherently problematical. Trademark rights are based on subjective criteria, involving factors such as interpretation, culture, and confusion. Everything depends on the context and the way the name is used. Rights in the domain name system, on the other hand, are based primarily on technical exclusivity. Furthermore, trademark rights are territorial, whereas domain names are inherently global in scope. It is therefore impossible to map DNS administration and trademark protection onto each other without fundamentally changing the nature of the rights involved.

And we *are* in the process of altering the nature of name rights. Much attention has been devoted to the threat of cybersquatting. Less attention has been paid to the danger that measures to control it are expanding property rights to names at the expense of free expression, privacy, and competition.

11.2.1 Mechanized Rights

Increasingly in the domain name space rights are established and defended not through *ex post facto* litigation that applies a legal standard to a particular situation, but by preemptive regulation. By "preemptive regulation" I mean techniques that protect name rights on an *ex ante* basis by hardwiring certain kinds of protection into the technical system. Rights become mechanized, the ultimate example of what Lessig (1999) calls regulation by Code.

The clearest examples of preemptive regulation are name exclusions. If one controls the root, one can insert into all contracts with domain name registries a list of prohibited names or words, and require all registries to check all applications for registrations against that list and block any registrations that match the words on the list. In other words, control of the DNS root can be exploited to make the assignment of certain names impossible, regardless of who uses them, the purpose of the use (e.g., commercial or noncommercial), or the impact of the use on the mark holder.

WIPO promoted the idea of across-the-board exclusions for major trademark holders during its first domain name process in 1999 (WIPO 1998; 1999). It advocated creating a list of globally famous trademarks that would then be excluded entirely from the DNS database. The list of famous marks would be compiled by WIPO through an application and review process that did not impose any fixed limit on the number of companies or marks to be granted this exclusive status. The proposal was a rather dramatic contradiction of WIPO's claim that it did not want to create new rights. An authoritative list of famous trademarks that is accepted on a global scale simply did not exist then, nor does it now. Had the ICANN process not blocked it, WIPO would have created a completely new kind of name right and implemented it via the domain name space.

But WIPO is not the only organization to advocate and use name exclusions. ICANN's staff unilaterally imposed a significant number of name exclusions upon the new generic top-level domain registries it created in 2001. Most of the affected names were acronyms and names associated with the Internet technical community and ICANN's own organizational subsidiaries.[3] Some of the excluded acronyms, however, were actually trademarked by private companies in various places in the world. Generic words like *ripe* and *museum* were excluded. The fact that global rights could be created by fiat, without any policy consultation or oversight, speaks to the potential power inherent in ICANN's position at the root.

Another form of preemptive regulation is simply the refusal to permit the creation of new top-level domains. Trademark holders fought success-fully against the creation of any new TLDs from 1997 to 2000 because it would raise their policing costs and increase the possibility that someone, somewhere, might register a name that a trademark owner finds objec-tionable. If there are no new TLDs, that can't happen and, of course, there is no need to judge whether a particular registration really is diluting or in-fringing a trademark. The situation is analogous to what might happen if photocopying machines were banned, or access to them tightly regulated by a copyright authority. Obviously, there would be fewer violations of the copyrights of book publishers and scholarly journal publishers. But all kinds of legitimate and legal activities would be curtailed, too.

There is, of course, nothing new about attempts by incumbent intellec-tual property holders to block the introduction of services or technologies that (they feel) threaten the exclusivity of intellectual property. Major copyright holders attempted to ban videocassette recorders on the grounds that someone might use them to make illegal copies.[4] In those cases, U.S. courts and legislators adhered to the commonsense principle that one must not prohibit an entire business simply because a small por-tion of the activity it generates might be violating copyright or trademark laws. In the domain name space, however, intellectual property interests have achieved the kind of prior restraint that they have sought but never been given in other new communication media. Intellectual property hold-ers have succeeded in gaining control, or a large amount of influence, over the point of market entry.

Preemptive regulation can also take the form of procedures regulating the initial assignment of names in new top-level domains. So-called "sunrise" procedures, for example, give trademark owners privileged access to do-main name registrations in the opening phase of new top-level domains. A proposal put forward by the Intellectual Property Constituency of the Domain Name Supporting Organization (DNSO), for example, demanded a 30-day period prior to the public launch of a new top-level domain dur-ing which registrations would only be available to trademark owners. The plan, dubbed "sunrise plus twenty," allowed a trademark owner whose mark was at least one year old to register 21 variations of a trademarked name within the new TLDs. It also asked registries to supply these "sunrise" registrations at a discount to normal domain name registration fees. Such procedures privilege trademark owners over other claimants regardless of whether classical infringement is involved. This is a completely new kind of trademark right; such preemptive privileges over the adoption of names by presumptively innocent third parties have never existed before. Indeed, the rights created both by the famous marks exclusion and the "sunrise-plus" proposals are so far afield of traditional trademark rights that they would bring many legitimate trademark holders into conflict with each other. Although the extreme version of "sunrise" sought by the International Trademark Association (INTA) and other large trademark holders was not implemented, many of the new TLDs licensed by ICANN did adopt milder variants of the "sunrise" proposal. Indeed, even the new *.name* top-level domain, which was supposed to be devoted exclusively to individual domain name holders who wanted their domain name to reflect their personal identity, adopted a "sunrise" procedure.

The problem with name exclusions, "sunrise" proposals, and other preemptive rights should be apparent. They substitute technical exclusivity and *ex ante* rules for what should be *ex post* legal judgments. Hence, they are completely insensitive to the boundaries and limitations that normally accompany trademark rights. Limitations on the ownership of words and names meant to protect freedom of speech and fair use can easily be squashed in a regime based on technical exclusivities. An across-the-board name exclusion doesn't distinguish between the name *ford.sucks,* which might be used legitimately for a protest site about the automobile company, and a deceptive or infringing registration of the domain name *ford.com.* It cannot make a distinction between the many legitimate concurrent uses that might be made of trademarked words, such as the Ford Theatre, the Ford Modeling agency, and the Ford Motor Company.

Neither WIPO nor the trademark interests have succeeded in getting all the preemptive rights they wanted out of the new regime. But it is significant that such rights are constantly being sought and that it is fairly easy to implement them as long as artificial scarcity is maintained and ICANN continues to link technical coordination to policymaking. The new regime encourages and rewards such expansion. Fighting against it, on the other hand, is costly and difficult.

11.2.2 Expanding Surveillance Rights

A critical part of maintaining any property right is the need to monitor its boundaries, that is, to identify perceived violations of the right and take effective enforcement action against them. Under traditional trademark practice, the owner of a mark is responsible for all policing and monitoring activity and costs. In the physical world, there is no single, integrated, global database of company, product, or brand names in which everyone must register. Trademark policing relies on a variety of activities: monitoring official trademark registers, checking telephone directories and Yellow Pages, searching industrial directories, and physically examining products in stores, to name a few. A number of specialized firms supply this surveillance function on a commercial basis to major brand holders.

As discussed in chapter 9, the creation of an institutional regime based on control of the DNS root has made it possible for intellectual property interests to claim new and expansive rights of surveillance over the adoption of names by users. The vehicle for these new rights is the WHOIS database.

The WHOIS database allows one to type in a domain name and pull up the name and address of the individual or company that registered the domain. It also shows the dates on which the domain was created, when it expires, and when it was last updated. It includes the name, address, and contact numbers of the domain technical administrator as well as technical information, such as the domain name and IP addresses of the name servers to used to resolve a name. The protocol was invented by the original creators of the Internet to provide information that might be needed to resolve technical problems involving a domain or an IP address. Later, the information proved to be useful in tracing the source of spam or hacking attacks. As domain names became economically valuable, WHOIS also became a popular way of finding out which domain names were taken, who had registered them and when, and when the registration would expire.

With the emergence of domain name–trademark conflicts, the WHOIS protocol took on a new function. It became a surveillance tool for intellectual property holders. The intellectual property interests discovered that they could perform searches for character strings that matched trademarks, and pull up many of the domain name registrations in the generic top-level domains that matched or contained a trademark. This automated and universal searching function proved to be so valuable to the trademark interests that they began to demand that the WHOIS surveillance functions be institutionalized, expanded, and subsidized.

The first WIPO process recommended that the contact details in a WHOIS record be contractually required to be complete, accurate, and up-to-date, on penalty of forfeiture of the domain name (WIPO 1999, para. 73). The intellectual property interests also demanded "bulk access" to the WHOIS data of domain name registrars, that is, the right to purchase the complete list and contact data for all of a registrar's customers in one fell swoop. They now want WHOIS functionality to be expanded, so that data can be searchable by domain name, the registrants' name or postal address, technical or administrative contact name, NIC handles,[5] and IP addresses. They also want searches to be based on Boolean operators or incomplete matches, as well as exact string matches. Further, they are requesting that the results of searches not be limited to a certain number (Network Solutions can only return 50 records at a time). Moreover, they want this expanded capability to be subsidized, that is, they want it to be considered a part of the public Internet infrastructure and not a value-added service that they would have to pay for. Not content with the already massive reduction in transaction costs brought about by the mere existence of a single, integrated name space that can be searched using automated tools, they want to shift the costs of policing and monitoring the trademark–domain name interface onto users, registries, and registrars.

As noted in chapter 9, the issue is no longer exclusively one of trademark surveillance and protection. Copyright interests now view expanded WHOIS functionality as a way to identify and serve process upon the owners of allegedly infringing Web sites. That is, "technical coordination" of the domain name system is already being leveraged to police the *content* of Web sites as well as their domain names. Moreover, public law enforcement agencies, notably the U.S. Federal Bureau of Investigation, have become deeply interested in the use of WHOIS to supplement their law enforcement activities. Ultimately, the intent seems to be to make a domain name the cyberspace equivalent of a driver's license. Only, unlike the driver's licenses database, this one would be publicly accessible to anyone and everyone to rummage through as they pleased.

Whether one supports or opposes the intellectual property interests' agenda for the WHOIS service, it is incontestable that the surveillance rights they are seeking are more comprehensive than any that have existed before. A reduction of transaction costs per se is not bad; indeed, from an economic standpoint, lower transaction costs, almost by definition, contribute to greater efficiency. The problem is that the expansive and compulsory WHOIS functions sought by the intellectual property interests do not reduce transaction costs for all. They mostly shift cost and risks that used to be assumed by intellectual property owners onto end users, registries, and registrars, in order to make life easier for trademark owners. End users are being asked to sacrifice privacy and expose themselves to spam, slamming, and other unsavory practices that exploit the open availability of WHOIS data. Registrars are required to lose control of their customer lists. Both registries and registrars must make major investments in software and infrastructure to support the comprehensive global surveillance capabilities sought by the intellectual property interests.

To compel everyone in the domain name space to expose themselves to surveillance expands the strength and comprehensiveness of intellectual property owners' rights over names. To require that the system be funded by the subjects of the surveillance is the *coup de grâce*.

Just how radical a shift in the balance of power the intellectual property agenda for WHOIS represents was illustrated by an amusing exchange on a public email list between Judy Henslee, the U.S. trademark manager for Harley-Davidson motorcycles, and an intellectual property lawyer, John Berryhill. Ms. Henslee was complaining about the limitations of the current WHOIS protocol on the INTA email list, and she concluded, "The ability to produce (or at the very least, purchase) accurate lists of all domains owned by a single person or entity would be extremely helpful to the trademark owner." Mr. Berryhill replied,

Dear Ms. Henslee,
I was sitting on my back porch this evening, and someone drove by riding a Harley Davidson motorcycle with a defective exhaust system. My community has strictly enforced noise and smog ordinances, and this person was clearly in violation of both. This person was also not wearing a helmet, in violation of the law. I shouted at the rider, whereupon he rode across and damaged my lawn. I would like to bring a trespass action against him, but I could not identify him. However, I can identify the make, model, year and color of the hog. I went to your Web site, and I noticed that Harley Davidson does not provide a readily accessible database of warranty registrations or, indeed, any other information that will assist me to identify the violator. As you surely can appreciate based on your comments concerning the

WHOIS database, your provision of this information would certainly help in bringing this lawbreaker to justice, as well as anyone else who uses a Harley Davidson product to violate the law. As I'm sure you are aware, despite the fine reputation enjoyed by Harley, and my own admiration for your machines, there is an element of the subculture associated with your company's product which has been known to demonstrate a pattern of unlawful behavior such as gang activity and drug transportation. Many of them may own more than one motorcycle. So, I'm sure there is considerable demand for this data.

Since there doesn't appear to be a convenient database, is there some way that I can arrange to purchase the names, postal addresses, email addresses, and telephone and fax numbers of people who own Harley Davidson motorcycles? If I send the description to you, will you help me identify the owner?

The Harley-Davidson lawyer was not amused by the parallel. But she did not argue effectively against its validity. Under ICANN's contractual regime, the consumers and suppliers of domain name registration services are required to facilitate their own surveillance by intellectual property owners. If we apply the same logic to any other industry, it seems absurdly overreaching. Motorcycles can be used to break the law, but we do not require all vehicle manufacturers to create a publicly accessible, global database with complete and accurate contact information about all their customers. Even the official, state-issued licenses attached to such vehicles are not open to anyone who wants to search through them; one must go through official law enforcement channels and demonstrate some cause of action. The linkage of resource administration to policy and regulation in the domain name regime has given intellectual property interests much more extensive rights of surveillance than they had before.

11.3   New Rights in Names: WIPO 2

If there were any doubts about the intent of WIPO and certain other interests to take advantage of the ICANN regime to create new rights in names, they were resolved with the release of the Interim Report of WIPO's second domain name proceeding (WIPO 2001). The second WIPO proceeding advocated several new types of name exclusions and some modifications of the Uniform Dispute Resolution Policy (UDRP) to recognize new rights in domain names. The new rights involved names of international organizations, nonproprietary pharmaceutical names, geographical indicators, country codes, personal names, and trade names.

The new rights were proposed before ICANN had even begun to evaluate its UDRP.

11.3.1   INNs and IGOs: Taking Care of Your Own

One of the focal points of WIPO's report was the list of International Non-proprietary Names (INNs) for pharmaceutical substances, created by the World Health Organization (WHO). The INN list consists of 8,000 generic names of drugs, such as "ampicillin" or "penicillin." Over 100 new names are added to the list each year. The purpose of the list is to ensure that no one can claim proprietary rights to those terms. The INN list, therefore, is intended to preserve freedom of expression in the realm of drug development and medicine by ensuring that no company or individual can control or regulate the basic terms used to scientifically describe and define pharmaceutical substances. One would think, therefore, that those terms' use in the domain name space would be open to all, as it is in other contexts. WHO is concerned, however, that the registration of an INN as a domain name means that a private interest might "control" an INN. Indeed, it refers to the registration of a domain name as a "monopoly of association."

Monopoly? WHO's understanding of DNS is less than perfect. It does not seem to understand that an INN can show up in any one of more than 257 top-level domains; that the number of TLDs could be expanded to a million; that INNs could show up in third-, fourth, and fifth-level domains (or further down the hierarchy) or on the right-hand side of a Uniform Resource Locator (URL). In fact, the report admits that "evidence of actual damage resulting from the registration and use of INNs as domain names is lacking" (WIPO 2001 para. 45).

None of these facts deterred WIPO from proposing to mint a new global right. It recommended that all character strings identical to INNs, in five official languages, be excluded from the DNS database. WIPO would like the exclusion to apply in all open generic TLDs, and urges all country code TLD registries to adopt it, too. Moreover, it proposes to expropriate holders of existing registrations by canceling their domain name registrations.

The WIPO report also recommends special treatment of the names of international intergovernmental organizations (IGOs). Under current treaties, IGOs are protected against registration of their names or acronyms as trademarks or service marks. WIPO proposed to exclude the exact names and acronyms of official IGOs from all gTLDs, regardless of how they were used. As in the case of INNs, it did not document a significant social problem caused by abusive registration of IGO names. Indeed, the only statements in support of the exclusion came from the IGOs themselves. The following comment, submitted to WIPO by the Preparatory Commission for the Comprehensive Nuclear-Test-Ban Treaty Organization, was typical of the rationale put forward: "[I]t is important to have only one authentic source of information in the Internet and to prevent the establishment of competing, unofficial Internet sites that may contain misleading, inaccurate, or prejudicial information, or that may lead the viewer to believe that he or she is using the official Web site of the organization."

This statement makes it abundantly clear that by regulating DNS labels, we are regulating speech and content as well. The treaty organization wanted to leverage the administration of DNS to ensure that there is "only one authentic source of information" about itself on the Internet and to prevent the formation of "competing, unofficial" sites. Few would object to measures aimed at eliminating fraudulent or deceptive Web sites, whether they target international organizations or any other type of organization. But fraud of that sort does not require a global name exclusion; it can be addressed by existing treaties and by the existing Uniform Dispute Resolution Policy. A more likely scenario is that the names of IGOs would be used not by frauds but by parodists or political critics to operate Web sites with critical or humorous content. An across-the-board exclusion seems intended only to prevent these critics from attracting the attention of the public by incorporating the IGO's name into their domain name label.

11.3.2   Geographical Designations

Geographical designations include the names of cities, nations, regions, or locations. Often, geographic names are used as indicators of the source of agricultural or manufactured products. Because of this type of usage, an extensive body of intellectual property law has grown up around them.[6] But neither the geographical indications themselves nor the legal principles governing them are uniform across territorial jurisdictions. As one legal scholar put it, "The same word can, in different contexts, constitute fully or partially a geographical indication, an indication of source, a geographic term, a descriptive term, a personal name, and a trademark. In other words, merely because a certain word functions as a geographical indication in one market, jurisdiction, and language, does not mean that the word is inherently a geographical indication."[7] Terms such as "champagne" or "bourbon," which have specific and regulated applications in France, may not be protected at all in the United States.

Nevertheless, the second WIPO report recommended the adoption of new measures to protect geographic indicators and indications of source in the open top-level domains. It proposed to do this by broadening the scope of ICANN's UDRP to include abusive registrations of geographical indications and indications of source. The result of such a move would be to vastly complicate the definition and application of the UDRP, and to foment hundreds if not thousands of new disputes as different territorial norms began to collide with each other. Even the International Trademark Association recognized that extending the UDRP to geographical terms would require "extensive adjustments" in the UDRP's language. "The number of required amendments would transform the UDRP from a relatively easy-to-understand process to a more complex legal regimen that may not be readily understandable, especially to respondents who are presented with a cause of action against them."[8] It is difficult to understand why WIPO would propose this other than as part of an ambitious attempt to exploit the leverage of the domain name system to carve out a new global system of name rights with itself at the center.

It is interesting to speculate on what would have happened if WIPO's proposed regime had been in place back in November 1994, when a start-up company with no real connection to Brazil registered the name *amazon.com*. Most likely, the claims of a small U.S. company with no political clout would have been brushed aside as an "inauthentic" use of an important geographical indicator.

11.3.3 Rights of Personality

Common pool conditions in the domain name space allowed anyone to register personal names as well as trademarked product names. Entertainers, celebrities, politicians, and some not-so-famous people found that their names had been registered by someone else. Frequently they did not like the use to which it was put. One activity in particular got the attention of politicians: the registration of the names of elected politicians and political candidates as domains. The names became the address of Web sites critical of the candidates' political views. Or they were offered to the candidates for a higher price.[9] While the Republican and Democratic parties' national committees expressed valid concerns about the use of domain name registrations to extort payments from campaign committees, they also raised troubling issues about the overlap between domain name regulation and free expression. The Democratic party's national committee, for example, complained about the "voter confusion arising from a multiplicity of sites with domain names including the candidate's name, when such sites are created by individuals or organizations in order to criticize or parody the candidate, rather than for profit." Was their concern really the abusive registration of names, or simply a desire to make their political opponents and critics a bit harder to find?

Because of the power of Hollywood, strong national legislation in the United States has already addressed personality rights in the domain name space. The so-called Anticybersquatting Consumer Protection Act (ACPA) allows civil lawsuits against people who register the domain name of a person "without that person's consent, with the specific intent to profit from such name by selling the domain name for financial gain to that person or any third party." Even before ACPA, several U.S. court cases stripped domain name speculators of registrations of the names of celebrities and performers.[10]

In general, personal names are not protected as marks unless they are used or registered as an identifier of a product or service. There are laws against defamation, libel, and slander, but they pertain to content rather than labels. Within the ICANN regime, several UDRP decisions have recognized and upheld personality rights when the name in question is associated with famous performers and effectively functions as a trademark.[11] The results, however, are mixed. Several cases uphold the right of third parties to register someone else's name if they are fans or have something to say about the person and wish to identify the site using a direct nominative reference.[12]

The second WIPO process considered some of these issues and raised the possibility of amending ICANN's dispute resolution policy to strengthen personality rights. The new right WIPO proposes would apply when the name is distinctive and the domain name registration is commercially exploited by an unauthorized party. The definition of "bad faith registration" would be modified to include practices that take advantage of the reputation or goodwill in a person's identity. The WIPO wording does not sound all that unreasonable, but it constitutes yet another step in the direction of an expanded, global regime of rights to names with WIPO at its center. The report was weak in documenting abuses, and particularly weak in demonstrating that the abuses that exist in this area are not being handled by existing remedies. If the UDRP is modified, thousands of new disputes will be created, as people around the world would be encouraged to bring claims against anyone who registers their personal name as a domain name. There are no guarantees about the results of a UDRP case, so the risk of registering such a name will rise. "Taking advantage of the reputation or goodwill in a person's identity" can be an all-encompassing claim. If someone writes a book about a famous person and uses the name in the title, are they taking advantage of someone else's reputation? Probably.

11.3.4   Country Names: Semantics and Sovereignty

An especially potent subset of the controversy over geographical designators concerns country names, including both the words themselves and the two-letter country codes of the ISO-3166-1 list. In this case, the rights being asserted are not derived from commercial trademark rights but are put forward as extensions of national sovereignty.

The ISO list of country codes embodied the pre-Internet international communication regime. It reflected a world of territorial nation-states where international relations were coordinated by treaty-based intergovernmental institutions. By incorporating this artifact into the domain name space, Jon Postel inadvertently helped to reproduce the political geography of the *ancien régime* in cyberspace. The ISO codes were originally part of a private name space and were intended to be nothing more than an identifier of what country a domain administrator was in. Remarkably, these casual delegations of top-level domains were transmuted into the basis of a sovereignty claim by national governments. According to the ICANN Governmental Advisory Committee (GAC), the "relevant national government or public authority" should determine who receives the right to operate a country code registry, the duration of the license, and any review or revocation processes.[13] This claim should not be confused with the simple and unexceptional notion that a registry located in a country must conform to the law of the country. Rather, nation-states via GAC are claiming that they should have the authority to determine who is *assigned* the country code top-level domain for their country. That is, they are asserting a right to share with ICANN the power to make top-level delegations. The claim is based on the flimsiest of grounds: an arbitrary semantic relationship, the notion that the ccTLD string "stands for" or "represents" the country, and that that semantic relationship is somehow exclusive and privileged. In fact, there could be many different TLDs referring to a specific country (e.g., *.us, .usa, .america,* and so on). The arbitrariness of the relationship becomes evident from countries with ccTLDs such as *.tv, .cc,* or *.md* that exploit the semantic properties of their country code to generate domain name registration business unrelated to the country itself, and that contract out the registry operation to companies in the United States or Britain.

But political factors have overridden technical and business facts in this case. The GAC has lobbied to make sure that ccTLD delegations are exclusive by warning ICANN not to delegate any new TLDs with the names of countries or that use the three-letter country codes. The director-general of the European Commission, Robert Verrue, expressed support for the idea of giving governments the opportunity to register or assign in advance the two-letter and three-letter ISO country codes in the new TLDs.[14] In its second process WIPO proposed to exclude all two-letter country codes from the second level of all new generic TLDs.

Elisabeth Porteneuve, an adviser to France's *.fr* registry, said that ccTLDs are "attached to the reputation of the country. It's important, like a brand name."[15] The government of the Republic of South Africa has taken an even stronger stance. It has objected to the common practice of registering country names in the second-level domain space, when the registrants "have no association or tie with that country." It goes on to say, "It is the position of the Republic of South Africa that second-level domain names the same as Country Names are valuable national assets belonging to the respective sovereign nations. The country names in the gTLDs, particularly the dot-com TLD, have the potential to be of substantial political and economic value, particularly to developing nations."[16]

Clearly, by adjusting the UDRP to recognize geographical indicators, WIPO opens the door to claims that *any* registration of the name of a country is "abusive." As the WIPO report recognizes, the same logic could also be used to support protecting the names of provinces, counties, cities, towns, and national parks. It also raises, but does not resolve, questions about rights to register the names of subnational groups, ethnic groups, and the names of tribes or indigenous peoples.

One can only wonder when the demand for protecting religious terms will surface. The current regime offers exclusive protection for the names of cookies, laundry detergents, and thirty-six different misspellings of "Yahoo." But it allows sacred names and profound concepts to be appropriated by anyone who wants them. Shouldn't our regulatory apparatus make sure that the registrant of *allah.org* (or its equivalent in Arabic script) is a devout Muslim, that *jesuschrist.com* is in authentic hands,[17] that the registrant of *truth.com* lives up to the name?

11.4   Free Expression vs. Controlled Vocabulary

At the heart of the controversy over global rights to names are two distinct and incompatible ideas about domain names and the function of the domain name system. One view sees domain names as a highly flexible naming framework that gives users tremendous freedom to adopt names and naming conventions, and use them to express and advertise messages and identities in a public space. In this view, the DNS protocol is just a framework for coordination. It is the users who autonomously select the names and give them meaning through their uses; the protocol merely ensures that they are unique. The naming regime this produces has no overall organization—it is self-organizing—and offers no guarantees of authenticity. The results are sometimes confusing. But the system as a whole leaves room for creativity and innovation and, more important, is highly responsive to what the broad masses of Internet users want to do with names. It was this freedom, after all, that created the global market for domain names.

The opposing view—the one that animates WIPO and other international organizations, many trademark holders, and national governments—strives to make domain names into what information scientists call a controlled vocabulary. A controlled vocabulary is a system of classification and naming wherein each term has an official and precise meaning. A controlled vocabulary presupposes an authority with the ability to make binding determinations as to what names are associated with what entities. The Library of Congress index or scientific taxonomies for classifying plants or chemical elements are examples of controlled vocabularies. As the examples suggest, controlled vocabularies can be extremely useful for a specific purpose. They are also rigid and constraining, and cannot be used successfully for anything other than the purpose for which they were designed.

Which approach to domain names—coordinated free expression or controlled vocabulary—is better suited to the Internet? I argue in the following sections that the DNS protocol answers this question for us. The DNS *is* a system of coordinated free expression; it cannot be made into a controlled vocabulary without drastically altering its functions.

11.4.1 Seven Deadly Assumptions

The effort to turn domain names into a controlled vocabulary is founded on a series of assumptions about how domain names are used, what they signify, and how they are interpreted by ordinary Internet users. Those assumptions are given in the following list. (The supporting commentary and footnotes refer to legal decisions and statements that show that these assumptions are widely held and commonly asserted.)

1. *The DNS is a directory.* This assumption posits that the purpose of DNS is to guide users to specific kinds of content, Web sites, or services. As a corollary, end users search for what they seek on the Internet primarily by consulting lists of domain names or by guessing domain names.

2. *Authenticity.* Domain names are (or should be) "authentic." To possess a domain name is to posses an official, authorized relationship to the named person, place, organization, or thing. A stronger form of this assumption holds that for any given name, it is possible to know which applicant has the most valid claim to it.

3. *Hierarchy doesn't matter.* Domain names are not really hierarchical. It does not matter whether a character string is registered under *.com, .to, .net, .org, .blat, .xxx,* or anything else. A name must be protected in *all* top-level domains; otherwise it has no meaningful protection at all.

4. *Nonuniqueness.* Domain names need not be unique. If a registered name looks something like a name that someone has rights to, including misspellings or words in combination with a trademark, then it ought to be held by the rights holder, or at the very least, not held by someone else.

5. *Domain names are trademarks.* Every domain name points to an e-commerce Web site, an offering of goods or services. Domain names are not used to express ideas or refer to things.

6. *Domain names strongly influence content interpretation.* Internet users' interpretation of what they encounter on the Internet and the Web is closely linked to the semantics of the domain name. Thus, if a domain name address leads users to information or content different from what they expected to find, they will be hopelessly confused. As a corollary, in adjudicating domain name disputes the actual content of a Web site is not as important as an analysis of the text of the domain name itself and whether it can be construed, in isolation, as somehow impinging on the scope of a mark.

7. *Global visibility.* The mere registration of a domain name guarantees the registrant a substantial public audience. The name or site does not have to be advertised or promoted to have a significant impact; indeed, it does not even have to be visible on the Internet or associated with an operational Web site or email account. Millions of users will spontaneously type the name into their browsers, without any prompting or advertising.

All the preceding assumptions are problematical. Many are simply false. Some are half-truths, while others stand in direct contradiction to how domain names function technically. Taken together as a package, they constitute an attempt to reconstruct domain names into a controlled vocabulary.

Consider, first, assumptions 1, 2, and 6: that the DNS is a directory, and the purpose of the directory is to steer users to officially sanctioned information correlated with the name. This set of assumptions is the most fundamental one behind the push to make DNS into a controlled vocabulary.

It is embedded in many court and UDRP decisions. The second WIPO report boldly states, "The placing on the domain name register of a distinctive name, such as *gretagarbo.com,* makes a representation to persons who consult the register that the registrant actually is, or is associated with, the person whose name is registered and thus is entitled to use the goodwill in the name" (WIPO 2001, para. 139).

This view of domain names is fundamentally inaccurate. The WIPO statement, for example, contradicts what we have already established about users' adoption of identities on the Net. The many AOL users who chose some variant of the name Greta Garbo are making a statement about *themselves*—their personality, likes, and dislikes—not representations to others that they *are* Garbo. Nor is it likely that many users who see the name interpret it as such, given the context.

Moreover, the theory that the DNS is an authoritative directory reveals a basic ignorance of how the protocol actually functions. People do not find things on the Internet by "consult[ing] the register of domain names." The domain name "register" consists of resource records scattered around half a million name servers in different parts of the planet. To compile and consult that list, one must pull out zone files using complicated software, and the resulting list would consist of nearly 35 *million* second-level domain names; the *.com* zone file alone would contain over 23 million. That simply is not how ordinary users find things on the Internet. The notion that domain names are used for "searching" confuses searching techniques with locators, two completely different functions.

When users type in a domain name to locate a site, it is usually because they already know the domain name and the nature of the site they are headed to. That is, they are using the domain name simply as a lookup tool. Although some users try to find sites by guessing an organization's domain name, this is done as a last resort after other methods have failed. The vast majority of users rely on search engines and portals. They locate content through hyperlinks that they receive from email or see on other sites. They bookmark links in their "favorites" file. Or they copy down or remember specific names that they have seen advertised.

As for assumption 6, the words "Greta Garbo" typed into the popular Google search engine bring over 38,400 hits. Interestingly, *none* of the top ten listings returned by Google have domain names that include the labels "gretagarbo," "garbo," or "greta." The URL that arrives at the top of the heap is <http://www.mdle.com/ClassicFilms/FeaturedStar/star53.htm>, a tribute to Garbo put up by a fan club for silent movies.[18] Similarly, on Yahoo! and HotBot, the most highly ranked content on Garbo is under domain names like *netcomuk.co.uk, home.hiwaay.net*, or *bombshells.com*. In the majority of cases, there is no correlation between the content of a Web site and the semantics of the domain name. At *gretagarbo.com*, on the other hand, ownership appears to rest in the hands of Garbo's heirs or licensees. At that site one finds a rather slow and poorly organized site selling jewelry. Although the connection to Garbo is "authentic," is it valid to assume that anyone using "Greta Garbo" as a keyword for searching, is looking for that particular line of jewelry?

Users who employ "Greta Garbo" as a keyword may be interested in communicating with other people who are fans of Garbo. They may want to buy a book about her, find a picture of her, or find out which retail stores sell copies of her movies. For all we know, a user may be trying to find out whether MTV has produced an episode of Celebrity Death Match (a cartoon using animated clay figures) that pits Garbo against Madonna. Given what we know about the Internet and the incredible variety of content and materials available there, it is presumptuous to claim that we *know* what people who type names into their browsers are looking for. There are at least as many different objectives for searches as there are searchers.

Consider, next, assumption 3 on the list. It is a fact that DNS names are hierarchical. Nevertheless, the assumption that the semantics of the top level do not matter is becoming an increasingly common part of the jurisprudence of domain name law and the UDRP. If one has a legal right to a name in one TLD, the theory goes, that right should extend across multiple TLDs, because users cannot be expected to differentiate among different top-level domains.

WIPO used this argument to support its policy of name exclusions for international organizations. A special top-level domain, *.int*, is reserved for legitimate international treaty organizations. WIPO recognized that Internet users "can have reasonable confidence and trust as to the genuine identity of the organizations registered in *.int*, and of the validity of the information provided by those organizations" (WIPO 2001, para. 102). The WIPO report also argued, however, that the mere existence of valid registrations in the *.int* domain is not sufficient because abusive registrations can still take place in other top-level domains. In essence, WIPO is arguing that the top level of a domain name doesn't matter. The same assumption shows up frequently in UDRP cases and domain name litigation. In one well-known British case, a judge took away the *bt.org* domain name from speculators and awarded it to British Telecom even though British Telecom already had the *bt.com* domain and the acronym BT could be used by many different legitimate organizations.

The assault on hierarchy is now being pushed into the second and third levels. The second WIPO report, for example, argued for excluding country codes from the second level on all new top-level domains, because users are unable to distinguish between domain names like *company.uk.com* and *company.co.uk*. And some trademark hawks are beginning to seek to assert rights in third-level delegations.

Consider, next, assumption 4. Uniqueness is the most significant requirement of domain name assignment under the standard protocol. But to DNS, "unique" means any difference in a character string that can be recognized by a machine. Uniqueness to a machine is not the same as differentiation by a human being. People might use any one of several different names to denote an organization, idea, or product, and they may not be able to distinguish between different spellings of the same word. In response to this problem, many brand holders have attempted to register every possible permutation of their names, multiple misspellings, as well as domain names that include the trademarked term along with generic terms, such as *fordcars.com, fordmotors.com, ford-source,* and so on. Both UDRP panelists and courts have often upheld their right to reclaim such domains.

Here again, however, the desires of trademark owners are fundamentally at odds with the nature of DNS. The protocol allows any unique character string to be registered. The giant telephone company Verizon, formed via a merger of GTE and Bell Atlantic, learned the futility of resisting DNS's reliance on uniqueness. Just before announcing its merger and new name, Verizon purchased close to 500 domain names, including not only *verizon.com* and *verizonlongdistance.com*, but also *verizon-*

sucks.com, and several misspellings of the brand. Later, the publishers of the hacker magazine 2600 tried to register *verizonsucks.com* to operate a site for consumer venting. Upon discovering that the name was not available they registered *verizonreallysucks.com.* The humorless telephone company sent them a cease-and-desist letter accusing them of trademark violation. Undeterred, the 2600 group went on to register *VerizonShould SpendMoreTimeFixingItsNetworkAndLessMoneyOnLawyers.com.*

The point of this story is that it is impossible for a company to prevent someone from incorporating its name into a domain name in some way. Registering a few common misspellings (or using the UDRP to recover them if they have been registered by others in bad faith) makes some sense. But the DNS supports too many variations to make it possible to preempt criticism or capture all possible references to a company or product. Any attempt to protect massive "clouds" of names will be pointless unless draconian and undesirable restrictions are placed on the use of DNS.

All this assumes, of course, that the possession of these domain names is important and valuable. Here, too, the case for a controlled vocabulary is based on highly questionable premises. As noted, the idea that the majority of Internet users find their way around the Internet by typing hundreds of different variations of domain names into their browses flies in the face of everything we know about user searching behavior. Contrary to assumption 7, the registration of a domain name is no guarantee that a significant number of users will be attracted. Popular Web sites that make money require expensive promotion, high-quality content, lots of links from other sites, and good word of mouth in the press and among users. What evidence we have suggests that simple, generic terms in the *.com* space do generate traffic, but there is also ample evidence that that type of random traffic by itself cannot sustain an online business.[19]

Controlled vocabulary advocates also assume that users who type in the domain name of a company and find something they did not expect—say, a protest site rather than the company—will not be smart enough to look elsewhere. They will become completely diverted and lost to the company forever. This notion is implausible on its face. It is like saying that someone who has incorrectly dialed a telephone number will not correct the error and redial.

11.5   DNS vs. WIPO

To conclude, common pool conditions in the domain name space upset existing institutional methods of controlling how and by whom names can be used. This was true not just of trademark owners but also of celebrities, political candidates, governments, and various organizations (mostly in Europe) supporting controlled appellations of origin. What started as a conservative reaction aimed at safeguarding older systems of control over names established by territorial institutions, however, has mutated into a radical program to create a new, global regime for the protection of new property rights in names. WIPO, and to a lesser extent ICANN, believes that control of the root of the domain name system has created a historic opportunity to define and implement such a regime. Their objective is to curtail the free adoption of names and transform domain names into a controlled vocabulary that gives a handful of privileged players—major trademark holders, international organizations, governments—sweeping rights over Internet identifiers.

This much is clear: the DNS protocol as it was traditionally implemented encourages and supports free expression. The protocol was designed merely to *coordinate* the assignment and resolution of multifarious name adoptions on the Internet. It was not structured to regulate their semantics or to provide users with a directory. The whole point of the protocol was to allow users to create their own semantics while ensuring that the names remained unique. DNS's hierarchical delegation of authority allows the same label to show up in thousands if not millions of different places, under different top-level domains or second-level domains or third-level domains or even or the right-hand side of a URL. Because responsibility is distributed down the levels of the hierarchy, there is room for vast amounts of variation in the policies and practices used to create naming conventions and assign names. Moreover, since the DNS name space is virtually inexhaustible, users have an extraordinary amount of flexibility to adopt whatever label they like. As long as it is unique it is available. DNS doesn't care whether the label is "confusingly similar" to a trademark or whether the person who adopted it has any authoritative connection to the referent. And the costs of entering a registration and propagating it throughout the Internet's intricate web of name servers are so low that anyone who can afford a PC and Internet access can probably afford to have their own domain name(s) as well.

To turn domain names into a controlled vocabulary is like pushing a heavy rock uphill. One must constantly work against nature. One must supplement the mechanical uniqueness enforced by DNS with exclusions, rules, and dispute resolution procedures to create what Jon Postel called a kind of "higher-order uniqueness"; one must undermine or abolish its hierarchical structure. In a fundamental sense, the ICANN-WIPO regime is at war with the DNS protocol itself.

12

Property Rights and Institutional Change: Some Musings on Theory

Douglass C. North (1990, 84) identifies only two sources of institutional change: changes in relative prices and changes in tastes. To that we can add a third: the creation of new resources in technical systems. When North attempts to reduce technological change to "changes in relative prices," he assumes that technology only enables us to do the same things more cheaply, e.g., to make transportation faster, weapons more deadly, information less expensive. That perspective overlooks technology's ability to create new collective action problems by throwing into the economy new resource spaces that must be allocated, regulated, and traded.

The preceding narrative about the Internet root makes it clear that resource creation is a significant and disruptive source of institutional change. The close historical parallel with radio spectrum management bolsters the significance of the argument.

12.1 Artificial Scarcity: "Positive Feedback" and Path Dependence

The most striking feature of the ICANN regime is its perpetuation of scarcity at the top level of the name space. According to Paul Vixie, the keeper of the BIND software that implements DNS on almost all the world's name servers, millions of new top-level domains are technically feasible. The root zone is just a zone file, after all, and if the DNS protocol can support the *.com, .net, .uk,* or *.de* zones with millions of registrations in them, there is no reason to believe that it could not also support a root zone with millions of unique names. Beneath each top-level domain, of course, there can be tens of millions of second-level names, and below that, millions more third-level names (think of the number of members and user names under *aol.com*). The name space created by the DNS protocol is practically inexhaustible.

There is, however, a tremendous disjunction between the capabilities of the technical system and the behavior of the new institution. The new regime has been able to authorize only seven new top-level names over the better part of a four-year period. The abundance of the technology is stringently limited by rules and procedures imposed by a central authority. This has occurred despite numerous demonstrations of consumer demand for new names at the top level and the existence of many businesses eager to supply them.

What accounts for the artificial scarcity? It is the product of a vicious cycle that, while lamentable from a public policy perspective, neatly corroborates some of the recent, more pessimistic theories about institutions and institutional change. North's (1990) foray into the development of a new theory of institutional change was motivated largely by an attempt to explain how societies could settle upon and retain institutional forms that were inefficient and even destructive. To solve that riddle, North called attention to the "symbiotic relationship" that exists between institutions— the rules constraining human action—and the organizations and human perceptions that evolve as a result of the incentives provided by the rules. He suggested that a society can get locked into a dysfunctional institutional framework when the rules reward people and organizations for acting in ways that perpetuate its inefficiencies.[1] This mutual reinforcement or "positive feedback" can explain why "natural selection" and competition don't eliminate inefficient institutions.

In the case of domain names, a Northian vicious cycle is clearly identifiable. We can spell out the stages as follows:

1. As the Internet was commercialized, the availability of only one global commercial top-level domain gave second-level domain names under *.com* a special value as an economic resource.

2. With common pool conditions in force, that special value stimulated hundreds of thousands of speculative, defensive, and abusive registrations.

3. The speculative and abusive registrations in turn provoked those with preexisting rights in names (mostly, but not exclusively, trademark holders)

to lobby politically against further expansion of the name space. Other vested interests, such as incumbent registries and speculators with large holdings in the *.com* space, also benefited from closing off new entry.

4. Failure to expand the name space further enhanced the value and power of names in *.com*. This fueled more speculation, more hardening of the attitudes of trademark owners, more politicization of the DNS, and continued the cycle.

Although the restrictive attitude of the trademark holders was in many ways irrational, in that it enhanced the speculative value of names, it is probably unrealistic to expect a brand manager or trademark lawyer to understand the long-term benefit of standing by idly while their names are left unprotected in thousands of new spaces. (Indeed, it is precisely these kinds of "mental constructs" that North tries to invoke in his theory of institutional change.)

Thus it should come as no surprise that almost all domain name disputes involve *.com* names. We need to be clear about what exactly is being disputed in these cases. Domain name disputes are rarely about actual trademark infringement as that term is normally understood in the law.[2] They are not really about the public use as an Internet address of words or marks similar to a trademark per se, because, as noted in chapter 11, trademarked character strings can appear anywhere in a Web site's URL: at the third or fourth level, after the slash, in other top-level domains, and on the Web site itself. In reality, the vast majority of domain name disputes are motivated by conflict over the right to get a favorable position in the second-level of the *.com* space. Conflict occurs because the second level of *.com* is reputedly the one most likely to be found, guessed, typed in, or remembered by users. What is disputed, therefore, is the ability of a name to attract traffic and attention. In that regard, not all domains are created equal: *.com* is the premium real estate. The problem of its dominance is exacerbated by high switching costs. Any business or organization that establishes an identity and a presence under *.com* is not going to want to change it.

The obvious solution to this is (or was) to blow away *.com*'s special status by authorizing thousands of new names in the top-level space and encouraging users to distribute their registrations over a much broader array of TLDs. Most of the economic basis for name speculation and cyber-squatting would be instantly eliminated by such a policy. It would also address the market dominance of Verisign/Network Solutions and the dangerous centralization of control over the Internet in a single entity's hands. Competing registries would offer customers a far more favorable set of contractual conditions, at least as long as the registration market continued to grow (FTC 1998).

That solution was apparent—and eminently possible—in 1996, when Jon Postel proposed to create 300 new TLDs. There were (and still are) hundreds of entrepreneurs willing to operate new registries, and thousands of ideas for new TLD strings. Yet the confusion and contested authority surrounding the root in 1996 prevented action and gave way to a period of intense politicization that allowed the vicious cycle to kick in. The cycle prevented the addition of *any* new open TLD for nearly seven years after the problems began.

The failure of draft-postel was a critical branching point in the evolution of Internet governance. When the new institutional regime finally was able to act, political consensus limited it to policies that perpetuated the cycle instead of eliminating it. The cycle was perpetuated in the following ways:

5. The value and dominance of *.com* was enhanced by opening it up to multiple, competing registrars. The lower price and more active marketing of *.com* names increased speculation.

6. The Internet governance process could not get large numbers of new TLDs past the trademark interests and other groups with a vested interest in a restricted name space; on the other hand, it could not avoid creating *some* new TLDs because of the demands of potential entrants. So it opened up a small number of new TLDs, two of which (*.biz* and *.info*) are put forward as alternatives or substitutes for *.com*.

7. With that restrictive policy in place, trademark holders will rush to register their existing *.com* names in the new generic TLDs to preempt any competition with their *.com* holdings. The mad desire to protect existing names also magnifies the opportunity for speculation.

In other words, a restricted name space reinforces the land rush mentality and potential for abuse that created the conflicts to begin with. And by reinforcing the problems, it rationalizes the continued existence of a restrictive regime that regulates the conflicts via collective action.[3] If there is artificial scarcity, there will be a land rush; if there is a land rush, there will be speculators, disputes, and preemptive registrations; those problems in turn create a political demand for rules and protections governing entry into the name space: "sunrise" policies, exclusions, gradual and slow expansion, and so on. Stability is the new regime's leitmotif, and in practice, stability means *all change is guilty until proven innocent.*

This is not a deliberate result. No one wanted it to happen this way. That is precisely what makes it interesting from the standpoint of institutional economics. A form of "positive feedback" led to the formation and entrenchment of an inefficient regime, just as North described. It is the product of social processes locked into a dysfunctional pattern by a kind of recursive political logic that no one knows how to break out of.

12.2 Who Owns the Name Space?

The analysis in this book relies heavily on concepts of property rights. But readers should not confuse recognition and enforcement of property claims with the creation of an efficient marketplace, or with market-oriented policies. Both Libecap (1989) and North (1990) emphasize the sensitivity of institutional change to political bargains affecting the distribution of wealth. The institutionalization process can produce highly restricted, inefficient property regimes as well as open, unregulated, or efficient ones. The argument here is that when resources are contested, some form of propertization or assertion of exclusive authority is inevitable. The only issue is what type of property regime emerges, and how the rights are distributed.

Clearly, the objective of the ICANN regime was not to facilitate a free market in DNS. It was, rather, part of a concerted effort to *regulate* and *limit* the market for domain names, and to *prevent* the creation of private property rights in certain areas, notably top-level domain names.

In the new Internet governance regime, private and intergovernmental conflict over the ownership of the root was resolved through the establishment of a central authority that, in effect, owns the entire name space and grants limited privileges of use to suppliers and consumers. Instead of the classical DNS model of hierarchical delegation, wherein the delegator yields control over what happens lower down in the hierarchy to the delegatee, the new regime gives the root administrator broad authority that extends beyond top-level delegations and includes second-level delegations (through UDRP, exclusions, and shared registry requirements, among other policies) and possibly even third-level delegations.[4]

Of course, these ownership rights are claimed on behalf of a mythical "Internet community." The ICANN regime borders on central planning in its policy approach to name and number resources. The model closely follows the pattern set by the nationalization of radio frequencies decades ago, except that in this case the central authority is global rather than national. The resource is "owned" by a quasi-governmental agency and the private sector receives licenses both limited in duration and restricted in use.

12.2.1 Property Rights in Top-Level Domains

The topic of property rights in TLDs needs to be taken up in more detail. In order to be able to recognize the claims and enforce the rights sought by members of the dominant coalition in the second level of the domain name hierarchy, ICANN has had to militantly oppose the establishment of any property rights in the top level of the hierarchy. This paradoxical result illustrates once again how path-dependent and sensitive to political strength institutional regimes are.

The question whether registry operators can establish a property right in their TLD string has arisen in a variety of contexts. One was Network Solutions' conflict with the U.S. Department of Commerce over the renewal of the InterNIC registry contract in 1998. Network Solutions initially asserted intellectual property rights over the TLD and its contents and indicated that it wanted to "brand" .*com*.[5] Another was the conflict between Image Online Design's claim to the .*web* top-level domain and the attempt by the Generic Top-Level Domain Memorandum of Understanding (gTLD-MoU) group to appropriate the .*web* string as one of its seven proposed new TLDs in 1997. After a long legal battle, a U.S. District Court judge summarily dismissed the .*web* proprietor's claim that it had common-law trademark rights in the .*web* top-level domain.[6]

Additionally, the ICANN Governmental Advisory Committee (GAC) has made one of its core principles the notion that Internet domain names are a "public resource" and that "no private intellectual or other property rights inhere in the TLD itself nor accrue to the delegated manager of the TLD as a result of such delegation."[7] (However, it should be noted that GAC members, in seeking authority over delegation of "their" country code, are actually claiming a kind of property right over a TLD.)

In September 1999 the U.S. Patent and Trademark Office issued an examination guide stating that a domain name, when used as a registry under which lower-level domain names are registered, does not function as a source identifier subject to service mark rights but is merely an informational description of the names being registered.[8] The doctrine that no property rights can inhere in top-level domains has made its way into McCarthy's authoritative *Trademarks and Unfair Competition* law book.[9]

The legal reasoning behind the doctrine is contradictory and insupportable. The legal profession has been led astray by its lack of knowledge of the workings of the domain name system. The doctrine elevates an accident of DNS's implementation into a permanent feature and draws false legal conclusions accordingly. Without a better understanding of the technical system, it is difficult to project alternative scenarios that might alter the way the principles are applied.

The reason trademark conflicts only take place over second-level names, not top-level names, is simply that the original implementation of DNS provided a fixed and limited number of top-level domains that were nothing but highly generic categories (*.com, .net, .org, .edu, .mil*). Users were unable to freely register new top-level domains (except in alternative roots). But there is nothing permanent about the original top-level domains. If the top level is opened up to first-come/first-served registration like the second level, then the same kinds of conflicts over property rights will occur. There is no doubt that open appropriation could have occurred at the top level; as noted in chapter 6, alternative root operators started the process in 1996, and the *.web* court case is one of their legacies. It seems probable that any registry operator who tried to occupy the *.aol, .att, or .mci* top-level domains would receive letters asserting intellectual property rights in TLDs rather quickly. The lawyers sending the letters would not be amused by citations to McCarthy holding that "only the second-level domain points to source." The issue is relevant because ICANN is adding new top-level domains to the root, and alternative roots still exist; indeed, they are thriving in the wake of the delay and artificial scarcity fostered by the ICANN regime.

The judge in the Image Online case displayed ignorance of the domain name industry and the workings of the DNS protocol. His comments reveal that he did not understand the economic relationship between a registry and a registrar. The opinion states that because many different registrars can register names in a shared top-level domain, "a gTLD is useless for the purpose of indicating source of registry." This is quite an interesting assertion. It is like saying that the availability of SONY products in many different retail stores means that the trademark SONY cannot indicate the source of a manufactured good. Registrars, like retailers, are merely intermediaries who deliver a registry's service to the public.[10]

If one actually understands the domain name registration industry, and applies traditional trademark principles to it, it is difficult to understand why registry services cannot be "branded" like any other service, and why the TLD string cannot be used as its brand, either directly or through the acquisition of secondary meaning. A top-level domain name must be a unique character string. As a result, top-level domains are by their very nature strong indicators of the source of the registry service. Before any company can operate a top-level registry, a top-level domain name must have been exclusively assigned to it. Thus, top-level domain name assignments are directly linked to a responsible party; they tell you who is assigning second-level names in that domain and who is publishing authoritative information about those assignments to other name servers on the Internet. The distinction between *.com* and *.web,* for example, indicates whether the registry is operated by Network Solutions, Inc. or Image Online Design. That distinction is just as significant as whether one's Internet service provider is Earthlink or AT&T. If two different registries adopt the same TLD string, then customers of either registry are likely to suffer from confusion. Why couldn't traditional trademark principles, which give weight to first use in commerce, be applied?

The real reason property rights in TLDs are being avoided is political, not legal. If registry operators had property rights in TLDs, top-level domain name owners would have stronger legal rights vis-à-vis the root authority. Governments could, of course, still regulate registry operators, but to do so they would have to pass legislation and follow formal regulatory processes.

12.2.2 Transaction Costs and the Uniform Dispute Resolution Policy

Despite serious procedural flaws, the Uniform Dispute Resolution Policy (UDRP) could be seen as one aspect of the institutional innovation that represents an advance in efficiency. The arbitration procedure greatly reduces the transaction costs of resolving disputes over domain names. With a single, global "jurisdiction" and lightweight, online procedures that are much less expensive than court litigation, UDRP allows thousands of cases to be resolved annually. Usually, the transaction cost reduction works in favor of the trademark holders who want to challenge a registration. But the lower costs can be very significant for domain name registrants as well, because most of them cannot afford to spend tens of thousands of dollars to defend a name. Respondents who contest a domain name challenge using a three-person panel have a reasonable chance of success. Although decisions are often inconsistent, via UDRP a global "common law" on what constitutes abusive and defensible domain name registrations is evolving (Badgley 2001).

The most disturbing thing about the UDRP is its uniformity. Registries could adopt different types of dispute resolution procedures (indeed, they already do in the country code TLDs), giving end users more choice and providing a check on abuse by allowing users to vote with their feet. "Rogue" registries that encouraged cybersquatting would almost certainly face costly legal challenges from trademark owners. So why not allow registries to offer different rule sets? This would accommodate the natural diversity that prevails in the real world, and reduce the threat, noted in chapter 11, of an aggressively centralist regime being imposed on the Internet by an international organization like WIPO.

13

The Taming of the Net

Governments of the Industrial World, you weary giants of flesh and steel, I come from Cyberspace, the new home of Mind. On behalf of the future, I ask you of the past to leave us alone. You are not welcome among us. You have no sovereignty where we gather. . . . I declare the global social space we are building to be naturally independent of the tyrannies you seek to impose on us.
—John Perry Barlow, 1996

Sometime during the early 1990s, the Internet acquired its status as a reference point for public discourse about utopia. Cyberspace was a new frontier that seemed to the highly educated and articulate people who first colonized it like a *tabula rasa* onto which they could project their own dreams and theories about how society should function. John Perry Barlow's "Declaration of the Independence of Cyberspace," was a bold expression of this attitude, written, appropriately enough, by the former lyricist for the Grateful Dead.

Libertarians looked at the Internet and rejoiced, because they saw in it a world without the state, an environment without taxation, censorship, or regulation. The Internet was the epitome of Jeffersonian decentralization. Computer technologists rejoiced because the Internet was free of formality and politics; it was the antithesis of the regulated and monopolistic telecommunication regime. Standards were made in informal, open working groups; decisions were based on consensus; the process of standards-setting was governed by a hierarchy of respected elders who had achieved their position through technical wizardry. Many on the democratic left were happy too, seeing in the Internet an arena of open communication, communitarianism, and equality. The Internet was free of the impediments of property rights, advertisements, and commerce. It was simultaneously a democratic agora, a gigantic free library, and a vigorous new space for public interaction.

Despite their diverse viewpoints, all of these groups saw the Internet as a kind of Garden of Eden exempt from the corruption of worldly institutions. Even a fairly conservative U.S. Supreme Court showed a special solicitude for the new medium in its decision unanimously striking down the Communications Decency Act in 1997. The attempt by the U.S. Congress to censor the Net served as the galvanizing force for cyberspace utopians of all ideological stripes in their confrontation with established institutions and norms.

Now, of course, the world is starting to close in on cyberspace. Formal organization, property rights and commerce, regulation and geopolitics are reasserting themselves systematically. Of course, the institutionalization of the Internet is taking place on a variety of fronts. Debates over taxation of e-commerce, regulation of content, and technical standardization are underway in a variety of national and international forums. But the administration of the Internet's name and address root was the first to produce a global solution.

Institutions affect both economic efficiency and equity. They provide the channels through which the fluid of everyday activity takes the path of least resistance. Institutional regimes, particularly at the international level, are not based on ideas or efficiency but on political bargains over the distribution of wealth. Institutional structures are not necessarily self-correcting; they are costly to establish and, once established, very costly to change. Thus, the small steps of the historical process recounted here matter greatly; cumulatively, they have led down a path that will take years to alter. The ICANN–WIPO–Commerce Department regime may yet prove to be the most significant institutional innovation produced by the Internet's rise.

Barlow's declaration hasn't aged well. His belief in the special status of cyberspace, however, was not entirely naive. The internetworking of computers did in fact break free of established institutional constraints. The whiff of possibility and autonomy was not an illusion. Many of the Internet's benefits and innovations occurred precisely because it had slipped out of the grasp of the old rules and organizations.

There is a life cycle in the evolution of technical systems. Systems that create new resources and new arenas of economic and social activity can escape institutional regimes and create moments of disequilibrating freedom and social innovation. But eventually a new equilibrium is established. The absolute freedom of a global common pool becomes too costly to maintain. It requires us to solve problems *de novo* constantly. It is cheaper to classify problems into a few distinct types and establish regular norms and procedures for handling them. The development of new forms of social organization is curbed in order to solve the problems posed by the initial spurt of innovative growth.

Despite its stated rationale, the formation of ICANN utterly failed to preserve the "self-governing" or "self-regulatory" character of the Internet. On the contrary, it is part of the process by which established economic players and arrangements assimilate internetworking. Both the Internet and the old order are changed in the process, of course—the influence is not entirely one way. What is surprising about the institutionalization of the Internet's name and address spaces, however, is the stark contrast between the new regime and the old spirit of the Internet. ICANN's practices and policies are rooted in some of the most conservative and constraining aspects of the old order: the International Telecommunication Union and its notion that the name and address spaces are "public resources" subject to centralized regulation; concepts of "public trusteeship" taken from broadcast and utility regulation; deference to copyright and trademark interests, long known for their hostility to new media; the engineer's propensity to favor tightly controlled, "rational" central planning over messy commercial, competitive, and heterogeneous systems. On the whole, it is a conservative, corporatist regime founded on artificial scarcity and regulatory control. Anyone interested in retaining or reinvigorating the revolutionary character of the Internet will be obliged to find ways to bypass it.

More likely, institutionalization under ICANN means that the Internet's role as a site of radical business and technology innovation, and its status as a revolutionary force that disrupts existing social and regulatory regimes, is coming to an end. Its status as an entropic source of change in the social and political order is winding down. That means that its capacity for continued technical evolution is being restricted as well. There are simply too many vested interests now, and too many points of control for them to exert leverage over the industry.

But no doubt there are other technologies and systems hatching somewhere, ready to take the world by surprise.

Selected Acronyms

ACLU	American Civil Liberties Union
ACPA	Anticybersquatting Consumer Protection Act
ACM	Association for Computing Machinery
AIM	European Brands Association
AP-NIC	Asia-Pacific—Network Information Center
ARIN	American Registry for Internet Numbers
ARPA	Advanced Projects Research Administration (U.S. Defense Department)
ATIS	Association for Telecommunications Industry Solutions
BBN	Bolt, Beranek and Newman
BIND	Berkeley Internet Name Domain
BWG	Boston Working Group
ccTLD	country code top-level domain
CIDR	classless interdomain routing
CIX	Commercial Internet eXchange
CLNP	Connectionless Network Protocol
CNRI	Corporation for National Research Initiatives
CORE	Council of Registrars
CPSR	Computer Professionals for Social Responsibility
DARPA	*See* ARPA
DDN	Defense Data Network
DDN-NIC	Defense Data Network—Network Information Center

DNRC	Domain Name Rights Coalition
DNS	domain name system
DNSO	Domain Name Supporting Organization
EC	European Commission
eDNS	Enhanced Domain Name Service
EFF	Electronic Frontier Foundation
ETSI	European Telecommunications Standards Institute
FCC	Federal Communications Commission
FICPI	Fédération Internationale des Conseils en Propriété Industrielle
FNC	Federal Networking Council
FRICC	Federal Research Internet Coordinating Committee
ftp	file transfer protocol
GAC	Governmental Advisory Committee (ICANN)
GIP	Global Internet Project
gTLD	generic top-level domain
gTLD-MoU	Generic Top-Level Domain Memorandum of Understanding
http	hypertext transfer protocol
IAB	Internet Activities Board; Internet Architecture Board
IAHC	International Ad Hoc Committee
IANA	Internet Assigned Numbers Authority
ICANN	Internet Corporation for Assigned Names and Numbers
IEEE	Institute of Electrical and Electronics Engineers
IESG	Internet Engineering Steering Group
IETF	Internet Engineering Task Force
IFWP	International Forum on the White Paper
IGO	international intergovernmental organization
INN	International Nonproprietary Name
INTA	International Trademark Association
IP	Internet Protocol
IPng	Internet Protocol next generation

IPTO	Information Processing Techniques Office (ARPA)
IR	Internet address registry
IRTF	Internet Research Task Force
ISI	Information Sciences Institute (USC)
ISO	International Standardization Organization
ISOC	Internet Society
ISP	Internet service provider
ITAA	Information Technology Association of America
ITAG	IANA Transition Advisory Group
ITU	International Telecommunication Union
JDRP	Jones, Day, Reavis & Pogue (law firm)
LAN	local area network
LINX	London Internet Exchange
MIT	Massachusetts Institute of Technology
MPAA	Motion Picture Association of America
NAP	network access point
NASA	National Aeronautics and Space Administration
NAT	network address translator
NIC	Network Information Center
NREN NIS	National Research and Education Network, Network Information Services
NSF	National Science Foundation
NSI	Network Solutions, Inc.
NTIA	National Telecommunications and Information Administration (U.S. Commerce Department)
OECD	Organization for Economic Cooperation & Development
ORSC	Open Root Server Confederation
OSI	Open Systems Interconnection
POC	Policy Oversight Committee (gTLD-MoU)
POISED	Process for Organization of Internet Standards working group
RFC	Request for Comments

RIPE   Réseaux IP Européens
RIPE-NCC   Réseaux IP Européens—Network Coordination Center
SAIC   Science Applications International Corporation
SITA   Société Internationale Télécommunications Aéronautiques
SLD   second-level domain
SO   Supporting Organization of ICANN
SRI   Stanford Research Institute
SRS   shared registration system
TCP   Transport Control Protocol
TLD   top-level domain
UCLA   University of California at Los Angeles
UDRP   Uniform Dispute Resolution Policy
UNIX   a computer operating system
URL   Uniform Resource Locator
USC   University of Southern California
W3C   World Wide Web Consortium
WIPO   World Intellectual Property Organization
WITSA   World Information Technology and Services Alliance
WWW   World Wide Web

Notes

Chapter 1: Introduction: The Problem of the Root

Many of the documenting sources are available on Internet sites. The addresses provided are accurate at time of publication of this book, but electronic addresses may change. If readers cannot reach them as cited, they should search further.

1. The IFWP call for participation, June 1998. Some materials from the original IFWP has been archived by Ellen Rony at <http://www.domainhandbook.com/ifwp.html>.

2. Ira Magaziner, introductory comments at the first IFWP meeting, July 1, 1998.

3. Mo Krochmal, "Magaziner, Lessig Spar over Domain Name Plan" *Techweb News,* June 11, 1998.

4. See Christopher Hill (1958) for an account of the Long Parliament and its role in English history.

5. TCP stands for Transport Control Protocol; IP stands for Internet Protocol. Both work together to guide the movement of packets across networks.

6. Internet purists may object to this label. Usually, *root* refers only to the un-named space at the top of the domain name hierarchy and does not include the IP address space. I have chosen to use *root* as a generic term that applies to both, for three reasons. First, even though the IP address and domain name spaces are distinct entities technically, there are structural similarities that are important institutionally and economically. IP address blocks are delegated in a hierarchical fashion just as domain names are, and the question of who controls the initial delegation—the top of the hierarchy—poses many of the same institutional issues in either case. Second, domain name root management and IP address management are technically interrelated in important ways (such as in the *in-addr.arpa* domain). Although this does not necessarily mean that responsibility for both should be combined in the same organization, historically they have been, and ICANN continues this practice. Indeed, the White Paper explicitly rejected appeals from some members of the technical community to place the two functions in separate organizations (NTIA 1998b, 31744). So in that respect it makes sense to speak of a generalized root that embraces both. Third, if the two previous points are valid, for reasons of

readability and style it make sense to use a single word to refer to both in many instances. When the term is used in that fashion, it means *the centrally coordinated naming and addressing functions required to ensure universal connectivity on the Internet.* When there is cause to discuss the root of the domain name system specifically, I refer to the "DNS root" or the "name space." When there is a need to refer exclusively to IP numbering, I refer to "IP address space" or "IP number allocation."

7. Esther Dyson, letter to Ralph Nader and Jamie Love, June 15, 1999.

Chapter 2: The Basic Political Economy of Identifiers

1. The uniqueness requirement is not so stringent in nonautomated networks. There may still be postal arrangements in various locales where a workable address would be "give this to Bob Smith." There may be many different Bob Smiths in the world, but a human delivery agent who is sensitive to context may still be able to deliver the message effectively.

2. The telephone system used to know the difference between an area code and any other part of the number, because area codes took the form NZN, where N is any number from 2 to 9, and Z is either 1 or 0. That syntax restricted the number of available area codes. Now area codes take the form NXX, and one must dial 1 to get into the toll network.

3. The new codes are 888, 877, 866, and 855.

4. FCC CC Docket No. 95-155 Toll Free Service Access Codes, Fourth Report and Order and Memorandum Opinion and Order. Adopted: March 27, 1998. Released: March 31, 1998. Paragraph 7: "Although we recognize commenters' concerns regarding trademark infringement and unfair competition, we find that those issues properly should be addressed by the courts under the trademark protection and unfair competition laws, rather than by the Commission."

5. I prefer to speak of "switching costs" rather than "lock-in" because the latter is less precise and somewhat judgmental. "Switching costs" connotes that there are costs associated with change. In some cases these costs are extremely high, in other cases they are not. "Lock-in" implies that switching is impossible. But businesses incur substantial switching costs all the time. Office headquarters are moved to new addresses, resulting in new phone numbers and new stationery, and generating significant short-term expenses such as confusion and moving expenses. The presence of these switching costs does not necessarily mean that the business is perpetually locked in to a particular landlord. Even something as central to corporate identity as brand names and corporate logos change. Just recently, for example, telephone company giants Bell Atlantic and GTE adopted an entirely new name, Verizon, following their merger. The costs associated with this change probably run in the hundreds of millions of dollars.

6. A 1991 FCC order required the industry to make 800 numbers portable by 1993.

7. EUI designations are trademarked by IEEE. The classical 48-bit address space (known as EUI-48) is being phased out in favor of a new, 64-bit address space known as EUI-64.

8. IEEE, Registration Authority Committee, Guidelines for 64-bit Global Identifier (EUI-64), and Guidelines for Use of a 48-bit Global Identifier (EUI-48), March 2000.

Chapter 3: The Internet Name and Address Spaces

1. Class A assignments used only the first 8 bits to identify the class and the network, providing for a relatively small number (126) of very large networks accommodating up to 16.7 million hosts. Class B assignments used the first 16 bits to identify the class and the network prefix, providing for 16,384 intermediate-sized networks accommodating up to 65,536 hosts. Class C assignments provided for a very large number of small networks with only 256 unique identifiers for hosts. There were also two additional classes, D and E, one for multicasting and the other for experimental uses.

2. Class C networks, with room for only 256 hosts, were too small for most organizations, and few applications were received for them; The huge class A assignments were massively underutilized by those lucky enough to get them. Class B assignments began to run out rapidly.

3. RFC 950 (1985). Subnetting allowed organizations with larger enterprise networks to turn the two-part IP address structure into a three-level hierarchy. This facilitated route aggregation at the organizational level.

4. RFCs 1517, 1518, 1519, and 1520 (1993).

5. Email to author from Karl Auerbach, May 18, 2000.

6. Office of the Manager, National Communications System, "Internet Protocol Next Generation (IPv6): A Tutorial for IT Managers." Technical Information Bulletin 97-1, January 1997.

7. Currently, only the letters A–Z, numerals 0–9, and the hyphen character (-) can be used in a domain name, and the hyphen cannot be used as the first or last character in a domain name. Efforts are underway to internationalize domain names so that they can utilize non-Roman characters such as Chinese characters or various European alphabets. Domain names can be a maximum of 67 characters long, including the top-level domain.

8. Of course, not all of them are meaningful, and as was noted in chapter 2, the value attributed by users to different names will vary greatly.

9. ISO-3166-1. Maintained by Deutsches Institut für Normung in Germany.

10. BIND stands for Berkeley Internet Name Domain. It is a software implementation of DNS protocols that includes a DNS server, a DNS library resolver, and tools for verifying the proper operation of the DNS server. BIND is currently maintained and distributed by the Internet Software Consortium, <http://www.isc.org/>.

11. On August 23, 2000, four root name servers—*b.root-servers.net, g.root-servers.net, j.root-servers.net,* and *m.root-servers.net*—had no name server records for the entire *.com* zone. The problem occurred because the BIND software interacted with Network Solutions' zone generation procedures in an unexpected way, causing the name server to remove the *.com* zone delegation information from the root zone held in memory. This means that the entire *.com* zone did not exist for about 4/13 of all the resolvers in the world that needed to refresh their *.com* pointers during the interval in question.

12. RFC 2826 (2000), "IAB Technical Comment on the Unique DNS Root," is often cited in the policy debates over alternative roots as if it were the last word on the subject. The basic point of the statement is simply that "there must be a generally agreed single set of rules for the root." This is a good starting point for policy discussion. However, to assert that the root zone needs to be coordinated is both uncontroversial and not dispositive of the policy problem posed by competing roots. Advocates of a "single authoritative root" need to face the reality that portions of the Internet community can and do defect from or supplement the so-called authoritative root. Asserting that a particular root server system "should be" authoritative and singular does not make it so. One can agree on the need for coordination at the root level without necessarily agreeing on who is the sole or proper source of those rules. Nor does the general need for a single set of rules eliminate the legitimacy and benefit of competition over what those rules should be.

13. But I will give my personal opinion. The value added by alternative roots that only offer new top-level domains is minimal relative to the compatibility risks unless some other innovative functionalities are added. Large providers with the ability to overcome the critical mass problem are more likely to choose strategies that work over or around DNS rather than replacing it.

14. Joe Baptista, 2000, root server estimates.

15. Karen Kaplan, "Start-up Offers Alternative System for Net Addresses," *Los Angeles Times,* March 6, 2001.

Chapter 4: The Root and Institutional Change: Analytical Framework

1. Economists normally use the term *endowment* in a static sense to describe a given state of resource distribution. When economists use the term in this way, the specific endowment is exogenous to whatever it is they are trying to explain. I am using *endowment* in a dynamic and historical sense, to describe something that *happens to* a resource.

2. Property rights economics is a branch of institutional economics. The theory draws on classical political economy, neoclassical microeconomics, transaction cost economics, institutionalism, and noncooperative game theory. For a thorough exploration of its components, see Furubotn and Richter (1997). Rutherford's (1994) contrast of the "old" and "new" institutionalism is also a useful summary of the methods and theories of institutional economics. Ostrom, Gardner, and

Walker (1994, 25–26), provide a summary of what they call institutional analysis and development literature.

3. A review of research on the economics of property rights by DeAlessi (1980) concludes, "The effects of alternate systems of property rights on behavior, and welfare, are substantial and pervasive" (40).

4. The definition of transaction costs also includes costs associated with the contractual transfer of property rights, such as search costs, expenditures on negotiation, and the costs of monitoring and enforcing contracts.

5. Ostrom (1990) explores some of these cases, showing how collective action can establish and enforce rules governing access to and use of the shared resource. These cooperative property regimes may succeed by sharing some of the monitoring and enforcement costs, and by eliminating the costs created by the need to define and measure individual claims. But they also raise some of the classic problems associated with collective action, such as free-rider problems and other kinds of opportunistic behaviors that occur when the incentives of individual actors diverge from the interests of the group. Ostrom sees this as a problem that can be overcome with the appropriate institutional design.

6. The new institutional economics does not afford any special attention to the role of technology in institutional change. In contrast, Rutherford (1994) notes that the older institutionalist literature "contains many suggestive ideas on . . . the unintended impact on institutions of intentionally introduced alterations to the technical and material means through which individuals make their living" (180). See Bush (1987) for an overview.

7. "Because of the scarcity of radio frequencies, the Government is permitted to put restraints on licensees in favor of others whose views should be expressed on this unique medium." U.S. Supreme Court, *Red Lion Broadcasting* v. *FCC*, 395 U.S. 367 (1969). See also B. Schmidt, Jr., *Freedom of the Press vs. Public Access* (New York: Praeger, 1976) for a characterization of broadcasters as "public trustees" because of their privileged use of scarce spectrum rights.

8. For example, Libecap (1989, 94) cites evidence from the time period 1910–1914 that common pool losses in the oil industry amounted to 25 percent of the total value of production. Estimated oil recovery rates of only 20 to 25 percent were achieved with competitive extraction, whereas recovery rates of 85 to 90 percent were thought possible with controlled withdrawal.

9. It should be noted that "gains" and "losses" are subjective constructs. In many cases, the true economic impact of property rights changes cannot be foreseen. Industry lobbyists may fight against some regulatory or legal change only to discover that in the longer run they have benefited from new opportunities or conditions created by the change. The Motion Picture Association of America, for example, attempted to ban the video cassette recorder as a threat to copyright protection, but now motion picture producers make more profit from videotape rental and purchase than from theatrical releases. Political bargaining over property rights, however, tends to be driven by short-term extrapolations of the expected gains and losses of deviating from current practices.

Chapter 5: Growing the Root

1. *Matrix News,* 9 (December 1999).

2. Robert Braden, later a major figure in the Internet Activities Board, worked at the UCLA campus computing center at the time and was active in the Network Working Group. Another contemporary UCLA graduate computer science student, Kilnom Chon, returned to his native Korea in 1981 to establish the first TCP/IP network in Asia and later became one of the leaders of the Asia-Pacific top-level domain administrators.

3. A history of the Network Working Group and the origins of the RFC series is contained in RFC 1000.

4. An interview with Keith Uncapher, OH174, conducted by Arthur Norberg on July 10, 1989, Los Angeles, California. Charles Babbage Institute, Center for the History of Information Processing, University of Minnesota, Minneapolis.

5. Cerf and Kahn, *IEEE Transactions on Communication* 22 (5): 637–648.

6. RFC 791, "DARPA Internet Program Protocol Specification," September 1981.

7. Joyce Reynolds, Jon Postel, RFC 870, "Assigned Numbers," October 1983.

8. Clark projected a future "upper limit of about 1,000 networks." RFC 814 (July 1982).

9. "[A] reasonable programming strategy would be to make the name table accessible only through a subroutine interface, rather than by scattering direct references to the table all through the code. In this way, it will be possible, at a later date, to replace the subroutine with one capable of making calls on remote name servers." David Clark, RFC 814 (July 1982).

10. Archives of it still exist at <http://www.tcm.org/msggroup/>.

11. Jon Postel, "Namedroppers Policy," November 2, 1983, <http://ittf.vlsm.org/ietf/129.txt>.

12. "The general guideline for a second-level domain is that it have over 50 hosts. This is a very soft 'requirement.' It makes sense that any major organization, such as a university or corporation, be allowed as a second-level domain—even if it has just a few hosts." Postel, RFC 881 (November 1983).

13. "Top-level domains," Postel wrote in RFC 881, "must be specially authorized. In general, they will only be authorized for domains expected to have over 500 hosts."

14. This May 11, 1984, draft of what became RFC 920 is available at <http://ittf.vlsm.org/ietf/132.txt>.

15. Einar Stefferud to *namedroppers* list, May 13, 1984.

16. Mark Horton, *namedroppers* list, November 2, 1985.

17. Yet, Postel still faced criticism that the Internet administration was "U.S.-centric" because some thought other countries had to use their country code as a top-level domain, whereas people in the United States didn't. Postel to *namedrop-*

pers list, May 20, 1984, <http://ittf.vlsm.org/ietf/131.txt>. In arguing against this notion, Postel observed that anyone could register in *.com, .edu,* or *.org.*

18. Ibid.

19. An X.400 address has an eight-layer hierarchy, starting with a country code. Moreover, each X.400 messaging system is an independent domain and can only be interconnected by agreement among the implementing service providers. The features of the X.400 standard reflect its origins in a telephone monopoly–dominated world.

20. Jon Postel to *msggroup,* November 15, 1985.

21. Steve Kille to *namedroppers* list, November 15, 1985.

22. "Hi. The namedroppers list is for the discussion of the technical issues in the DARPA domain name system. The actual spelling of the name strings, and especially the semantics that people attach to those strings are not part of these technical issues. So please, no messages in this mailing list about the merits of EDU vs US (etc.) as a top-level domain name. Clearly, the choices of top-level names is a highly charged political issue. Please discuss it in the appropriate forum (msggroup?, poli-sci??).—jon."

23. Jon Postel, Namedroppers Policy, August 2, 1987, <http://ittf.vlsm.org/ietf/165.txt>.

24. "There was a contract executed in 1988 with DARPA, which I have seen. It contains a set of about 5 or 6 work items which are recognizable as the IANA functions plus the RFC editor and the Internet Monthly Report (which Postel also did). The term "IANA" was not used in the contract. It's my recollection that this contract was preceded by another long-term contract between DARPA and ISI that included the same functions, but I've never seen that one." Brian Kahin, email to author, December 19, 2000.

25. By maintaining both the DNS root and several different top-level domains (*.arpa, .com, .edu, .org, .gov, and .mil*) the DDN-NIC combined functions that, in a strict implementation of a hierarchical name space, should have been separate. Postel and other members of the technical community recognized this and didn't particularly like it, but accepted it because there was no one else to do the task. See Postel to *namedroppers* list, May 20, 1984, <http://ittf.vlsm.org/ietf/131.txt>.

26. As an example, responsibility for ARPANET management was transferred from ARPA to the Defense Communications Agency in 1975. See NAS (1994), 238, and Abbate (2000), 136.

27. Interview with Charles Brownstein, former NSF division chief, June 2000. See also NAS (1994), 238.

28. NSFNET cooperative agreement, <http://www.merit.edu/merit/archive/nsfnet/>.

29. NSFNET Backbone Services Acceptable Use Policy, June 1992, <http://www.merit.edu/merit/archive/nsfnet/acceptable.use.policy>.

30. RIPE Terms of Reference, November 29, 1989, <http://www.ripe.net/ripe/docs/ripe-001.html>.

31. Interview with Daniel Karrenberg, June 20, 2000.

32. Interview with David Conrad, August 23, 2000.

33. The proposal was formatted as a recommendation from the Internet Activities Board to the Federal Networking Council and was eventually approved. See sections 5.4.1 and 5.5.1 for more detail about the institutional environment in which these decisions were made.

34. Jon Postel to *msggroup*, November 15, 1985.

35. Interview with John Klensin, November 13, 2000.

36. The committee was known as the Internet Configuration Control Board (RFC 1160).

37. Craig Partridge, email communication with author, July 2001.

38. Steve Crocker, cited in RFC 1000 (August 1987).

39. Cited in Hofmann (1998, 14).

40. RFC 1083 (December 1988); RFC 1111 (August 1989); RFC 1120 (September 1989); RFC 1160 (May 1990); RFC 1200 (April 1991); RFC 1250 (August 1991).

41. An "Internet FAQ" written by ISI staff members claimed, "The task of coordinating the assignment of values to the parameters of protocols is delegated by the Internet Activities Board (IAB) to the Internet Assigned Numbers Authority (IANA)." This document seems to have evolved into RFC 1207 (February 1991).

42. Interestingly, though, Cerf's major RFC documenting the IAB does not mention name and address assignment as one of its key functions. RFC 1160 defines the IAB functions as "(1) Sets Internet Standards; (2) manages the RFC publication process; (3) reviews the operation of the IETF and IRTF; (4) performs strategic planning for the Internet, identifying long-range problems and opportunities; (5) acts as a technical policy liaison and representative for the Internet community; and (6) resolves technical issues which cannot be treated within the IETF or IRTF frameworks."

43. Jon Postel to *msggroup*, November 15, 1985. See also email, Cerf to Aiken, March 17, 1995; RFC 1174 (August 1990); RFC 1207 (February 1991). The actual RFCs (1032 and 1020) announcing the transfer in 1987 were not written by Postel and do not mention IANA or any delegation from Postel or the IAB.

44. Email, Cerf to Rutkowski, November 6, 1990, <http://www.wia.org/ISOC/901106.htm>.

45. Interview with Don Mitchell, December 19, 2000.

46. Email, Cerf to Rutkowski, November 6, 1990, <http://www.wia.org/ISOC/901106.htm>.

47. The case of Daniel Bernstein, who contended that his RFC submission had not been handled according to the IETF's documented processes, was another key event in instilling the fear of lawsuits among the IAB/IETF hierarchy. See <http://ittf.vlsm.org/ietf/16.txt>.

48. Email, Rutkowski to Cerf, April 5, 1991, <http://www.wia.org/ISOC/910405.htm>.

49. Interview with Charles Brownstein, May 18, 2000.

50. Hofmann (1998, 12, 16) does an excellent job of analyzing the mixture of technical, political, and organizational factors that led the bulk of the IETF participants to greet the decision with such revulsion.

51. The National Research and Education Network Program, A Report to Congress, December 1992. Submitted by the Director, Office of Science and Technology Policy, in response to a requirement of The High Performance Computing Act of 1991 (P.L. 102–194), http://www.eff.org/pub/Legislation/nren_congress.report.

52. Email, Cerf to Rutkowski, April 3, 1991. See <http://www.wia.org>.

53. National Science Foundation, Network Information Services, Manager(s) for NSFNET and the NREN, Project Solicitation, March 19, 1992, <http://www.cavebear.com/nsf-dns/internic-solicitation.htm>. NREN stands for National Research and Education Network.

54. NSI Project Solicitation, October 1992, <http://www.networksolutions.com/en_US/legal/internic/nsf-solicitation/>.

55. Ibid, section M.

56. NSF Cooperative Agreement No. NCR-9218742, available at <http://www.networksolutions.com/en_US/legal/internic/cooperative-agreement/index.html>.

57. David Conrad's description of the Internet technical community, interview with author, August 23, 2000.

Chapter 6: Appropriating the Root: Property Rights Conflicts

1. Nysernet formed PSINet, other regionals formed Cerfnet, and UUNet. Later, these three joined with Sprint to form the Commercial Internet eXchange (CIX) in 1991.

2. Email, Steve Wolff, director, NSF CISE, to Eric Aupperle, president, Merit Network, May 24, 1991, <http://www.merit.edu/merit/archive/nsfnet/nsf.agreements/commercial.traffic>.

3. Project Solicitation 93–52, Network Access Point Manager, Routing Arbiter, Regional Network Providers, and Very High Speed Backbone Network Services Provider for NSFNET and the NREN Program.

4. NSF also supported a "routing arbiter" to provide a database and other information needed by the NAPs to exchange traffic in an orderly fashion, as well as some transitional funding for the regional networks.

5. Mosaic was the outgrowth of a program written by the Software Development Group at the NCSA called Collage, designed to enable researchers to collaborate over networks. As the project neared completion, programmers at the group got wind of the World Wide Web project and quickly realized that Web compatibility

could turn the Collage project into something much broader than a collaboration tool. See <http://www.webhistory.org/historyday/abstracts.html>.

6. NSFNET backbone statistics are archived at the Georgia Tech Graphics, Visualization and Usability Center, <http://www.cc.gatech.edu/gvu/stats/NSF/merit.html>.

7. Minutes, October 13, 1994, IAB Meeting, <ftp://ftp.iab.org/in-notes/IAB/IABmins/IABmins.941013>.

8. "It is clear from the materials presented by NSI that a primary culprit in the RS work load is the .COM domain. . . . At present, the management of .COM is paid for by the NSF, and hence increasing demand for .COM registrations will require increasing support from the NSF. The panel recommends that NSI begin charging for .COM domain name registrations, and later charge for name registrations in all domains." InterNIC Midterm Evaluation and Recommendations: A Panel Report to the National Science Foundation, December 1994, <http://www.networksolutions.com/en_US/legal/internic/midterm/index.html>.

9. <http://www.networksolutions.com/en_US/legal/internic/cooperative-agreement/amendment4.html>.

10. Global Domain Names Status Report, NetNames, London, March 1997.

11. Email, August 17, 1998, from former NSI employee to newslist.

12. In July 1993, Brian Reid, who at the time worked for Digital Equipment Corporation, received an email from InterNIC stating, "We try to register only one name per "organization." DEC.COM has been around since day-one. Do you intend to replace DEC.COM with DIGITAL.COM?" <domreg@internic.net> to Brian Reid, July 16, 1993; on file with author.

13. According to Kim Hubbard, former director of ARIN, an early employee of Network Solutions, and a worker at the InterNIC from 1991 to 1996, it was Jon Postel who decided that it was a "waste of time" to attempt to segregate *.com, .net,* and *.org* registrations.

14. Network Solutions did not threaten to deactivate domain names for nonpayment of the fees until June 1996. A copy of a June 17 news release is archived at <http://www.iiia.org/lists/newdom/1996q2/0295.html>.

15. The French ccTLD, for example, in 1996 required users to fit into one of eight categories: *.asso, .barreau, .cci, .cesi, .dxxx, .gouv, .presse,* and *.tm.*

16. Internet Domain Survey, July 1995, <http://www.isc.org/ds/WWW-9507/distbynum.html>.

17. For U.K. statistics, see <http://www.nominet.org.uk/news/stats/stats.1996.html>; for U.S. statistics see <http://www.networksolutions.com/en_US/legal/internic/coop-stats/>.

18. *Panavision International* v. *Toeppen,* 46 U.S.P.Q.2d 1511, 1998 WL 178553 (9th Cir. April 17, 1998); *Intermatic Inc.* v. *Toeppen,* 947 F. Supp. 1227 (N.D.Ill. 1996).

19. *Marks & Spencer PLC, British Telecommunications PLC, Virgin Enterprises, Ltd., J. Sainsbury PLC, Ladbroke Group PLC v. One in a Million, et al.*, Judgment (On Appeal in the High Court of Justice, Supreme Court of Judicature Chani, 98/ 0025/B-July 23, 1998); *British Telecommunications Ltd. and Others v. One in a Million, Ltd.* (1999), FSR 1 (C.A.).

20. As of mid-2000, Yahoo! was a complainant in four UDRP cases involving 99 domain names; AOL was a complainant in nine UDRP cases involving 34 domain names.

21. "Online Legal Issues," *New York Law Journal*, February 15, 1995.

22. *People for the Ethical Treatment of Animals v. Doughney*, CA No. 99–1336-A, E.D. Va., June 12, 2000.

23. *Planned Parenthood Fed'n of America, Inc. v. Bucci*, 42 U.S.P.Q.2d 1430, 1432 (S.D.N.Y. 1997).

24. Chet Flippo, "Country Artists Sue 'Cybersquatter.'" *Billboard*, April 25, 1998, p. 82.

25. Amended Complaint, *KnowledgeNet, Inc. v. D.L. Boone & Co., Network Solutions, Inc., and Digital Express Group, Inc.*, U.S. District Court for the Northern District of Illinois, Eastern Division, No. 94-C-7195.

26. In the first six weeks after adoption of the new policy, the rate of domain name registration fell from about 20,000 per month to 6,000 per month. But the effect was temporary, and growth in the number of registrations resumed at the previous rate shortly thereafter. *Investor's Business Daily*, October 17, 1995, p. A10.

27. Because of public pressure, Prema backed down from its claim.

28. *Roadrunner Computer Systems v. Network Solutions, Inc*, Civil Action No. 96-413 (E.D. Va., March 26, 1996); *Giacalone v. Network Solutions, Inc.*, Case No. 96-20434 (N.D. California, June 14, 1996); *Network Solutions, Inc. v. Clue Computing*, Case No. 96-CV-694 (D. Colorado June 21, 1996).

29. *Lockheed Martin Corp. v. NSI*, 43 U.S.P.Q.2d 1056, 1997 U.S. Dist. Lexis 10314, 1997 WL 381967 (C.D. Cal. 1997).

30. *Oggi Advertising Ltd. v. McKenzie and others*, CP.147/98 (High Court of New Zealand, Auckland Registry), June 2, 1998. See also Domainz Media Statement, November 13, 1998, <http://www.domainz.net.nz/newsstand/stories/court4.html>.

31. An English company from Manchester, Fast-net Developments Ltd., applied to IANA for the top-level domain for Libya, *.ly*. Fast-net Development's owner, Kalil Elwiheishi, was listed as the administrative contact for the *.ly* domain with an address in Tripoli, which appears to fulfill IANA's residency requirement. The owner's real residence was England, but IANA lacked the capacity to monitor such things. A British company, NetNames, acted as collector of registration fees for *.ly*, which it split with the administrative contact. Such arrangements were not at all uncommon with other developing country ccTLDs.

32. The small nation of Niue (.*nu*), for example, allows its ccTLD to be administered and marketed by a "nonprofit" foundation. Both .*nu* and the ccTLD for the Cocos and Keeling islands (.*cc*) are marketed commercially and globally as an alternative to generic TLDs. In a few cases, a happy coincidence allows the ccTLD to function as a kind of generic TLD. The ISO code for Tuvalu, for example, is .*tv;* for Moldova, the code is .*md.* .*tv* was subdelegated to Idealab, Inc. and marketed commercially.

33. For an account of the Haiti (.*ht*) delegation crisis, see John S. Quarterman, *Matrix News* 7 (December 1997).

34. It was not unusual to see on various email lists disapproval of the idea that "everyone wants their own domain" and the opinion that DNS was "never designed" to provide that. See, for example, Joe Provo: "The problem is—and always has been—inappropriate registering. The "joes-bar-and-grill.com"–style registering is wildly inappropriate and was (mostly) avoided by ordinary pressures until the 'anything for a buck' providers entered the game." Email to *newdom* list, October 25, 1995, <http://www.iiia.org/lists/newdom/>.

35. See IAB minutes, August 1995, <ftp://ftp.iab.org/in-notes/IAB/IABmins/IABmins.950808>.

36. "No one has really objected to paying reasonable fees for registration. EVERYONE (almost) has objected to paying fees set arbitrarily by a group which contains and considers little or no input from the community in the process and is not restricted to any public comment period or public regulation regarding future fee levels." Owen DeLong, email to *newdom* list, September 20, 1995, <http://www.iiia. org/lists/newdom/1995q3/0323.html>. However, the Internet Architecture Board minutes for October 13, 1994, note, "There was an NSF-sponsored meeting on this issue [charging], which concluded that a charging model should be developed for registration services (on a yearly maintenance basis).

37. Email, Postel to isoc-trustees@linus.isoc.org, September 15, 1995, <http://www.wia.org/pub/postel-iana-draft13.htm>.

38. "So I would suggest we proceed on two fronts in parallel: (1) to look at ways a single TLD could be shared between two or more registries without a single central mechanism, and (2) to look at the procedures we would set up to establish new registries and new TLDs without such sharing. If we find a good way to support the sharing we will update the procedures to include it." Email, Postel to *newdom,* October 19, 1995, <http://www.iiia.org/lists/newdom/1995q4/0009.html>.

39. An IETF Working Group on shared TLDs was formed and met at the Dallas meeting in December 1995, producing a draft.

40. Draft-postel is unfortunately vague about how it would handle conflicting applications for the same character strings; rather than specifying an auction procedure it implies that IANA would use its own discretion (Postel 1996, 19).

41. The $10,000 fee varied across different drafts, starting at $100,000 and going down to $2,000 in one iteration.

42. The significance of this exchange is disputed. Ambler maintains that Manning watched him write the check and understood that it and the accompanying paperwork constituted a formal application for permission from IANA to run an experimental registry. Postel and Manning strongly disputed this statement, contending that the envelope was presented to Manning in a manila folder along with other papers from Ambler and that he did not discover it until after Ambler left the meeting.

43. The fact that the envelope was unopened tends to support Ambler's version of the story—how could the IANA staff have known that it contained money if they never opened it?

44. From Thom Stark, "The New Domain Name Game," 1997, <http://www.starkrealities.com/iahc.html>.

45. IAB minutes, October 1994, <ftp://ftp.iab.org/in-notes/IAB/IABmins/IABmins.941013>.

46. Interview with Scott Bradner, July 19, 2000. Bradner blames Rutkowski for many of the tensions, claiming that he acted as if the IETF was a "wholly owned subsidiary of the Internet Society" during his tenure as director.

47. IAB minutes, December 1994, <ftp://ftp.iab.org/in-notes/IAB/IABmins/IABmins.941209>.

48. IAB minutes, January 1995.

49. L. Landweber, B. Carpenter, J. Postel, and N. Trio, "Proposal for an ISOC Role in DNS Name Space Management," November 1995, <http://www.iiia.org/lists/newdom/1995q4/0154.html>.

50. Email, Aiken to ISOC Board, March 17, 1995, <http://www.wia.org/pub/postel-iana-draft5.htm>.

51. Email, Cerf to Aiken, March 18, 1995, <http://www.wia.org/pub/postel-iana-draft9.htm>.

52. National Science Foundation and Harvard Information Infrastructure Project, "Internet Names, Numbers, and Beyond: Issues in the Coordination, Privatization, and Internationalization of the Internet," November 20, 1995, <http://www.ksg.harvard.edu/iip/GIIconf/nsfmin1.html>.

53. M. St. Johns, "FNC's Role in the DNS Issue," Internet Numbering Issues, Kennedy School at Annenberg Program Offices, Washington, D.C., November 20, 1995.

54. Minutes of the NSF/Harvard conference, <http://www.ksg.harvard.edu/iip/GIIconf/nsfmin1.html>.

55. G. Lawton, "New Top-Level Domains Promise Descriptive Names," *SunWorld Online*, September 1996.

56. IANA's critics charged that it had moved forward with implementation of draft-postel without obtaining IETF approval of it as an RFC and also that it proposed to create an ad hoc working group appointed by Postel rather than an open, IETF working group.

57. Karl Denninger, *newdom* post, October 28, 1996.

58. Email, Vixie to *newdom*, October 28, 1996.

59. "The FNCAC reiterates and underscores the urgency of transferring responsibility for supporting U.S. commercial interests in iTLD administration from the NSF to an appropriate agency." Draft Minutes of the Federal Networking Council Advisory Committee Meeting, October 1996, <http://www.itrd.gov/fnc/FNCAC_10_96_minutes.html>. According to Mike Roberts of Educom, "The motion we passed expressed the strong desire that the FNC work hard NOW to develop a sound future foundation for the domain name system when the NSI agreement ends in less than 18 months, and further, that an 'appropriate entity' be identified to hold responsibility for those parts of the DNS that are found to require permanent stewardship, i.e., not to be handed over for dissection by the greedy private sector types that lust after the alleged NSI monopoly profits." Mike Roberts to IETF list, November 10, 1996.

Chapter 7: The Root in Play

1. "The chief technical officers of two of the largest ISPs on the planet indicated privately to me that unless something happened soon, they were going to point to AlterNIC." David Conrad, email to author, February 18, 1997.

2. News Release, ISOC, Washington, D.C., October 22, 1996, "Blue Ribbon International Panel to Examine Enhancements to Internet Domain Name System."

3. Interview with Don Heath, June 19, 2000; interview with David Conrad, August 23, 2000.

4. Interview with Scott Bradner, July 19, 2000.

5. Heath later stated that he had wanted to add a CIX representative to the group (Simon 1998).

6. The seven proposed gTLDs were *.web, .info, .nom, .firm, .rec, .arts, .store.*

7. Pekka Tarjanne, "Internet Governance: Toward Voluntary Multilateralism," Keynote address, Meeting of Signatories and Potential Signatories of the Generic Top-Level Domain Memorandum of Understanding (gTLD-MoU), ITU, Geneva, April 29–May 1, 1997.

8. Network Solutions' Preliminary Response to the IAHC's Draft Specifications for the Administration and Management of gTLDs, January 17, 1997.

9. Cited in *Wired News,* April 24, 1997, <http://www.wired.com/news/politics/0,1283,3395,00.html>.

10. <ftp://www.sec.gov/edgar/data/1030341/0000950133–97–002418.txt>.

11. Jay Fenello, the would-be proprietor of a *.per* top-level domain for personal names, criticized "the chaos the entire IAHC process has created in the Internet community. Their arrogance about their dominion over the root, and their claim to rightful ownership of such valuable properties like .com and .web have created

the conflicts we are now experiencing. A fundamental question is why the IANA, a U.S. government funded contractor, should be allowed to "give" seven new gTLDs to its self-selected representatives (especially when it negotiates behind closed doors, sets up a Swiss-based cartel, ignores prior Internet precedents, and is generally regarded as an inappropriate power grab). Why should the IANA be allowed to **exclude** already operational [alternative] TLDs and registries?" <http://www.ntia.doc.gov/ntiahome/domainname/130dftmail/02_13_98.htm>.

12. *Imagine Online Design v. IANA,* Superior and Municipal Court of the State of California, for the County of San Luis Obispo, Case CV080380, February 27, 1997, <http://www.jmls.edu/cyber/cases/iod1.html>.

13. John Fontana, "Net Domain Plan Draws Fire," *CMP News,* Issue 644, January 6, 1997.

14. Comments of Computer Professionals for Social Responsibility in the NTIA proceeding, August 18, 1997, <http://www.cpsr.org/dns/cpsr_dns1.html>.

15. "EU Commission Meeting with TLD Registry Representatives," report by Niall O'Reilly, University College Dublin Computing Services, April 1997, archived at <http://www.fitug.de/debate/9704/msg00078.html>.

16. Kent Cukier, "EC Urges Halt to IAHC Plan." *Communications Week International,* April 21, 1997.

17. Comments of AT&T in the NTIA Notice of Inquiry, August 18, 1997, <http://www.ntia.doc.gov/ntiahome/domainname/email/8_18_97comments.htm>.

18. *P.G. Media Inc., dba Name.Space, v. Network Solutions Inc.,* 97 CV 1946, March 20, 1997, <http://name-space.com/law/litigation_cont.html>. The original complaint also named the Internet Society and the IAHC as "non-party co-conspirators" for their role in forming the gTLD-MoU, but this aspect of the complaint was later withdrawn.

19. D. Mitchell, NSF, to David Graves, Internet Business Manager, Network Solutions, Inc., June 25, 1997.

20. *PgMedia d/b/a Name.Space v. Network Solutions Inc and the National Science Foundation,* 97 Civ. 1946 (RPP), second amended complaint, September 17, 1997, <http://www.name-space.com/law/litigation_nsf.html>.

21. "By redirecting the domain name 'www.internic.net,' we are protesting the recent InterNIC claim to ownership of '.com,' '.org,' and '.net,' which they were supposed to be running in the public trust. Our apologies for any trouble this DNS protest has caused you. . . . We think we exercised restraint in the use of our latest DNS technology for this protest. We terminated the protest configuration at 8 a.m. Monday, July 14." Cited in Courtney Macavinta, "AlterNIC takes over InterNIC Traffic," *CNET News,* July 14, 1997, <http://news.cnet.com/news/0-1004-200-320460.html?cnet.tkr>.

22. Ibid.

23. Interview with Brian Kahin, May 17, 2000.

24. "The Administration of Internet Addresses," Office of the Inspector General, National Science Foundation, February 7, 1997. The report argued that "the public interest requires that Internet address administration remain a governmental activity" and that the government should impose fees on domain name and IP address registrations and use the money to supplement the government's investment in the Internet.

25. W. Bordogna, NSF, memo in response to OIG report, April 17, 1997.

26. Ibid.

27. "US Federal Gov't Decides to Solve DNS Problem—Rug Pulled out from under NSF," *Cook Report*, March 28, 1997.

28. Karl Auerbach statement in Freed collection.

29. David Conrad, interview with author, August 23, 2000. Conrad, as head of APNIC at the time, committed US$50,000 to IANA support and reported that RIPE-NCC had committed US$25,000.

30. Magaziner had also been in charge of the Clinton administration's abortive health care reform initiative. That initiative had received a brutal response in part because it attempted to socialize a larger part of the U.S. health care system. More than one internal observer of Magaziner's role in the creation of ICANN felt that he was motivated in part by a need to redeem himself for the health care fiasco. Magaziner went to extraordinary lengths to actively consult with as many actors in the private sector as possible.

31. Gordon Cook, transcript of interview with Ira Magaziner, September 24, 1998.

32. The original co-chair was Bruce McConnell of the Office of Management and Budget, but he became an inactive member and was replaced by Burr in July 1997.

33. State Dept cable; on file with author.

34. Interview with Brian Kahin, May 17, 2000.

35. Presidential Directive on Electronic Commerce, memorandum for the heads of executive departments and agencies, July 1, 1997.

36. Request for Comments in the Matter of Registration and Administration of Internet Domain Names, U.S. Dept of Commerce, Doc. No. 970613137-7137-01, July 1, 1997.

37. "US Rejects Net Name Plan," May 2, 1997, <http://yahoo.cnet.com/news/0-1005-200-318681.html>.

38. Email to *gtld-discuss* mailing list, October 1997.

39. Email, Gordon Cook to *com-priv* list, November 14, 1997; on file with author.

40. U.S. Congress, House Science Committee, Subcommittee on Basic Research, Hearing on Internet Domain Names, September 30, 1997, <http://www.house.gov/science/pickering_9-30.html>.

41. Stability, competition, private, bottom-up coordination, and representation were adopted as the basic principles to guide the transition.

42. Three would be appointed by the Regional Address Registries, two by the Internet Architecture Board, and two by an as-yet-nonexistent "membership association of registries and registrars." The remaining seven members would represent Internet users, to be elected by an (also nonexistent) Internet users' members association.

43. The minimum requirements involved a searchable database, accurate contact information, selection of a "readily available and convenient dispute resolution process that requires no involvement by registrars," and suspension of a domain name during a dispute if a trademark owner objected to it within 30 days of its registration. Green Paper (NTIA 1998a), Appendix 2, p. 8833.

44. Email, Cook to author, August 12, 2000, with quotations from Magaziner interview, December 10, 1997.

45. Interview with Paul Vixie, July 18, 2000.

46. Email, Brian Reid to author, August 12, 2000.

47. For news coverage of this event, see Sandra Gittlen, "Taking the Wrong Root?" *Network World,* February 4, 1998; Ted Bridis, "Clinton Administration Says Internet Reconfiguration Was Rogue Test," Associated Press, February 5, 1998.

Chapter 8: Institutionalizing the Root: The Formation of ICANN

1. Comments on the Green Paper are still posted at <http://www.ntia.doc.gov/ntiahome/domainname/130dftmail/>.

2. For a detailed legal discussion of the implications of the Administrative Procedures Act and its avoidance in the creation of ICANN, see Froomkin (2000). Ultimately the Commerce Department chose a mode of action designed to avoid the APA, but at the Green Paper stage, there was still the possibility that the privatization process would occur under the Act. See the comments of J. Beckwith Burr, Transcript of a Public Hearing with Ira Magaziner, White House Advisor, and Beckwith Burr, Associate Administrator, NTIA, Department of Commerce, Washington, D.C., February 23, 1998, <http://www.ntia.doc.gov/ntiahome/domainname/130dftmail/feb23transcript.htm>.

3. Network Solutions and the alternative registries supported the general thrust of the proposal. IBM praised the Green Paper as "basically sound and workable." Educom commented that "the Green Paper provides a robust blueprint for addressing many current problems with management of Domain Names, and is strongly endorsed by the higher education networking community."

4. The Australian government's comments, for example, criticize the Green Paper for not mentioning the gTLD-MoU, even though they "do not necessarily support it." The Australian government's policy critique of the Green Paper followed the

same lines as the MoUvement's, insisting that registries should be administered as a monopoly, nonprofit "public trust" instead of by for-profit enterprises, and rejecting the nonuniform dispute resolution approach of the NTIA proposal.

5. Interview with Don Heath, June 19, 2000.

6. Of the 50-odd emailed comments filed on March 21 and 22, the second and third days before the deadline, nearly three-fourths came from individual ISOC members or CORE participants; 17 of the responses were identical. See note 1.

7. The CORE executive committee at this time consisted of Werner Staub (Switzerland), Siegfried Langenbach (Germany), Ivan Pope (U.K.), Leni Mayo (Australia), and Trevor Hayes (Australia).

8. Council of the European Union, European Commission: "Internet Governance: Reply of the European Commission and Its Member States to the U.S. Green Paper," March 16, 1998.

9. Response of the Commonwealth Government of Australia to the Proposed Rule of the United States Department of Commerce, <http://www.ntia.doc.gov/ntiahome/domainname/130dftmail/Australia.htm>.

10. The issue of for-profit registries and the uniformity of the dispute resolution procedure were both points of substantive policy difference between the two proposals.

11. Its founding members were Netscape (acquired by AOL by 1999), MCI, IBM, AT&T, Deutsche Telekom, Oracle, Visa International, NEC, Fujitsu, Sun Microsystems, BBN Planet, and EDS.

12. From the GIP Web site, <http://www.gip.org/>. Compare this to Barlow's "Governments of the Industrial World, you weary giants of flesh and steel, I come from Cyberspace, the new home of Mind. On behalf of the future, I ask you of the past to leave us alone. You are not welcome among us. You have no sovereignty where we gather. . . . Where there are real conflicts, where there are wrongs, we will identify them and address them by our means. We are forming our own Social Contract. This governance will arise according to the conditions of our world, not yours."

13. In June 1999, when ICANN was desperate for funds, Vint Cerf and Mike Nelson mounted an appeal to the Internet industry for US$1 million in "bridge funding." According to Cerf, "I would then launch a campaign with GIP, ITAA, Internet Society, and other interested groups on the basis that ICANN must succeed or Internet will be in jeopardy." Despite fund-raising appeals to Silicon Valley, only MCI WorldCom and Cisco were willing to provide loans for US$500,000 and US$150,000, respectively. Email, Gordon Cook to Telecom Digest email list, September 1, 1999; on file with author.

14. Interview with Roger Cochetti, June 2, 2001. A group of major IBM executives had been treated to a presentation by the IAHC members at a very early stage, either late December 1996 or early January 1997. They came out of the meeting, according to Cochetti, unimpressed with the claims of the IAHC that they already

controlled the root and convinced that the brash IAHC members failed to comprehend the need to cultivate the needed political support.

15. Interview with Scott Bradner, July 19, 2000.

16. The IAB had not, however, completely abandoned the gTLD-MoU. Its meeting minutes reveal that it continued to nominate representatives to the MoU's Policy Oversight Committee as late as June 1998. IAB Minutes for June 9, 1998.

17. A source at WIPO who wishes to remain anonymous thinks that Magaziner really did believe that technical coordination concerns were paramount and that trademark issues were a distraction. After agreeing (thanks to European pressure) to permit WIPO to perform its role, he expected to bury or sidestep the issue in that way.

18. A revealing public statement by Magaziner shortly after the release of the Green Paper provides insight into the motivation behind the U.S. Government's approach to the White Paper: "The easiest thing for us would be if we could punt on this. That is, if we could say, 'We're lame ducks. We're getting out of this. Let's wait for this new organization, and we're not going to change anything until that comes into being.' And that would certainly make our job easier. [But we are convinced] that it would delay the onset of competition. And so that's why [in the Green Paper] we went against our better visceral judgment about what was in our own best interests, and said, we'll go ahead and try to create this transition. . . . But if there was an overwhelming set of opinions from the broad community that said, 'No, just wait,' then I'm sure we would be amenable to listening to that." Transcript of a Public Hearing with Ira Magaziner, White House Advisor, and Beckwith Burr, Associate Administrator NTIA, Department of Commerce, Washington, D.C., February 23, 1998.

19. Internet Architecture Board minutes, June 9, 1998.

20. Don Heath told the press that "the final policy represents a victory for the Internet Society–influenced Generic Top-Level Domain Memorandum of Understanding (MoU). 'It's excellent,' he said, that government had decided to leave Internet governance to users and the private sector instead of governments." Will Rodger, "Government Hands Domain Name Reins to Private Sector," *ZDNet News*, June 5, 1998.

21. A European Commission Council meeting dated May 19—several weeks before the publication of the White Paper—noted, "The U.S. authorities are now in the process of drafting a White Paper which, according to Commissioner Bangemann, seems to take into account many of the concerns expressed in [Commission's response to the Green Paper]." Minutes of European Commission 2096th Council Meeting, Brussels, May 19, 1998, 8529/98 (Presse 149).

22. John Sopko, Chief Counsel for Special Matters, U.S. Commerce Department, to Rep. Thomas J. Bliley, November 5, 1998.

23. Rutkowski's June 9, 1998 email to Jon Postel, Vint Cerf, Dave Farber, Scott Bradner, and John Gilmore, entitled "Incorporation Workshop," said in part, "It's critical now to really bring everyone together to construct a corporation or trust

with the right attributes—that provides for diversity, balance, safeguards, and meets the interests and expectations of everyone. This workshop happened because a lot of people were talking with a lot of other people about how to proceed if the government wasn't going to itself form a corporation, and what form of legal creature should be brought into existence."

24. ISP/C news release, June 18, 1998.

25. The IFWP steering committee included representatives of the following organizations: Catalonian Foundation for Research (ES), Image Online Design (US), Information Technology Association of America (US), Canadian Association of Internet Providers (CA), Association for Interactive Media (US), Camara Argentina de Bases de Datos y Servicios en Linea (AR), Association Usarias de Internet (ES), Open Root Server Confederation (US), EuroISP Association—UK, EuroISP Association—Germany, Council of Internet Registrars (CH), ISOC Australia, Mexican TLD, Domain Name Rights Coalition (US), Harvard Berkman Center (US), ISP/C (US), DENIC (DE), Internet Society (US), Commercial Internet eXchange (US), European Telecommunications Standards Institute (EU), Asia Pacific Internet Association (AP), EDUCAUSE (US), ISOC-Geneva (CH), Asia Pacific Networking Group (SG), International Chamber of Commerce (UK).

26. Einar Stefferud raised procedural and substantive objections to the plenary's actions. See Stefferud to IETF list, September 2, 1998, "Tamar's IETF appearance."

27. Stefferud's report, corroborated by others present, notes that he stood up and asked the plenary attendees, Who has read the proposals? Only about one-quarter of the attendees raised their hands.

28. Email, Lawrence Lessig to Michael Sondow, September 6, 2000; on file with author.

29. A widely publicized, caustic email from Mike Roberts announcing his refusal to participate in the ratification meeting signaled the demise of the final meeting proposals. Mike Roberts to IFWP-discuss list, August 28, 1998, "Ratification—the IFWP Emperor Has No Clothes."

30. Paul Festa, "Raising Funds for New Names Body," CNET News, September 9, 1998.

31. The first subclause stated that the new corporation must recognize any agreements between the U.S. government and IANA or Network Solutions. The second subclause stated that the corporation should not knowingly destroy any contractual or property right of a particular party.

32. The BWG members included Karl Auerbach, Internet technologist since 1974, IETF participant since the mid-1980s, California attorney, and chief technical officer of InterWorking Labs; Peter Dengate Thrush, patent attorney, solicitor, and barrister, counsel to ISOCNZ (New Zealand) and its subsidiary, the NZ registry, Domainz; David Schutt, chief information systems manager for a manufacturing company; Patrick O'Brien, CEO of Domainz, the NZ registry; Eric Weisberg, principal and general counsel for a rural Texas ISP, Internet Texoma; Diane Cabell, of the law firm Fausett, Gaeta & Lund; Jorge Contreras, Hale & Dorr (host, repre-

senting the Berkman Center for Internet and Society at Harvard Law School). Most had purchased nonrefundable airline tickets to Boston.

33. Letter from the Boston Working Group to Ira Magaziner, senior advisor to the President for policy development, September 28, 1998.

34. The Open Root Server Confederation was formed in July 1997 by Richard Sexton, Einar Stefferud, and Brian Reid. It was incorporated in Delaware in the summer of 1998.

35. The Electronic Frontier Foundation urged IANA to include protections for freedom of expression in the articles, and a proposal submitted by the European ISP Association proposed a structure similar to ORSC's.

36. "I am assuming that by midweek at the latest, there will be some names of board members emerging. I am assuming this because we will need to have some broad public discussion of those names before October first." Gordon Cook, interview with Ira Magaziner, September 21, 1998, posted to Domain Policy list, September 22, 1998.

37. John Sopko, Chief Counsel for Special Matters, U.S. Commerce Department, to Rep. Thomas J. Bliley, November 5, 1998.

38. Ibid.

39. Comments responding to the ICANN incorporation proposal are still posted at <http://www.ntia.doc.gov/ntiahome/domainname/proposals/comments/comments. html>.

40. "Overall, the submissions we received supported moving forward with the ICANN structure. We note, however, that the public comments received on the ICANN submission reflect significant concerns about substantive and operational aspects of ICANN. The submissions of the Boston Working Group and the Open Root Server Confederation, among others, articulate specific concerns, many of which we share. As you refine your proposal, we urge you to consult with these groups and others who commented critically on your proposal to try to broaden the consensus." Burr letter to ISI, October 20, 1998.

41. Letter of Esther Dyson, interim board chair, to J. Beckwith Burr, Department of Commerce, November 6, 1998.

42. Memorandum of Understanding, Department of Commerce and ICANN, November 28, 1998.

43. Letter from Esther Dyson, ICANN, to J. Beckwith Burr, Department of Commerce, July 19, 1999.

Chapter 9: The New Regime

1. ICANN's management and staff had prepared draft guidelines for accreditation by February 8, 1999, even before it was officially designated "NewCo" by the Commerce Department. The board adopted the draft a month later.

2. Among other things, accredited registrars committed themselves to 11 WIPO recommendations, including contractual features requiring transfer of a disputed domain name, agreement to exclude second-level names designated by ICANN, payment for registrations in advance, and the domain name holder's consent to jurisdiction. ICANN, "Guidelines for Accreditation of Internet Domain Name Registrars and for the Selection of Registrars for the Shared Registry System Testbed for *.com, .net,* and *.org* Domains," February 8, 1999, Section II.K, "Intellectual Property Issues."

3. CORE, the organization of registrars left over from the gTLD-MoU, was accredited as one registrar despite the fact that it consisted of a consortium of 88 different registration service providers. France Telecom, a gTLD-MoU signatory, and AOL, a GIP member, had both donated US$25,000 in start-up funding to ICANN and were vocal supporters of it in the final stages of the Commerce Department proceeding. Melbourne IT was also a CORE member and was closely tied to the Australian National Office of the Information Economy.

4. Amendment 13 to the Commerce Department–Network Solutions Cooperative Agreement, NCR 92-189742, <http://www.ntia.doc.gov/ntiahome/domainname/amendment13.htm>.

5. Andrew Pincus, General Counsel, Commerce Department, to Thomas Bliley, Chairman, House Commerce Committee, July 8, 1999, p. 15.

6. ICANN News Release, "ICANN Names Competitive Domain-Name Registrars," April 21, 1999, <http://www.icann.org/registrars/icann-pr21apr99.htm>.

7. "Network Solutions Announces 14th Consecutive Quarter of Record Profitability—Cash from Operations Exceeds $118 million," *Business Wire,* April 27, 2000.

8. Ibid.

9. See, e.g., House Committee on Commerce News Release, "Bliley Blasts ICANN Management of Domain Names, Questions Authority to Levy Domain Name Tax," June 22, 1999. Bliley chaired the House Commerce Committee.

10. Section II(K) of ICANN's Registrar Accreditation Agreement, <http://www.icann.org/nsi/icann-raa-04nov99.htm>.

11. In a case involving the domain name *corinthians.com,* Judge Young (Massachusetts District Court) held that no declaratory judgment was available to the registrant, not even under the Anticybersquatting Consumer Protection Act, if the victorious party in the UDRP (the trademark holder) disclaimed any intention to file a trademark lawsuit of its own. There being exactly that disclaimer, he then dismissed the case for failure to state a claim.

12. A "Petition to ICANN and the U.S. Department of Commerce," May 1999, objecting to the adoption of WIPO recommendations without any action by the DNSO was signed by 86 prominent people from the legal, technical, and policy communities, including four members of WIPO's panel of experts. <http://www.domainhandbook.com/petition-0599.html>.

13. Michael Palage, chair, "Working Group B Report," submitted to the DNSO Names Council April 17, 2000. In its summary of consensus points, the report noted, "There does not appear to be the need for the creation of a universally famous marks list at this point in time," and "There appears to be a consensus that protection afforded to trademark owners will depend upon the type of top-level domain."

14. WIPO actively promoted adoption of the UDRP among ccTLD administrators. ICANN attempted to tax the ccTLDs, and the Commerce Department, in GAC meetings, urged that the "quasi-generic" ccTLDs be regulated like Network Solutions. <http://www.dnso.org/dnso/notes/20000417.NCwgb-report.html>.

15. U.S. Congress, House of Representatives, Committee on Commerce, Subcommittee on Oversight and Investigations, July 22, 1999, Thomas Bliley (R., Virginia), Chairman.

16. In late August 1999, MCI loaned ICANN US$500,000 and Cisco Systems loaned it US$150,000. See J. Niccolai, "ICANN Survives on Corporate Dole," *The Industry Standard*, August 20, 1999, <http://thestandard.com/article/0,1902, 6037,00.html>.

17. The July 22, 1999, hearings were a disaster for Network Solutions, as Democratic representatives spotlighted its monopoly rather than ICANN's authority. Leading up to it, ICANN officers initiated meetings with White House aide Thomas Kalil, seeking help raising funds, and FTC antitrust probes against NSI were initiated.

18. "Approved Agreements among ICANN, the U.S. Department of Commerce, and Network Solutions, Inc.," November 10, 1999, <http://www.icann.org/nsi/nsi-agreements.htm>.

19. Revised Verisign registry agreements, April 16, 2001.

20. NTIA, "Domain Name Agreements between the U.S. Department of Commerce, Network Solutions, Inc., and the Internet Corporation for Assigned Names and Numbers (ICANN)," fact sheet, September 28, 1999, <http://www.ntia.doc. gov/ntiahome/domainname/agreements/summary-factsheet.htm>.

21. The Green Paper, in discussing "representation," referred to "membership associations" representing "Internet users" as deserving representation on the board of a new corporation. The White Paper has said that the new organization should be "representative of Internet users around the globe."

22. "Application to Become the Domain Name Support Organization, pursuant to Art. I, Section 3(b) of the Bylaws of Internet Corporation for Assigned Names and Numbers (the "Corporation")," February 9, 1999. The organizations submitting the proposal to ICANN were listed as Electronic Commerce Europe (ECE), European ISP Association (EuroISPA), Information Technology Association of America (ITAA), International Chamber of Commerce (ICC), Internet Council of Registrars (CORE), International Trademark Association (INTA), Internet Society (ISOC), Policy Oversight Committee (POC), World Information Technology and Services Alliance (WITSA).

23. Individual Domain Name Holders Constituency, April 23, 1999, petition to ICANN board for recognition, <http://www.democracy.org.nz/idno/petition.htm>.

24. In her October 20 letter to the ICANN management, Commerce Department official J. Beckwith Burr noted, "Many commenters expressed the view that the principles of private, bottom-up coordination and representation set out in the White Paper are unlikely to be achieved in the absence of some type of membership-based structure. We believe ICANN should resolve this issue in a way that ensures greater accountability of the board of directors to the Internet community."

25. The report adduced the following reasons for an at-large membership: to reflect the global diversity of users (membership should not be limited to IP address or domain name holders); to ensure that ICANN's corporate structure operates for the benefit of the Internet community as a whole, is not captured, and continues to provide fair and proportional representation of the entire user community; to provide input from the user community to the ICANN directors and management. MAC Report, Berlin meeting, May 26, 1999.

26. ICANN Staff Report, "Statutory Members vs. Nonstatutory Members for the ICANN At-large Membership," August 11, 1999.

27. ICANN Bylaws, Article II, §{\!s}1.

28. Axel Steuerwald, "Mueller-Maguhn CANN; From Anarchist-in-the-making to Euro Net Lord," USC Annenberg Online Journalism Review, November 7, 2000, <http://ojr.usc.edu/content/story.cfm?request=479>.

Kieren McCarthy, "Anarchist Hacker voted onto ICANN Board," *The Register,* November 10, 2000, <http://www.theregister.co.uk/content/archive/13899.html>.

29. The Names Council itself was unable to agree on the numbers proposed by the working group. Its resolution called for "introduction of new gTLDs in a measured and responsible manner, giving due regard in the implementation of that policy to (a) promoting orderly registration of names during the initial phases; (b) minimizing the use of gTLDs to carry out infringements of intellectual property rights; and (c) recognizing the need for ensuring user confidence in the technical operation of the new TLD and the DNS as a whole."

30. ICANN staff, "Criteria for assessing TLD proposals," August 15, 2000, <http://www.icann.org/tlds/tld-criteria-15aug00.htm>.

31. U.S. Congress, House of Representatives, Committee on Energy and Commerce, Subcommittee on Telecommunications, W. J. Tauzin, Chairman, February 8, 2001, Hearings on "Is ICANN's New Generation of Internet Domain Name Selection Process Thwarting Competition?"

32. Australian Senator Alston, in the final comment period on the ICANN proposal, expressed concerns about "the authority of national governments to manage or establish policy for their own ccTLDs." Letter, Senator Richard Alston to William Daley, Secretary of Commerce, October 8, 1998. In her October 20 letter to the interim board designees, Commerce Department official J. Beckwith Burr asked ICANN to provide assurances about their intentions regarding ccTLD man-

agement. ICANN's response confirmed that governments would have such authority but cautioned that the "details of implementation . . . may be complex" and implied that it would look to guidance from the GAC on that question. Dyson to Burr, November 6, 1998.

33. Leadership of the GAC came primarily from representatives of governments and intergovernmental organizations activated either by the gTLD-MoU or by the Green Paper: Paul Twomey of Australia, Robert Shaw of the ITU, Christopher Wilkinson of the EC, and Francis Gurry of WIPO. The initial list of names inviting governments to send representatives to meetings was drawn from the ITU.

34. At the Berlin meeting of ICANN in May 1999, the GAC communiqué asked ICANN to reassign "with the utmost promptness" ccTLD delegations of "external and dependent territories" upon request of the "relevant public authority or government." GAC communiqué, May 25, 1999. "The GAC also reaffirmed that the delegation of a ccTLD Registry is subject to the ultimate authority of the relevant public authority or government," GAC communiqué, August 24, 1999.

35. Interview with Dennis Jennings, June 28, 2000, "Best Practice Guidelines for ccTLD Managers," ccTLD Constituency of the DNSO, June 12, 2000, section 3.1.

36. ICANN, Draft Final Report, President's Task Force on Funding, October 31, 1999.

Chapter 10: ICANN as Global Regulatory Regime

1. U.S. Congress, Hearings of the House Committee on Energy and Commerce, "Is ICANN's New Generation of Internet Domain Name Selection Process Thwarting Competition?" February 8, 2001.

2. Of course, the IETF originated as an extension of government research contracts, and received funding from the National Science Foundation and other government agencies (see chapter 5).

3. The registries and registrars regulated by ICANN, for example, "would not voluntarily agree to contracts that submit decision-making to voting by an unpredictable populace of those who may or may not have a significant stake in (or even pay much attention to) the resulting rules" (Johnson and Crawford 2000, 2).

4. International regimes are defined by Krasner (1984, 2) as "arrangements that pertain to well-defined activities, resources or geographical areas," consisting of "principles, rules, norms and decision-making procedures, around which actors' expectations converge."

5. Internationally, radio spectrum management through the International Telecommunication Union is mostly confined to technical coordination. Allocation and assignment of frequencies at the international level is not leveraged to exert policy control over national telecommunication regimes because the ITU is subordinate to national governments and they (or at least, the most powerful ones) would never relinquish such authority.

6. Paul Twomey, National Office for the Information Economy (Australia), Minutes of the *.au* Domain Administration Board Meeting, Melbourne, January 10, 1999, <http://www.auda.org.au/minutes/2000–01.html>.

7. The IETF's Internationalized Domain Name (idn) Working Group first met in November 1999. Beginning in August 2000 it began to miss its deadlines. Its work also was affected by the opening of working "testbeds" by major industry players, notably Verisign. See <http://www.ietf.org/html.charters/idn-charter.html>.

8. A spokesman for China's Internet Network Information Center (CNNIC), reacting to the announcement by the U.S. company Verisign that it would begin testbed registration of Chinese-character domain names under *.com,* said, "A company shouldn't be allowed to provide Chinese domain name registration services in China without the approval of the Chinese government." He added, "Related Chinese departments have protested to the Internet Corporation for Assigned Names and Numbers (ICANN) that Chinese-character domain names are quite different from the ASCII (English) ones, since they have unique . . . cultural and historic implications. China is seeking to participate in the formulation of the international standard for Chinese character domain names." *China Online,* November 3, 2000.

9. John Klensin, IAB chair, urged ICANN to "start warning the relevant domains" of the harm being caused by the testbeds and accompany the warning with a threat to "start a redelegation process" of their domain. Cited in "Status Report of the Internationalized Domain Name Internal Working Group of the ICANN Board of Directors," June 1, 2001, <http://www.icann.org/committees/idn/status-report-05jul01.htm>.

10. In a January 22, 2001, email to Roger Cochetti initiating negotiations on revision of the Verisign–NSI divestiture agreement, Sims refers to "revision of the registry agreement to make it clearer that ICANN has the right and power to set technical standards (a current example would be multilingual)." Posted on ICANNWatch site, "Text of Joe Sims' 'Willing to Advocate' Email," May 17, 2001, <http://www.icannwatch.org/article.php?sid=156>.

11. "Provisional IPv6 Assignment and Allocation Policy Document," version released May 28, 1999, and amended July 14, 1999, <http://www.apnic.net/drafts/ipv6-policy-280599.txt>.

Chapter 11: Global Rights to Names

1. Guidelines on Usenet Newsgroup Names, <http://www.faqs.org/faqs/usenet/creating-newsgroups/naming/part1/>.

2. Guidelines for Usenet Group Creation, January 31, 1997. See Hardy (1993) for a discussion of some of the controversies that arose over the formation of new top-level domains in the Usenet name space.

3. The following names are reserved at the second level and at all other levels within the TLD at which an ICANN-accredited registry operator makes registra-

tions: *.aso, .dnso, .icann, .internic, .pso, .afrinic, .apnic, .arin, .example, .gtld-servers, .iab, .iana, .iana-servers, .iesg, .ietf, .irtf, .istf, .lacnic, .latnic, .rfc-editor, .ripe, .root-servers.* The following names are reserved at the second level: *.aero, .arpa, .biz, .com, .coop, .edu, .gov, .info, .int, .mil, .museum, .name, .net, .org, .pro.*

4. *Sony Corp. of Am. v. Universal City Studios, Inc.,* 464 U.S. 417 (1984).

5. The NIC handle is a short, unique alphanumeric code that a registry assigns to a domain name holder when the registrant registers a name. People who use different names might use the same NIC handle in the WHOIS record.

6. The Paris Convention, Article 10 (1), states that its provision on seizure of goods traded across national boundaries shall apply to instances where false indications of the source of the goods or the identity of the producer are used. The Madrid (Indications of Source) Agreement broadens the application of the Paris convention to "deceptive" indications of source. The Lisbon Agreement regulates "appellations of origin," requiring participating states to protect registered appellations against any "usurpation or imitation." Geographical indications are also covered by Articles 22 and 23 of the TRIPS Agreement.

7. Christine Haight Farley, assistant professor of law, American University, Response to the Interim Report of the Second WIPO Internet Domain Name Process, Washington D.C. Regional Consultation, May 29, 2001.

8. Letter from International Trademark Association to Francis Gurry, May 24, 2001, <http://wipo2.wipo.int/process2/rfc/rfc3/comments/msg00034.html>.

9. Terry Allen, "Squatting for Dollars: A Political Cybersquatter Makes Mischief, and a Few Dollars, by Registering Candidate Domain Names," June 12, 2000, <http://www.salon.com/>.

10. A group of country music artists sued Jim Salmon, who registered around 450 personal names, in 1998. Jim Hu, "Country Music Artists Sue over Domains," *CNET News,* April 8, 1998.

11. Julia Fiona Roberts -v- Russell Boyd, re: *juliaroberts.com* (WIPO case no. D2000-0210), and Daniel C Mario Jnr -v- Video Images Productions, re: *danmarino.com* (WIPO case no. D2000-0598), and several other cases recognized common law trademark rights in personal names and transferred domain name registrations to celebrities.

12. In Bruce Springsteen -v- Jeff Burgar and Bruce Springsteen Club, re: *brucespringsteen.com* (WIPO case no. D2000-1532), the majority holds that "the users of the internet do not expect all sites bearing the name of celebrities or famous historical figures or politicians, to be authorized or in some way connected with the figure themselves." In Jules I. Kendall -v- Donald Mayer, re: *skipkendall.com* (WIPO case no. D2000-0868), the panelists unanimously permitted a relative of the golfer Skip Kendall to continue to use the name as the address of a Web site airing grievances about a personal debt.

13. GAC, Principles for the Delegation and Administration of ccTLDs, February 23, 2000, Sec. 9.

14. Letter from Robert Verrue, European Commission, to Mike Roberts, President of ICANN, December 1, 2000, <http://wipo2.wipo.int/process2/rfc/rfc3/comments/msg00034.html>.

15. Kenneth Neil Cukier, "Governments Stake Claim for Control over Country-Specific Domain Names," *Communications Week International,* June 7, 1999, p. 1.

16. Submission by Republic of South Africa in Response to World Intellectual Property Organization's WIPO2 RFC-2 Process, March 1, 2001.

17. In a rather delicious irony, *jesus.com* has been registered by a Washington D.C. area man with an uncanny resemblance to the stereotypical Bible school picture of Jesus. The Web site at that address is an extended personal ad: "Golden-haired, blue-eyed Jesus seeks loving young woman (22–29), preferably of recent Norse-Germanic heritage, who wishes to live in the spirit of the eternal. Innocence, or re-birth into innocence, and a desire to transcend the material mendacity of this world are essential! I offer a pure and spiritual existence of life's essence, free of fear, free of despair. I will reveal the bliss, power, and endless rewards of faith and belief. The right woman who is ready for my love, blessings, and unforgettable spiritual exploration will be given the world, but will also want to give me her world in the mutual quest to share the infinite. I offer you the ability to experience the fulfillment of your dreams and all you seek. Prospective respondents should read 1 John 4:18. True to artistic depictions, I have a lean swimmer's body and a six-pack, and if you have sought your best in life you will also be in good shape." Where is WIPO when we need it?

18. The domain name in this URL, *mdle.com,* refers to M. David Lewis Enterprises, an organization that has no official relationship to Garbo or her estate.

19. Cecily Barnes, "Catchy Domain Names Lose Their Luster," *CNET News,* October 16, 2000.

Chapter 12: Property Rights and Institutional Change: Some Musings on Theory

1. "The path of institutional change is shaped by (1) the lock-in that comes from the symbiotic relationship between institutions and the organizations that have evolved as a consequence of the incentive structure provided by those institutions, and (2) the feedback process by which human beings perceive and react to changes in the opportunity set" (North 1990, 7). I consider this aspect of North's theory to be suggestive and interesting but not very well articulated and badly in need of further development and testing.

2. The vast majority of cybersquatting cases involve domain name registrations that are not being used, and hence cannot confuse or deceive customers.

3. For more than a year after the new domains were authorized, ICANN was still presenting them to the public as a "proof of concept," an experiment, a step into unknown territory. This despite the fact that over 100 country code TLDs had been

added to the root since 1994 and that there is nothing unknown or experimental about the process of adding a new name to a name server's zone files (it happens thousands of times a day in the *.com* zone).

4. WIPO notes that in the case of third-level names registered under commercial second-level domain name holders, such as *.uk.com,* the UDRP may not be applicable. It considers this to be a bad thing. Also, in authorizing the *.name* top-level domain, ICANN encouraged the registry to impose controls and exclusions on third- and fourth-level assignments in order to prevent trademark conflicts.

5. Network Solutions backed away from a strong assertion of property rights over *.com,* however, choosing to allow its generic TLDs to be shared in exchange for avoiding litigation with the U.S. government and the continuation of its registry contract. As Libecap's (1989) model suggests, it would be highly unlikely for an public institutionalization process to recognize Network Solutions' claim because of the extreme concentration of the share distribution (about 75 percent of the total global market) and the fact that Network Solutions' original control of *.com, .net,* and *.org* was the product of a U.S. government contract.

6. *Image Online Design v. CORE Association and Ken Stubbs,* U.S. District Court, Central District of California, CV 99-11347 RJK, June 22, 2000.

7. GAC communiqué, August 1999.

8. PTO Examination Guide No. 2-99, "Marks Composed, in Whole or Part, of Domain Names," September 29, 1999.

9. J. Thomas McCarthy, *Trademarks and Unfair Competition,* 4th ed. (1996) and Supplement (2000), Section 7:17.1 at 7-27. West Group.

10. There is nothing about the technology or economics of DNS that requires a registry to be shared. Indeed, a registry with recognized property rights in its string could choose whether or not to open its registry up to multiple registrars. Many of the world's domain name registries are not shared.

References

The text of many of these references may be found on the Internet.

Abbate, J. 2000. *Inventing the Internet*. Cambridge, Mass.: MIT Press.

Adams, J., and A. E. Scaperlanda, eds. 1996. *The Institutional Economics of the International Economy*. Boston: Kluwer.

Albitz, P., and C. Liu. 1998. *DNS and BIND*. 3d ed. Sebastopol, Calif.: O'Reilly.

Alston, L. J., T. Eggertsson, and D. C. North, eds. 1996. *Empirical Studies in Institutional Change*. New York: Cambridge University Press.

Amin, A., and J. Hausner, eds. 1997. *Beyond Market and Hierarchy: Interactive Governance and Social Complexity*. Cheltenham, U.K.: Edward Elgar.

Aupperle, E. 1998. Merit's History: Three Decades of Growth, Innovation, and Achievement at Michigan's Leading ISP. *Library Hi-Tech* 16 (1).

Badgley, R. 2001. Internet Domain Names and ICANN Arbitration: The Emerging "Law" of Domain Name Custody Disputes. *Texas Review of Law and Politics* 5 (2): 343–392.

Ballon, I. 2000. E-Commerce and Internet Law: A Primer. Paper presented at meeting of New York Bar State Association Intellectual Property Section, Bolton Landing, October. Also published by Glasser LegalWorks, Little Falls, N.J.

Berners-Lee, T. 1994. Uniform Resource Locators. Internet-Draft (March).

Bertelsmann Foundation. 2001. *Wer Regiert das Internet? ICANN als Fallbeispiel in Global Internet Governance*. Gütersloh, Germany: Bertelsmann Foundation.

Besen, S. 1992. AM vs. FM: The Battle of the Bands. *Industrial and Corporate Change* 1: 375.

Bradner, S. 1998. Institutionalizing the IANA Functions to Deliver a Stable and Accessible Global Internet.

Brock, G. 1981. *The Telecommunications Industry: The Dynamics of Market Structure*. Cambridge, Mass.: Harvard University Press.

Brunel, A. 1996. Trademark Protection for Internet Domain Names. In *The Internet and Business: A Lawyer's Guide to the Emerging Legal Issues*, ed. Joseph F. Ruh, Jr. Fairfax, Va.: Computer Law Association.

Burk, D. L. 1995. Trademarks Along the Infobahn: A First Look at the Emerging Law of Cybermarks. *Richmond Journal of Law and Technology* 1: 1.

Bush, P. D. 1987. The Theory of Institutional Change. *Journal of Economic Issues* 21 (September): 1075–1116.

Cailliau, R. 1995. A Short History of the Web. Speech presented at World Wide Web Consortium ceremony, Paris, November.

Cerf, V. 1995. IETF and ISOC. Internet Society (ISOC).

Codding, G. A., Jr. 1964. *The Universal Postal Union: Coordinator of the International Mails.* New York: NYU Press.

Codding, G. A., Jr., and A. M. Rutkowski. 1982. *The International Telecommunication Union in a Changing World.* Dedham, Mass.: Artech House.

Comer, D. E. 1995. *Internetworking with TCP/IP.* Englewood Cliffs, N.J.: Prentice Hall.

Cook, G. 1992. NSFnet "Privatization" and the Public Interest: Can Misguided Policy Be Corrected? *The Cook Report on Internet.*

Cowhey, P. 1990. The International Telecommunications Regime: The Political Roots of Regimes for High Technology. *International Organization* 44 (2): 169–199.

David, P., and J. A. Bunn. 1988. The Economics of Gateway Technologies in Network Evolution: Lessons from Electricity Supply History. *Information Economics and Policy* 3 (2): 165–202.

Davidson, S. J., and N. Engisch. 1996. Applying the Trademark Misuse Doctrine to Domain Name Disputes. Minneapolis: Leonard, Street, and Deinard (law firm).

DeAlessi, L. 1980. The Economics of Property Rights: A Review of the Evidence. *Research in Law and Economics* 2: 1–47.

DeGidio, A. J., Jr. 1997. Internet Domain Names and the Federal Trademark Dilution Act: A Law for the Rich and Famous.

Diamond, D. 1998. Whose Internet Is It, Anyway? *Wired* 6 (April).

Drobak, J. N., and J. Nye. 1997. *The Frontiers of the New Institutional Economics.* San Diego: Academic Press.

Dueker, K. S. 1996. Trademark Law Lost in Cyberspace: Trademark Protection for Internet Addresses. *Harvard Journal of Law and Technology* 9 (Summer): 483.

Economides, N. 1996. The Economics of Networks. *International Journal of Industrial Organization* 16 (4): 673–699.

Farrell, J., and C. Shapiro. 1992. Standard Setting in High-Definition Television. Brookings Papers on Economic Activity: Microeconomics. Washington, D.C.: Brookings Institution.

Frankel, T. 1998. Analysis of the Proposed Structures for the New Corporation (ICANN).

Frey, D., and R. Adams. 1990. *A Directory of Electronic Mail and Addressing Networks.* 3d ed. Sebastopol, Calif.: O'Reilly.

Frezza, B. 1996. The Net Governance Cartel Begins to Crumble. *Communications Week* (October 28).

Friedlander, A. 1995. Emerging Infrastructure: The Growth of Railroads. Arlington, Va.: Corporation for National Research Initiatives (CNRI).

Froomkin, M. 1999. A Commentary on WIPO's "The Management of Internet Names and Addresses: Intellectual Property Issues."

———. 2000. Wrong Turn in Cyberspace: Using ICANN to Route Around the APA and the Constitution. *Duke Law Journal* 50: 17–184.

FTC. 1998. Comment of the Staffs of the Bureaus of Economics and Competition of the Federal Trade Commission in the Matter of Improvement of Technical Management of Internet Names and Addresses. Washington, D.C.: Federal Trade Commission, Bureaus of Economics and Competition.

Furubotn, E. G., and R. Richter. 1997. *Institutions and Economic Theory: The Contribution of the New Institutional Economics*. Ann Arbor: University of Michigan Press.

GAC. 2000. Principles for the Delegation and Administration of Country Code Top-Level Domains. ICANN Governmental Advisory Committee (February).

GAO. 1989. Computer Security: Virus Highlights Need for Improved Internet Management. Report to the Chairman, Subcommittee on Telecommunications and Finance, Committee on Energy and Commerce, House of Representatives. Washington, D.C.: General Accounting Office.

———. 1996. Telecommunications: Competition Issues in International Satellite Communications. RCED-97-1. Washington D.C.: General Accounting Office.

———. 2000. Department of Commerce: Relationship with the Internet Corporation for Assigned Names and Numbers. Washington, D.C.: General Accounting Office.

Green, B., and M. Bide. 1997. Unique Identifiers: A Brief Introduction. Book Industry Communication.

Hardy, H. E. 1993. The History of the Net. Master's thesis, School of Communications, Grand Valley State University, Allendale, Michigan.

Hazlett, T. 1990. The Rationality of U.S. Regulation of the Broadcast Spectrum. *Journal of Law and Economics* 33: 133–175.

Helfer, L. 2001. International Dispute Settlement at the Trademark–Domain Name Interface. Los Angeles: Loyola Law School.

Helmers, S., U. Hoffman, and J. Hofmann. 1998. Governing Technologies and Techniques of Government: Politics on the Net. In *Internet: The Final Frontier.* Berlin, Wissenschaftszentrum Berlin fur Sozialforschung (WZB).

Hill, C. 1958. *Puritanism and Revolution*. New York: Schocken Books.

Hofmann, J. 1998. Topological Ordering in Cyberspace. Paper presented at conference of European Association for the Study of Science and Technology (EASST), Lisbon, September.

Hughes, T. P. 1998. *Rescuing Prometheus: Four Monumental Projects that Changed the Modern World.* New York: Vintage Books.

Huston, G. 1994. Observations on the Management of Internet Address Space. RFC 1744 (December).

———. 2001. Analyzing the Internet's BGP Routing Table. *Internet Protocol Journal* 4 (March).

IAHC. 1997. Final Report of the International Ad Hoc Committee: Recommendations for Administration and Management of gTLDs. International Ad Hoc Committee.

INTA. 1997. INTA White Paper: Trademarks on the Internet. New York: International Trademark Association.

ITU. 1999. Trends in Telecommunication Reform: Convergence and Regulation. Geneva: International Telecommunication Union.

———. 2000. Report of IP-Telecoms Interworking Workshop (Numbering, Naming, Addressing, Routing). Geneva: International Telecommunication Union.

Johnson, D. R., and S. P. Crawford. 2000. Why Consensus Matters: The Theory Underlying ICANN's Mandate to Set Policy Standards for the Domain Name System. Available at http://www.icannwatch.org/.

———. 2001. The Idea of ICANN. Available at http://www.icannwatch.org/.

Johnson, D. R., and D. G. Post. 1996. Law and Borders—The Rise of Law in Cyberspace. *Stanford Law Review* 48: 1367.

———. 1997. The Rise of Law on the Global Network. In *Borders in Cyberspace,* ed. B. Kahin and C. Nesson, 3–47. Cambridge, Mass.: MIT Press.

———. 1998. The New "Civic Virtue" of the Internet. *First Monday* 3 (January 5): 22.

Kauffman, S. 1993. *The Origins of Order: Self-Organization and Selection in Evolution.* New York: Oxford University Press.

Kinsley, M. 1976. *Outer Space and Inner Sanctums: Government, Business, and Satellite Communications.* New York: Wiley.

Kleeman, M. J. 1999. *The Internet and Global Telecommunications: Exploring the Boundaries of International Coordination.* A Report of the Fourth Annual Aspen Institute Roundtable on International Telecommunications. Washington, D.C.: Aspen Institute.

Klensin, J. 2000. The Role of the Domain Name System. Internet-Draft (November).

———. 2001. Reflections on the DNS, RFC 1591, and Categories of Domains. RFC 3071 (February).

Krasner, S., ed. 1984. *International Regimes.* Ithaca, N.Y.: Cornell University Press.

Krasnow, E. G., L. D. Longley, and H. A. Terry. 1982. *The Politics of Broadcast Regulation.* 3d ed. New York, St. Martins Press.

Lemley, M. 1999. The Modern Lanham Act and the Death of Common Sense. *Yale Law Journal* 108: 1687.

Lessig, L. 1999. *Code and Other Laws of Cyberspace.* New York: Basic Books.

Levy, B., and P. Spiller. 1994. The Institutional Foundations of Regulatory Commitment: A Comparative Analysis of Telecommunications Regulation. *Journal of Law, Economics and Organization* 10 (2): 201–246.

Libecap, G. D. 1989. *Contracting for Property Rights.* New York: Cambridge University Press.

Maher, D. 1996. Trademarks on the Internet: Who's in Charge? CIX/ISOC Internet Infrastructure Workshop, Washington, D.C.

Malamud, C. 1992. *Exploring the Internet. A Technical Travelogue.* Englewood Cliffs, N.J.: Prentice Hall.

Mathiason, J. R., and C. C. Kuhlman. 1998. International Public Regulation of the Internet: Who Will Give You Your Domain Name? Paper presented at meeting of International Studies Association, Minneapolis, March.

McReary, S., and K. C. Claffy. 1998. IPv4 Address Space Utilization: How Much of the Internet Address Space Is Used? San Diego: Cooperative Association for Internet Data Analysis (CAIDA).

Mealling, M. 1998. Requirements for Human Friendly Identifiers. Internet-Draft (June).

Minasian, J. 1970. The Political Economy of Broadcasting in the 1920s. *Journal of Law and Economics* 12 (2): 391.

Mockapetris, P. 1987a. Domain Names: Concepts and Facilities. RFC 1034 (November).

———. 1987b. Domain Names: Implementation and Specification. RFC 1035 (November).

Mueller, M. 1997. *Universal Service: Competition, Interconnection and Monopoly in the Making of the American Telephone System.* Cambridge, Mass.: MIT Press.

———. 1998. The Battle over Internet Domain Names: Global or National TLDs? *Telecommunications Policy* 22 (2): 89–108.

———. 1999a. ICANN and Internet Governance: Sorting Through the Debris of "Self-Regulation." *Info* 1 (6): 477–500.

———. 1999b. Trademarks and Domain Names: Property Rights and Institutional Evolution in Cyberspace. In *Selected Papers from the 1998 Telecommunications Policy Research Conference,* ed. S. E. Gillett and I. Vogelsang. Mahwah, N.J.: LEA Publishers.

———. 2000. Rough Justice: An Analysis of ICANN's Uniform Dispute Resolution Policy. Convergence Center, School of Information Studies, Syracuse University, Syracuse, New York.

NAS. 1994. *Realizing the Information Future: The Internet and Beyond.* National Academy of Sciences. Washington, D.C.: National Academy Press.

Nathenson, I. S. 1997. Showdown at the Domain Name Corral: Property Rights and Personal Jurisdiction over Squatters, Poachers, and Other Parasites. *University of Pittsburgh Law Review* 58: 911.

North, D. C. 1981. *Structure and Change in Economic History.* New York: Norton.

North, D. C. 1990. *Institutions, Institutional Change, and Economic Performance.* New York: Cambridge University Press.

NTIA. 1997. National Telecommunications and Information Administration. U.S. Department of Commerce. Request for Comments. *Federal Register* 62: 35896.

———. 1998a. Improvement of Technical Management of Internet Names and Addresses. Green Paper. *Federal Register* 63: 8825.

———. 1998b. Management of Internet Names and Addresses. White Paper. *Federal Register* 63: 31741.

Olson, M. 1971. *The Logic of Collective Action: Public Goods and the Theory of Groups.* Cambridge, Mass.: Harvard University Press.

Oppedahl, C. 1996. Analysis and Suggestions Regarding NSI Domain Name Trademark Dispute Policy. *Fordham Property, Media and Entertainment Law Journal* 7: 73.

———. 1997. Remedies in Domain Name Lawsuits: How Is a Domain Name Like a Cow? *John Marshall Journal of Computer and Information Law* 15: 437.

———. 1999. Recent Trademark Cases Examine Reverse Domain Name Hijacking. *Hastings Communications and Entertainment (Comm/Ent) Law Journal* 21: 535.

Oslund, J. 1977. Open Shores to Open Skies: Sources and Directions of U.S. Satellite Policy. In *Economic and Policy Problems in Satellite Communication,* ed. J. Pelton and M. Snow. New York: Praeger.

Ostrom, E. 1990. *Governing the Commons: The Evolution of Institutions for Collective Action.* New York: Cambridge University Press.

Ostrom, E., R. Gardner, and J. Walker. 1994. *Rules, Games, and Common Pool Resources.* Ann Arbor: University of Michigan Press.

Paskin, N. 1999. Toward Unique Identifiers. *Proceedings of the IEEE* 87 (7): 1208.

Pearson, H. D. 1997. *Origins of Law and Economics: The Economists' New Science of Law, 1830–1930.* New York: Cambridge University Press.

Pejovich, S. 1998. *Economic Analysis of Institutions and Systems.* Boston: Kluwer.

Perritt, H. H., Jr. 1998. The Internet as Threat to Sovereignty? Thoughts on the Internet's Role in Strengthening National and Global Governance. *Indiana Journal of Global Legal Studies* 5 (2): 423.

Popp, N. 1998. The RealName System: A Human Friendly Naming Scheme. Internet-Draft (September).

Posner, R. 1972. *The Economic Analysis of Law.* Boston: Little, Brown.

Post, D. 1998. Cyberspace's Constitutional Moment. *American Lawyer* (November).

Postel, J. 1996. New Registries and the Delegation of International Top Level Domains. Internet-Draft (May).

Postel, J., and J. Reynolds. 1984. Domain Requirements. RFC 920 (October).

Quarterman, J. 1990. *The Matrix: Computer Networks and Conferencing Systems Worldwide.* Bedford, Mass.: Digital Press.

Quittner, J. 1994. Billions Registered. *Wired* 2 (October).

Ransom, R. L., R. Sutch, and G. M. Walton, eds. 1982. *Explorations in the New Economic History: Essays in Honor of Douglass C. North.* New York: Academic Press.

Rekhter, Y., P. Resnick, and S. Bellovin. 1997. Financial Incentives for Route Aggregation and Efficient Address Utilization in the Internet. In *Coordinating the Internet,* ed. B. Kahin and J. Keller, 273–287. Cambridge, Mass.: MIT Press.

Richards, J. E. 1999. Toward a Positive Theory of International Institutions: Regulating International Aviation Markets. *International Organization* 53 (1): 1–37.

Rohlfs, J. 1974. "A Theory of Interdependent Demand for a Communications Service." *The RAND Journal of Economics* 5 (1): 16–37.

Rony, E., and P. Rony. 1998. *The Domain Name Handbook.* Lawrence, Kans.: R&D Publications.

Rutherford, M. 1994. *Institutions in Economics: The Old and the New Institutionalism.* New York: Cambridge University Press.

Rutkowski, A. 1997. Statement Before the U.S. State Department, Bureau of Economic Affairs, Office of Telecommunications and Information Policy (October).

———. 2001. "The ENUM Golden Tree." *Info* 3(2): 97–100.

Shapiro, C., and H. Varian. 1998. *Information Rules: A Strategic Guide to the Network Economy.* Boston: Harvard Business School Press.

Shaw, R. 1997. Internet Domain Names: Whose Domain Is This? In *Coordinating the Internet,* ed. B. Kahin and J. Keller, 107–134. Cambridge, Mass.: MIT Press.

Simon, C. 1998. Overview of the DNS Controversy.

Slaughter, A.-M. 1995. International Law in a World of Liberal States. *European Journal of International Law* 6 (4): 1.

SOI (Subcommittee on Oversight and Investigations). 1999. Domain Name System Privatization: Is ICANN Out of Control? Hearing Before the Subcommittee on Oversight and Investigations of the Committee on Commerce, House of Representatives, One Hundred Sixth Congress, First Session, July 22, 1999. Washington, D.C.: Government Printing Office.

Stark, T. 1997. How Hard Is CIDR? *@internet.*

Su, Z., and J. Postel. 1982. The Domain Naming Convention for Internet User Applications. RFC 819 (August).

Turkle, S. 1995. *Life on the Screen: Identity in the Age of the Internet.* New York: Simon and Schuster.

Venditto, G. 1998. Netscape's Quiet Power Grab. *Internet World* (August 24).

Vixie, P. 1995. External Issues in DNS Scalability. Paper presented at Harvard Conference on the Internet and Society, Washington, D.C., November.

Vromen, J. J. 1994. *Evolution and Efficiency: An Inquiry into the Foundations of "New Institutional Economics."* Delft: Eburon.

Weinberg, J. 2000. ICANN and the Problem of Legitimacy. *Duke Law Journal* 50: 187–260.

Werle, R., and V. Leib. 1997. Private Organizations in the Governance of International Telecommunications: The Case of the Internet Society. Cologne, Germany: Max Planck Institute for the Study of Societies.

———. 2000. The Internet Society and Its Struggle for Recognition and Influence. In *Private Organizations in Global Politics,* ed. K. Ronit and V. Schneider. London: Routledge.

WIPO. 1998. The Management of Internet Names and Addresses: Intellectual Property Issues. RFC-3. Geneva: World Intellectual Property Organization.

———. 1999. Final Report: The Management of Internet Names and Addresses: Intellectual Property Issues. Geneva: World Intellectual Property Organization.

———. 2001. Second WIPO Internet Domain Name Process. RFC-3. Geneva: World Intellectual Property Organization.

Young, O. 1989. *International Cooperation: Building Regimes for Natural Resources and the Environment.* Ithaca, N.Y.: Cornell University Press.

Index